# NATIONS OF THE MODERN WORLD

AUSTRALIA
O. H. K. Spate
*Director, Research School of Pacific Studies,*
*Australian National University, Canberra*

CEYLON
S. A. Pakeman
*Formerly Professor of Modern History, Ceylon*
*University College; Appointed Member, House o*
*Representatives, Ceylon, 1947–52*

MODERN EGYPT
Tom Little
*Managing Director and General Manager of*
*Regional News Services (Middle East,) Ltd., London*

ENGLAND
A Portrait
John Bowle
*Professor of Political Theory, Collège d'Europe,*
*Bruges*

MODERN INDIA
Sir Percival Griffiths
*President of the India, Pakistan and Burma*
*Association*

MODERN IRAN
Peter Avery
*Lecturer in Persian and Fellow of King's College,*
*Cambridge*

ITALY
Muriel Grindrod
*Formerly Editor of* International Affairs *and*
The World Today
*Assistant Editor of* The Annual Register

JAPAN
Sir Esler Dening
*H.M. Ambassador to Japan, 1952–67*

KENYA
A. Marshall MacPhee
*Formerly Managing Editor of* The East African
Standard Group; *producer with British Broadcasting*
*Corporation*

MALAYA
J. M. Gullick
*Formerly of the Malayan Civil Service*

| | |
|---|---|
| MOROCCO | Mark I. Cohen<br>and<br>Lorna Hahn |
| NIGERIA | Sir Rex Niven<br>*Colonial Service, Nigeria, 1921–59; Member o*<br>*Northern House of Assembly, 1947–59* |
| NEW ZEALAND | James W. Rowe<br>*Director of New Zealand Institute of Economic*<br>*Research, Inc.*<br>Margaret A. Rowe<br>*Tutor in English, Victoria University, Wellington* |
| PAKISTAN | Ian Stephens<br>*Formerly Editor of* The Statesman *Calcutta and*<br>*Delhi; 1942–51; Fellow of King's College,*<br>*Cambridge, 1952–58* |
| SOUTH AFRICA | John Cope<br>*Formerly Editor-in-Chief of* The Forum; *South*<br>*African Correspondent of* The Guardian |
| SUDAN<br>REPUBLIC | K. D. D. Henderson<br>*Formerly of the Sudan Political Service; Governor of*<br>*Darfur Province, 1949–53* |
| TURKEY | Geoffrey Lewis<br>*Senior Lecturer in Islamic Studies, Oxford* |
| THE UNITED<br>STATES OF<br>AMERICA | H. C. Allen<br>*Commonwealth Fund Professor of American History,*<br>*University College, London* |
| WEST<br>GERMANY | Michael Balfour<br>*Reader in European History, University of*<br>*East Anglia* |
| YUGOSLAVIA | Muriel Heppell<br>and<br>F. B. Singleton |

# MODERN EGYPT

3

# MODERN EGYPT

*By*

TOM LITTLE

FREDERICK A. PRAEGER, *Publishers*

New York · Washington

# BOOKS THAT MATTER

Published in the United States of America in 1967
by Frederick A. Praeger, Inc., Publishers
111 Fourth Avenue, New York, N.Y. 10003

*Second printing 1968*

Library of Congress Catalog Card Number: 67-25303

Printed in Great Britain

TO
MOTHER
WITH LOVE

# Preface

IN MY book on Egypt which was published by Ernest Benn
Limited in their Nations of the Modern World Series in 1958,
I referred in my preface to the revolution in Iraq which had
taken place some months after the book was finished, and commented:

'. . . Everywhere in the Arab world the dream of unity, which is
the first aim of the Arab revolutionaries, has grown firm in outline.
They are impatient of talk of future differences and difficulties;
these, they say, are inevitable, but cannot any longer spell division;
the people of Egypt and Iraq have come together at last and they
have the people of Syria with them; from their unity will come the
unity of all the Arabs.

'The hopes men set their hearts upon are seldom entirely fulfilled. . . .'

This book substantially recasts and expands the earlier one and
in bringing it up-to-date it recounts the failure of hopes so far. The
governments of the United Arab Republic, Syria and Iraq are in
uneasy alliance, the division between them and the Arab monarchies was sharper than it had ever been since the formation of the Arab
League twenty-two years ago until the brief and sorry war with
Israel this month compelled them to close their ranks for a while.
As I remarked in 1958, the desire for unity remains constant and
military failure will doubtless have emphasised once again the need
for it, but the peoples of the various countries were bewildered and
often disillusioned by events even before defeat added its quota of
despair.

Events in Egypt have had their part in creating this state of
affairs, not least because President Nasser's conviction that he has
a duty to lead the Arab world to its revolutionary future has
hardened with his years of authority. He has done much for his
country but whether his purpose and the prosperity of Egypt can
be achieved together is a question yet to be answered. The loss of
blood and treasure in the war with Israel can only have enhanced
the problem and enlarged the doubt.

There are a few points I should make about the book itself. The spelling of Arabic words and names is arbitrary and conforms to most common usage. I have usually used Egypt in place of the United Arab Republic; I happen to like the old name better, the world knows it better, and most Egyptians will forgive me. The bibliography is a reading list confined to modern Egypt and is far from complete, so numerous are the books that have been published about the period. As for pre-modern Egypt, it hardly seemed worth-while picking a few titles from so rich a list. I have noted many sources in the course of the book but the primary source has been the day-to-day reporting of the region to which I have devoted a quarter of the century as correspondent and news agency chief. Finally, I would like to thank Mrs Peggy Ball and Miss Thelma Way for typing the manuscript under pressure of time.

If my account and judgement of events annoys any Egyptians, I assure them that neither was prompted by ill-will. I am very fond of them and their country.

TOM LITTLE

Whitchurch
Oxon.
24 June 1967

# Contents

# Map

---

# PART ONE

---

# The Land and the People

---

THE NORTH-EAST CORNER of the African continent is Egypt and it is linked to Asia by the triangular Sinai plateau. The Mediterranean and Red Seas give it natural boundaries to the north and east, and lines drawn at right angles to each other through the desert give it arbitrary western and southern frontiers on 25 degrees longitude and 27 degrees latitude. It is for the most part desert outside the valley of the Nile which, flowing from the south, forms a rich, verdant strip six miles wide until it reaches Cairo and widens into the fields and sand-spits of the delta.

The entire country lies on crystalline basement rock which sometimes breaks through to the surface. The Sinai slopes upward from the northern coast, tilting sharply in its apex between the gulfs of Suez and Aqaba to peaks ranging from 2,500 to 5,000 feet and reaching 8,660 feet at one point, Mount Catherina. These spectacular uplands are rent by gorges sometimes several thousand feet in depth, leaving sharp, isolated massifs, and they fall steeply at last into Aqaba gulf.

Stretching southwards along the western shore of the Gulf of Suez and the Red Sea coast are the eastern highlands, like a detached extension of Sinai but only half as high except at Mount Shayeb, which is over 7,000 feet. Deep narrow valleys running from the Red Sea to the Nile carve the highlands into jagged masses which are arid, harsh and inhospitable.

Most of the land is rainless. During about six months of the year there are rains along the Mediterranean coastal fringe and their sporadic overspill causes brief storms once every two or three years in the delta and valley for some distance to the south. Elsewhere there are only the lightest showers or no rain at all. The spring and summer are hot during the day and are very hot in the south where Egypt reaches into the tropics, but usually the temperature falls sharply after sunset. The autumn and winter are mild by day and cool at night, and there are sometimes short-lived cold spells bringing frost. During the early months of the year hot, dry winds, the *Khamsin*, carry dust from the desert and parch the cultivated

3

valley. By contrast, there are prevalent north-easterly winds off the sea which moderate the summer heat of the Mediterranean coast.

The northern coastal strip is broken by the lagoons, salt marshes and sand spits at the mouth of the Nile delta, but wherever there is soil and space there is some cultivation and habitation made possible by the rains and the more equable climate. The shore of the western desert receives about eight inches of rain a year, and the desert road from Alexandria runs through a number of villages from Alamein to Sollum. About six inches of rain a year fall on the broad plain stretching across northern Sinai from the isthmus of Suez through Gaza into Israel, and here too there are occasional areas of cultivation and small towns such as El-Arish and Gaza itself. The Red Sea coast, with greater heat and less rain and almost isolated from the rest of the country by the western mountains, is sparsely populated. There are people in the oases of the western desert, the biggest centre of population being at Fayoum, but the Qattara depression, the most extensive basin of them all, is covered with salt marshes caused by the evaporation of surface water from artesian sources and only a few nomads scratch a life from its useless earth. Bedawin tribes roam the three deserts, but the wilderness east of the Nile is harsh and forbidding territory even for them. Fayoum apart, the only major centre of population outside the Nile valley is on the isthmus of Suez itself, but this community is watered artificially from the Nile and is man-made to meet the needs of the Suez Canal.

Therefore, without the Nile there would be no Egypt. Its banks are cultivated for 800 of the 1,000 miles of its journey from the southern frontier to the sea, the valley drawing a sharp green line through the yellow of the wilderness. Of the country's 386,000 square miles only 15,000 are fit for people to live on. This simple fact of geography has been the limiting condition of Egypt through the thousands of years of her history and it remains so today. Nineteen out of every twenty people live on the Nile banks; Cairo, the national capital, lies astride the apex of the delta; and every other town of importance stands beside the river or lives because of it.

For 100 miles southwards from the first Nile cataract at Aswan there lived until 1964 about 35,000 Nubians, a people of different race. The region is rainless and the river flows roughly over its broken bed until it breaches the cataract and begins its sober journey to the south. The inhabitants scratched so poor a living from the small, fertile inlets in the rocky banks that most of the young men were forced to emigrate to the cities and towns of the delta to make a living as servants and porters. Nubia has now been submerged by the lake formed behind the new High Dam at Aswan and the people moved to New Nubia, which has been built for them on the Nile farther south at Kom Ombo.

The Nubians, who lived on the stretch of Nile from the first cataract to the third, 250 miles inside the Sudan, are a people of obscure origins, darker and physically different from the Egyptians. They spoke a language of their own, the script of which was lost about a thousand years ago, and now the Egyptian Nubian speaks Kenuzi while those in the Sudan speak Mahasi. They have always stood apart from their compatriots in Egypt, being regarded and regarding themselves as different, but their transfer south into close association with the Egyptians may at last terminate the many centuries of separation.

The source of the Nile in the central African mountains has been known for barely a century. Although a great civilisation had flourished on its banks for more than 2,000 years when Herodotus travelled along it for 600 miles from Alexandria, he could find only one man claiming any knowledge of its beginning, and according to him the waters issued from bottomless springs situated between two conical mountains named Crophi and Mophi in the Aswan cataract region, half to flow northward and half to the south. Herodotus did not take the story very seriously, but if oral tradition could have survived dimly through thousands of years preceding recorded history, the bottomless springs fancifully support a theory, advanced by some geographers, that in Miocene times the Mediterranean Sea reached inland to what is now Cairo and one of the small streams that drained into it was the 'proto-Nile'. The geographers state that at that time the rivers from the African highlands spent themselves in the Sudd, a lake of swamp and papyrus grass stretching for 250 miles across the path of the river in Southern Sudan, so that there were two 'Niles' divided by the cataract region between Khartoum and Aswan until about 21,000 years ago, when the lake spilled northwards, reached and breached the rocks to join the proto-Nile, and poured down a close-cut channel to the sea. With this union of the rivers, 'Egypt' began to take shape, and from that day to this an unfailing flood has fertilised and irrigated the valley of the Nile, sustaining life within its well-defined rhythm.

The rhythm begins with the rain-bearing winds of the South Atlantic, which, after journeying 2,200 miles across Africa, beat upon the central lake plateau and the highlands of Ethiopia in March and April. The water scores the hillsides into numerous streams which find their way to rivers, the Sobat, the Blue Nile and the Atbara; the rivers in turn plunge downwards, sometimes through canyons thousands of feet deep, and traverse swamps and desert to reach the Mediterranean Sea nearly 4,200 miles from the most remote source close to Lake Tanganyika. Fed by the rains of the Ethiopian highlands, the Blue Nile is well towards flood in June. In August and September it is, as part of the Nile proper, in rich red spate against the steep eastern bank of its Egyptian channel and is flooding the shallow western slope. The White Nile, fed by the Sobat, is steadied by the lakes Victoria and Albert, the great waters behind it, and loses the force of its flood in the swamps; but when the Blue Nile falls away, the White Nile maintains at least 40 per cent of the flow to serve Egypt in the low season. Not a single tributary joins the Nile on the final 1,700 miles to the sea.

While the upper Nile was breaching the cataracts, the icecap of Europe was receding northwards. When the Atlantic cyclone belt was driven southwards by the northern cold during the Ice Age it brought ample and continuous rains into North Africa and where there is desert now there were then rolling prairies of grass and parkland; but by the time the first glacial period was completed 15,000 years ago, the Atlantic rainstorms had been drawn away from the southern Mediterranean region and the grasslands of North Africa had dried out. Slowly but surely what is now Egypt had taken its present physical form.

As the rivers and grasslands withered in the waterless heat, the plentiful people who inhabited them must have moved away in search of life-giving rains, some perhaps traversing the sea into Europe or the Mediterranean islands, and others moving southwards to become, as some people believe, the Dinka and Shilluk of Southern Sudan. Others took a shorter but equally daring journey into the valley of the Nile, which at that time was a rank swamp, an impenetrable wilderness. There, in response to the challenge of new surroundings and a different way of life, they created the civilisation of ancient Egypt.

Manetho, scribe to the Ptolemies, set down on the eve of the Christian era the history of Egypt and began the catalogue of human kings with Menes more than 6,000 years ago. He records fabulous generations of gods and demi-gods who preceded Menes and possibly represent the oral tradition of peoples who had started on the road towards civilisation long before the Ist Dynasty. These shadowy inhabitants of the Nile valley could work in metal, sailed the seas on trading expeditions, cooked their food and domesticated their animals; they glazed their beads, stitched their clothes, lay on beds; they played games such as ninepins and enjoyed the artistry of shaping and decorating their pots. They seem to have had a nebulous concept of life after death.

These forefathers of the Egyptians must have penetrated the swampy bottom of the Nile slowly from the edges, probably beginning in Upper Egypt and pressing downwards to the delta. They lived at first as hunters of the hippopotamus, the wild boar, the crocodile, the ibis, the ox, the giraffe and other animals which were plentiful and are now found only on the river far beyond the southern frontier. At some time in the prehistoric period these people noticed the vegetation which grew where the Nile had watered its own banks, and advanced towards civilisation by planting their own edible crops.

The river was rising and falling through the years just as it does now. The people must at first have built their villages on the deserts close to the river-banks where they had access to the land enriched and watered by the floods. In time they learnt to make small mud retaining walls to trap flood-water for longer periods in order to grow better crops. Later still they must have banded together to enlarge the basin of water, to live on high ground which became an island in the flood and then to create artificial hills for their habitation. The systematic utilisation of the Nile in turn compelled the people to create an advanced social organisation, from which evolved the early kingdom, and they were united in the first nation-state.

The people congregated in villages, the villages were bound together in cantons, or nomes, as the Greeks named them, and the Nile imposed an overall unity. In due time, largely as a result of the need to define their eastern frontier, the rulers of Egypt fashioned the first imperial administration, applying to the control of conquered territories those principles of government they had learnt on the Nile.

## Chapter 2

# From Empire to Slavery

O NE STILL SPEAKS today of Upper and Lower Egypt. The
imaginary dividing line, drawn immediately south of Cairo,
with the alluvial delta to the north and the ribbon of Nile
valley to the south, had its origins in the 'two kingdoms' of Egyptian
pre-history, which were united by Menes who drove northwards
from the Upper Kingdom to conquer the delta about 5,500 years
ago. The history of Egypt began with his conquest.

Ancient Egyptian civilisation covered immense periods of time.
From Menes to the end of the Old Kingdom is as great a period as
the whole of British history since Alfred the Great; a single interlude
when Egypt was ruled by barbarian invaders called the Hyksos
was as long as American history since the War of Independence;
and from Menes to the conquest of Egypt by Alexander the Great
was 1,000 years more than the entire Christian era. No other civilisation has equalled its durability.

It was, inevitably, an uneven history through which dynasties
emerged and were overthrown, empires rose and fell, and ages of
spiritual and material progress collapsed in decadence and decay.
Historians have marked and named three main periods: the Old
Kingdom, in the third millennium B.C.; the Middle Kingdom, in
the first half of the second; and the New Kingdom, which occupied
the rest of that millennium, whereafter the civilisation ran its
unsteady course, with brief moments of recovery, until it succumbed
to other empires three centuries before the Christian era.*

The emergence of the civilisation was as rapid as its existence was

---

* A more detailed and usually acceptable breakdown of the approximate
chronology of ancient Egypt is as follows:
    I and II Dynasties: Archaic Period beginning with Menes, 3188–2815 B.C.
    III to VI Dynasties: Old Kingdom, 2815–2294 B.C.
    VII to X Dynasties: First Intermediate Period, 2294–2132 B.C.
    XI to XII Dynasties: Middle Kingdom, 2132–1777 B.C.
    XIII to XVII Dynasties: Second Intermediate Period, 1777–1573 B.C.
    XVIII to XX Dynasties: New Kingdom, 1573–1090 B.C.
    XXI to XXV Dynasties: Late New Kingdom, 1090–663 B.C.
    XXVI Dynasty: Saite Period, 663–525 B.C.
    XXVII to XXXI Dynasties: Late Period, 525–332 B.C.

durable. Less than 500 years from its beginning there was sufficient engineering skill to build the step pyramid at Saqqara, in the outlying desert of the Memphis area, and within another 250 years the Pharaoh Khufu had constructed the Great Pyramid at Giza and Khafre the Second Pyramid and carved the Sphinx out of solid rock. The science, skill and art of these monuments were not the only achievements of this early period. The Egyptians also created a government organisation of great complexity and cohesion.

The early struggle of the people of the Nile was against their natural environment, in the conquest of which they created their civilisation, but by the end of the IVth Dynasty the political organisation and social structure of the country were so advanced that the challenge of environment had little meaning. With the valley tamed and the sun warm and generous, they lost the discipline the Nile had formerly demanded of them. The collapse of the VIth Dynasty then brought to an end the first and most creative period of Egyptian history. The union of the Upper and Lower Kingdoms was lost in a struggle of princelings, and learning, which had precociously advanced to meet the challenge and the promise of existence on the Nile, became a certificate into a parasitical bureaucracy and priesthood.

Although the Egyptians were able to reach out tentatively to the Mediterranean and the nomad tribes, their society was sheltered by surrounding deserts and there was as yet no external pressure. It was still in this security that able pharaohs of the XIth and XIIth Dynasties united 'the two lands'. Despite primitive communications they were able to extend their rule both east and south of Egypt; but to the east the Sumerians had developed a comparable civilisation in the valleys of the Tigris and the Euphrates and between them and Egypt there were people whose rudeness, mobility and endurance could breach the deserts protecting the civilised societies. The Hyksos, peasant kings 'of an ignoble race' (as Manetho, the ancient chronicler, described them), crossed the Sinai with horse and chariot and subdued a degenerate Egypt without a battle. They were illiterate people, probably of Semitic stock, unskilled in all except warfare, but they were nevertheless prophetic of Egypt's fate. From the Hyksos to the final fall of Egypt no king could maintain his independence on the Nile without first subduing the forces arrayed against him. This was impossible in the long run. There were resources of manpower in Asia that Egypt could not equal and the waves of people who pressed against her desert bastions had their vigour replenished from many barbarian springs.

It was, therefore, in struggle against conquerors that the next great flowering of pharaonic civilisation began with the XVIIIth Dynasty. The Amenhoteps and Thotmeses of this period expelled the Hyksos, and they fought their way to the Orontes, the Euphrates and the Third Cataract on the Nile in Kush.* Now there was no rest. The XIXth Dynasty was committed to exhausting wars in Syria against the Hittites, a stronger power than Egypt had ever before faced. In the next dynasty arose Ramses III, the last of the great fighting pharaohs, who defeated a confederacy of Mediterranean peoples by land and sea, and again advanced to the Orontes and conquered Kush.

Internal decay was already present in the time of Ramses III, for his military power was based on slaves and mercenaries from Libya and Kush and a hard core of Greeks brought from the Mediterranean islands. The Egyptians were by this time an unwarlike and flaccid people and within twenty-five years of the death of Ramses III were held in contempt even by petty Syrian princelings. From the XXth Dynasty onwards the story is one of disintegration and defeat only occasionally relieved by the greatness of a king or the revolt of the people.

Before the great state tottered to its fall, Libyans, Nubians and Ethiopians took turns in conquering it, and then Assyrians fell upon the delta and pillaged it. For one last time the Egyptians rose against their enemies and the Saite Dynasty expelled the Assyrians in the middle of the seventh century B.C. This dynasty consciously sought to revive the glory of Egypt by turning away from the mercenary and foreign groups, who had been at the heart of delta governments for centuries, to look back 2,000 years to the achievements of the Old Kingdom, restoring and sometimes improving the classical art it reproduced; but with the fall of the last Saite king, Egypt 'belonged to a new world to which she had contributed much but in which she could no longer play an active part. Her great work was done. . .'.†

The work had indeed been great. From the primitive social groups of pre-history the Egyptians fashioned one of the first, if not the first, complex and civilised society. Professor Arnold Toynbee has described the IVth Dynasty, which ruled in Egypt 5,000 years ago, as 'the zenith of the characteristic achievement of Egyptian Society; the co-ordination of human labour in great engineering enterprises ranging from the reclamation of swamps to the construction of pyramids. It was also the zenith in the spheres of

---

* A region stretching from the present Egyptian frontier for about 250 miles southwards on the Nile.
† Professor James Breasted, *The History of Egypt*.

political administration and of art'. Using the most primitive communications, the Egyptians were able to extend their rule far beyond
their frontiers, so that before their final decline began in the XXth
Dynasty they had not only created an empire but fashioned, for the
first time in history, an imperial administration.

In ancient Egypt, Pharaoh was the peak of an administrative
pyramid, which broadened downwards through the Grand Vizier
and, in territories beyond the frontier such as Kush, the Viceroys, to
the princelings of the nomes and the mass of scribes and clerks.
Administration was detailed and complicated; able to lay down
regulations for the use of the Nile-waters in flood time, organise
taxation, and hold a biennial census of cattle. For the administration
of justice there were local courts, high courts and the right of appeal
to the pharaohs, who, if one may judge from the absence from the
tombs of pictures of Egyptians suffering torture, were more humane
than most rulers for centuries after. This experience of government
they bequeathed to civilisation.

In the course of their imperial mission, the Egyptians developed
maritime and military skills to an advanced stage. There were large
wooden boats before Menes, but in time they imported timber from
the Lebanon to build vessels with two banks of oars for voyages to
Mediterranean islands such as Crete and Malta, and to the Syrian
coast and Asia Minor. They possibly entered the Black Sea and,
sailing from their Red Sea coast, reached the shores of India.
Pharaonic fortifications in Kush were so far developed that they
were never equalled for another 2,500 years, providing for both
vertical and horizontal fields of fire from the apertures in the walls,
which formed, with the moats, an elaborate defence system.*

The Egyptians acquired in their domestic lives an astonishing
degree of sophistication. Although their homes, which were built of
wood, mud and reeds, have entirely disappeared, the wall paintings
surviving in tombs and temples give some idea of the graceful living
of the rich. They were gay people, not absorbed and overwhelmed
with the idea of death, as the mortuary relics suggest. They lived in
villas set back from patios and gardens, beautifying their homes with
the lotus, the forget-me-not, buttercups, daisies and flowering rushes,
and spending their leisure listening to music. Their food was rich,
consisting of meats, usually cooked on horizontal spits over charcoal
fires, fish, pastries, breads and fruits, and they often got drunk on
wine and beer. They played games, hunted, and fished in the Nile
from rafts of papyrus reeds which they propelled by oars and

* As discovered by Professor Walter B. Emery at Buhen, opposite Wadi Halfa
in the Sudan, in 1961.

paddles. They slept on beds with string mattresses and used chairs as early as the IInd Dynasty. Feminine influence was strong in domestic life, possibly because inheritance was on the female side, and the delicacy and good taste of the princesses can be judged by their jewellery in the Cairo Museum and the charming figures painted on the walls of tombs.

The Nile flood compelled the Egyptians to expand their knowledge far in advance of other ancient peoples. They lived by it and their intelligence was therefore directed towards predicting its coming, measuring it, controlling it and using it; and when this was done they needed to count the crops. They created a solar calendar of 365 days which required only slight adjustment to become the Gregorian calendar, and by their observations of the heavens they formulated a primitive astronomy. For their many enterprises in building and agriculture they devised a mathematical system, which was cumbersome but accurate enough to be the foundation of the Greek system later. In order to count crops and impose taxes they created the first system of accountancy and the need to record all these operations contributed in no small measure to the beginning of writing. Their methods of embalming the dead reveal considerable knowledge of the human body, and medicine, although compounded with magical formulas and popular remedies, was in many directions far advanced, as, for example, in the use of surgery even on the skull.

Their monuments, notably the Great Pyramid, bear witness to their contribution to architectural science and art. Massive structures such as the Giza pyramids were feats of engineering remarkable both in the mass and in their detailed exactness. Using simple methods upon imperishable materials, they produced a grand treatment of broad planes which has never since been equalled. They knew how to use the arch and vault, but relegated them to subsidiary positions, such as the granaries of Joseph behind the temple of Ramses at Luxor, preferring in their stead the impression of power obtained by suspending a flat roof on huge, yet often delicately proportioned, pillars and columns. The hypostyle hall of the XIXth Dynasty at Thebes is one of the finest architectural achievements of the world. They gardened the landscape in stone, usually with such an unerring sense of proportion in the management of large masses that even today among the ruins of an avenue of sphinxes it is easy to visualise the majesty and power of the temple scene.

The artist in ancient Egypt had an official mission: to register in stone and colour the events of a reign. 'He may add a beauty of his own,' remarks Maeterlinck, 'but this was not required or expected of him and will certainly not be paid for.'* The dimensions of the wall-paintings in the tombs and the size of some of the larger pieces of sculpture suggest that he worked usually as one of a team. Inevitably there are trivial and even puerile pieces; the surprising thing is the high proportion of pure art. From the masterpieces in the grand style of decorative art to the delicate integrity of the little figures there is a continuous range of beauty. The artist served the pharaoh by recording his master's victories, his service to the temple and to god, his wisdom, and the happiness of his people, but in doing so the artist served his own spirit, and his work marks the emergence of civilised man.

The ancient Egyptians also carried civilisation a long way forward, both in extension of religion to the people and in conception of the one God. Local gods were worshipped in prehistoric Egypt, having animal forms to suit the tribal, hunting communities of those days. Each one of the small states had its own god, and as the states merged so the deities merged with or were swallowed by each other. The relationships and meanings of the gods and goddesses were mutual and often incongruous. In the Old Kingdom the cult of Re was dominant; with the power of Thebes rose the power of the local god of Thebes; Amon, by origin a goose and by name 'the great cackler', grew to be the most important deity and was merged with Re to become Amon-Re. Amon advanced with the army of Thotmes III to be 'the supreme god of the known world'. There were other deities, not as powerful as Amon, which nevertheless expanded their frontiers. Thoth, for long trivial at Zehut, grew to be the Master of the Words of God, the god of all learning, and the recorder of the Last Judgement. The cat goddess, Bast, was worshipped at Bubastis for 2,000 years before a Libyan, Sheshak, became pharaoh and made her popular throughout Egypt and important into the Persian period. Finally, there was the significant ascendancy of the cult of Isis and Osiris.

In early pharaonic times, only the pharaoh could buy the intercession of Sun-God, Re, and as his wealth increased the price he paid for solar immortality mounted to the incredible proportions of the Great Pyramid. When rich people of the land trespassed on his exclusive right to salvation by building tombs and endowing priests to secure their immortality, the pharaoh climbed from the common ruck to become God himself, and from that unassailable position he was able to leave to mankind the comforts of redemption and the after-life. As kings were gods, worship was patriotism, and in time

* Maurice Maeterlinck, *Ancient Egypt*.

there seemed no advantage in restricting worship to powerful families whose ambition sometimes challenged the throne. Thus, later, the worship of Amon-Re was as splendid as ever, but its consolation was extended to the mass of pious peasants; Amon brought the souls of the poor to the harvest, was their Vizier, 'who takes no unrighteous reward, who speaks not to him who bears false witness nor looks upon him who only makes promises'. As the centuries unfolded the religion of the pharaohs became less and less remote, until in the cult of Osiris it was adjusted to the spiritual needs of the common people.

There was moral decay in the priesthood, which became more and more powerful and exclusive with every endowment of a tomb or temple until it was the dominant class in the state. By the time Thotmes III was extending the Egyptian empire to the Euphrates the priests of Amon were rivalling his power at home. The pharaohs were by this time not so much placating the gods with their temples and extravagant festivities as the priests whose support they must maintain. While Ramses III used slaves and mercenaries to revive Egypt's greatness in Asia, the priests ruled Egypt through lords and peasants alike, and it is reasonable to suppose that they preserved magical formulas and fetishism long after higher concepts of god prevailed in order to maintain their mastery over the minds of the common people. Their storehouses were bursting at the seams with treasure drawn alike from the labour of peasants and the conquests of kings; they owned 15 per cent of the land of Egypt, the income of 169 towns in Egypt, Syria and Kush; and about one in every fifty people was a slave to the temple. The position of the High Priest of Amon became hereditary in the XIXth Dynasty, and as the XXth Dynasty dribbled to its close the chief priest became pharaoh and therefore his own god, and every act of corrupt rule had divine sanction. The priests, supine and avaricious, ushered in a century and a half of economic decline from which it was too late for Egypt to recover.

Despite this abuse of religion, concepts of the grandeur of god and of eternal life emerged. The ancient gods of Egypt were the deification of the hopes and fears of the soul as it emerged from the primitive, and the key to their meanings was in the minds of the ancient Egyptians and is lost with them. Primitive superstition and totemism survived alongside sublime concepts, so that absurd rituals of magic can be found side by side with supreme hope of life after death in the Book of the Dead. Maeterlinck wrote: 'There is one chapter devoted to the Judgement of the Dead in which, probably for the first time in this world, the lofty idea of the drama of human consciousness and the survival of the soul is flung, like a ray of light, into the darkness of those prehistoric days.'* For the Egyptians were not so much concerned with death as with life after death and in the evolution of their religions the belief in the one God was distilled. In all Egyptian writings from the New Kingdom onwards there was manifest a growing tendency to monotheism. More than 1,300 years before the Gospel according to St. John, Ptah appears in Egyptian religion as pure reason wherein all creation takes place. Thus, dimly seeing that 'in the beginning was the word and the word was with God', the Egyptians reached towards Hellenised Christian thought.

This contribution of the Egyptians to civilised knowledge was transmitted to other peoples by the Egyptians on their wars of conquest or, perhaps to a greater extent, imbibed by those who conquered them. The Greeks acknowledged their debt and retransmitted the Egyptian inheritance to posterity, so that it is reasonable to doubt whether the flowering of art and knowledge in and from Greece could have been as rich without the contribution of Egypt.

The Egyptians were already a subject people when Alexander the Great conquered them in 332 B.C., but thereafter they were linked to the Hellenic civilisations of the Mediterranean for thirteen centuries. Cambyses, whose Persian Empire extended from the Indus to the Aegean, had conquered Egypt without much trouble in 525 B.C., and although the Egyptians had risen in rebellion from time to time and the Saite monarchs had secured their independence for sixty years, they had been cowed barbarously. Aware of the hatred of the entire population and without enough forces to resist, the Persian Satrap had hastened to submit when Alexander arrived.

Egypt's culture was itself, by this time, affected by centuries of contact with other peoples and civilisations, and with none more than Greece. Although the Saite dynasty looked backwards for inspiration to the classicism of the Old Kingdom and was consciously an upsurge of Egyptian nationalism against foreign minorities in the delta, its success increased rather than diminished Greek influence, for as the national revenue rose and business revived with the Mediterranean, Greek traders came in large numbers to the towns of the delta. The Egyptians protested against Greek influence, but Saite power had been secured largely with Greek mercenaries and depended on them for security and on the Greek communities for trade. Amasis, the greatest of the Saite kings, was conciliatory to Egyptian opinion but was himself at heart a Greek.

Although he remained in the country only a year, Alexander

* Maurice Maeterlinck, op. cit.

established a system of government which was wiser and more tolerant than that of the Persians. He reaffirmed the credibility of the Egyptian religion and, by proclaiming through the oracle of Amon at Siwa that he was the son of God, he secured the support of the priests and the temple oligarchies. He refurbished the administration of the Saite period under two controllers who, if not Egyptian in origin, were naturalised and known to the Egyptians. His purpose, nevertheless, was to secure the treasure and tribute of Egypt in order to pursue his conquests in Asia, where he had bitten deeply into the Persian Empire, and he made little secret of the part Egypt must play. The garrisons and central authority were in the hands of Greeks, and Alexandria, the new capital which he founded on the shores of the Mediterranean, was intended to be, and became, the city of the ruling caste of Greeks.

Under the Ptolemies, who succeeded Alexander, the court at Alexandria became the richest and most extravagant in the world, but also the most cultured. The kings preserved the temples of Egypt, often embellished them and sometimes added new monuments of great beauty. The museum at Alexandria, supported by royal patronage, became a great centre of teaching which attracted the finest thinkers of the day and made several great strides in knowledge, such as the geometrical system of Euclid and the surgical methods of Herophilos. The library, until it was destroyed by fire in Roman times, was the largest collection of written wisdom that had ever existed. A canal between the delta and the Red Sea, which a Saite ruler, Necho, had begun to build, was completed, and another route to the Red Sea at Kosseir from Upper Egypt was made safe. The frontiers of Egypt were extended once again into Nubia and Syria.

Even the early Ptolemies regarded Egypt as a Greek state, holding it for themselves and their compatriots. The land, except for the land of the temples, belonged to the ruler, and he gave it to Greeks, who were set aside in self-governing communities under laws intended to keep them apart from the Egyptians and superior. They were tried in their own courts and were forbidden to marry Egyptians, although this proscription came late in the day for families who had in some cases lived in the delta for many generations. The museum and the library were part of the Hellenic world from which the Egyptians, although they had 3,000 years of civilisation behind them, were excluded.

Neither want nor lawlessness existed in the land, but this advantage was lost when the dynasty declined in fratricidal strife after the third Ptolemy. The administration collapsed and towards the end authority rested solely with the generals commanding the garrisons, and Greek writ ran little beyond the garrison cities. Towards the end of the second century Polybius described the Egyptians as 'exposed to the fury of the soldiery' and wrote that Alexandria filled him with disgust. 'It is inhabited', he said, 'by three distinct races: native Egyptians, an acute and civilised race; secondly, mercenary soldiers who have learnt to rule rather than to obey; and ... a mongrel race of Alexandrians, originally Greek.' The 'mongrels' and the natives combined to form the bloodiest mob to be found in any city of the civilised world; in the countryside the roads were infested with criminals; and the southern frontier was harried and sometimes penetrated by the barbarians of Kush.

For centuries the Egyptian peasant had been taught to labour for his master and pay taxes to his king, but during the Greek period the middle class of farmer and craftsman also sank into the morass of general poverty. But, as Mahaffy remarks, 'it was comparatively easy to make them (the Egyptians) slaves but they were perpetually revolting slaves'.* It is probable that the third Ptolemy, at a time when the benefits of Greek rule were still manifest, had to abandon his invasion of Syria at the outset of his reign because of troubles at home, for shortly after his return the Treaty of Canopus suggested by its wording an agreement with the Egyptian people. Rebellion broke out before his death, and again in the next reign Thebes regained a period of separate independence. The formation of a native Egyptian army for wars in Syria during the middle period of Ptolemaic rule only made matters worse by revealing to the natives that they were not necessarily inferior as soldiers to the Greeks, with the result that Egyptian soldiery encouraged revolts they could not carry through. The history of the Ptolemaic period is punctuated by small and great rebellions, notably in the region of Thebes.

The dynasty slid, amid disorders and popular hate, into the arms of Rome. The weak and vicious Ptolemy Auletes was to all intents and purposes a vassal before Cleopatra gave herself and her country first to Julius Caesar and then to Antony; and as the son she bore to the great Caesar was murdered before her death and her sons by Antony were murdered or otherwise lost to history, she failed to preserve the dynasty or to found a new Greco-Roman one of her own. In the year 30 B.C. Augustus Caesar took possession of Egypt.

For six and a half centuries Egypt was subject to Rome and the successor-empire of Byzantium. It was valuable as a supplier of grain and as a defensible military base, and at the outset it prospered under Rome's firm rule. Egyptian trade was stimulated by the

* J. P. Mahaffy, *The Empire of the Ptolemies.*

3—ME

suppression of piracy in the Mediterranean and the discovery of the monsoon route to India, which replaced the tedious Arabian coastal caravans. Yet Rome was, in one important respect, worse than the Ptolemies. Whereas the latter were oppressive farmers living on their lands, the Romans were absentee landlords who drained the country of grain and money and taxed the people to the limit. Although the Emperor claimed to be pharaoh he was an absentee pharaoh, for whom a viceroy farmed the country in alliance with the ruling caste of Greeks and mercenary soldiers, who were separated from the Egyptians by privileges, such as the right to have their own popular assemblies and to pay lower taxes. It was military government. The country was divided into three provinces, each of which was ruled by a Roman, but the provincial administration collapsed in chaos, and the rulers were compelled to make provincial officials responsible with their own lives and properties for the collection of taxes: a system so onerous that the officials had to be conscripted for the work.

Rome fared no better than the Ptolemies at the hands of the natives. The first tour of the Roman tax collector was taken as the signal for revolt at Thebes. During the reign of Marcus Aurelius, in the second century A.D., there occurred the Bucolic Wars, a powerful revolt led by native troops which lasted for several years. Again, towards the end of the third century, the Egyptians revolted and chose a renegade Roman, Achilleus, as their commander and Emperor.

This brought to Egypt the Emperor Diocletian, who stormed through the delta and laid successful siege to Alexandria, where he was hailed as saviour because he diverted to the starving survivors of the siege the grain-ships intended for Rome. When he recognised the source of trouble he reformed the administration, but within a few years of his abdication the provincial organisations again collapsed. Land fell into disuse and was bought up by nobles very cheaply, until Egypt consisted of vast estates ruled by private armies, whereon every tenant, every artisan, every peasant was bound to his serf-like function through generations.

These oppressed people, prepared by the monotheist tendencies of their paganism, took readily to Christianity when Mark, the devoted follower of St. Paul, brought it to Egypt. The educated pagans of Alexandria still engaged their minds in neoplatonism, with the result that the ruling class was further separated from the Egyptians by religion, but towards the end of the second century Alexandria became a nursery of early fathers of the Church, and the school founded by Panteus produced Christian thinkers, such as

Clement, Origen, Plotinus and Longinus, who had been raised in
the Greek tradition. Christians were thus brought into collision with
the pagan Greeks of the capital and this led to the first major
persecution by Decius between 249 and 251. Christian Alexandria
survived the ordeal to become in the next century second only in
importance to now Christian Rome.

Nevertheless, Christianity was in the main the religion of the
Egyptians and gave cohesion to their national movement. Monastic-
ism, which had existed in embryo at the time of the pagan hermits,
probably had its origin in Egypt. St. Anthony is reputed to be its
founder and to have inspired hermits and monks to establish their
retreats along the Nile. The first monastery, properly so called, was
founded by St. Pachomius near Dendera, and before his death early
in the fourth century there were nine monasteries housing about
7,000 men and women. These monasteries led the resistance to
paganism and against the ruling class of foreigners who practised it,
sustaining in the process a national revolt all the way from ruined
Thebes to Alexandria.

The creation in A.D. 330 of Constantinople in the triangle of land
held by the waters of the Golden Horn heralded the birth of
Byzantium as an extension in time of the Roman Empire and of
Greek culture. By that time Christianity had overcome paganism
in the Mediterranean. At the Council of Chalcedon in 451, the
Egyptian Church clashed with that of Byzantium, which was busily
elevating Constantinople to leadership of the faith alongside Rome.
The dispute concerned the nature of Christ, the Alexandrians contending that He had only one nature, whereas the Nestorians of
Byzantium claimed He had two. Although the Council decided
against Alexandria, the Egyptians refused to abandon their monophysite beliefs and founded an heretical Church which became the
Coptic Church of Egypt. The first orthodox patriarch sent to rule
the rebellious Egyptian Church was murdered by the Alexandrians.
Thereafter Alexandria had two patriarchs, one the official representative who led the movement to sustain the empire, and the
other unofficial Coptic leader of the Egyptian struggle against it.
For the Copts it was a national rather than doctrinal dispute and
their attitude was clearly reflected in the name they gave to their
opponents: the Melkites, that is, the King's Party, or 'the imperialists'. The Byzantine rulers who had no doubt about the meaning
of the movement persecuted the Copts relentlessly, and the struggle
kept the country in such disorder that trade, agriculture and
administration all decayed, Alexandria ceased to be a centre of
learning, and Egypt lost its leading role in the civilised world.

Her contribution to civilisation in both mind and spirit had, in any case, been made. When the Persians were expelled by the Greeks it must have seemed a natural thing that Egypt should be delivered from Asia and live with the Mediterranean communities to which the Nile directly presented her. The Nile civilisation had been the creation of people whose line of life ran north and south along the river, linking the Mediterranean with black Africa, and the people of the delta had affinities and possibly common descent with the people of the Eastern Mediterranean islands. By contrast, the barbarians to the east had been enemies who threatened the peace and prosperity of the valley. Nevertheless, Egypt in her despair turned to the Arabs – to the East instead of the 'West' of Greece and Rome.

## Chapter 3

# Islam Ascendant

---

T HE PROPHET MOHAMMED began his mission at Mecca in the year 610 and, after a period of contempt and persecution there, he journeyed with his followers to Medina in 622. The date of their flight, the Hejira, marks the start of the Moslem era and calendar, and in an astonishingly short space of time an Arab empire was created that reached eventually from the Indus to the Atlantic. Amr ibn el-As, the conqueror of Palestine, crossed the frontier of Egypt with 4,000 camel riders in December 639 and took the coastal route across the Sinai to the eastern delta stronghold of Pelusium in January. The town fell within a month and then Babylon, a fortress city close to the present site of Cairo, submitted after a long siege. Reinforced with 10,000 men from Arabia, Amr invested the towering walls of Alexandria, and the Melkite Patriarch and Prefect yielded the capital to him, despite the Byzantine garrison of 50,000 men and the navy in the harbour. The Emperor Constans briefly recovered the city three years later, but when Amr reconquered it in 646, Alexandria, and with it Egypt, passed for ever from the possession of Christian kings.

Arab rule lasted for 500 years. During that period Egypt was for long periods a subject province and at others the dominant state in a restless empire, but never at any time did the Egyptians rule themselves. Soon after the death of Mohammed the Ummayad caliphs established their command of the empire from Damascus and were dominant for a century. They were followed by the Abbasid caliphs of Baghdad, who ruled for another century before their power began to disintegrate. During this period of disintegration Egypt broke free from the Abbasid empire, but independence was again won for her by a foreign conqueror. A new line of descendants from the Prophet through his daughter Fatima dominated north-west Africa, and Gohar, their viceroy and general, led his army through Libya into Egypt, where the people, wearied as usual by misrule, opened the gates of Alexandria to him, and by 969 the whole country was in his possession. Gohar founded Cairo and from this secure base he marched to the conquest of Syria and to the Tigris, to start 200 years of rule by Fatimid caliphs.

The Christian crusaders made inroads into the power of the Fatimids, holding at times the Syrian heartland of the empire, but they were never able to conquer Egypt, and the last Crusade, led by Louis IX of France, was decimated by plague and war in the delta and utterly defeated. Saint Louis did not, however, succumb to the Fatimids; they had themselves already fallen before the same Kurdish force that had defeated the Christians in the Holy Land. The second Kurdish viceroy in Egypt, Salah el-Din al-Ayyoub, the Saladin of Western romance, had proclaimed himself Sultan of Egypt, and with an army of Kurdish mercenaries and slaves had driven the Crusaders from Jerusalem and extended his rule to the Tigris.

The empire of Salah el-Din crumbled after his death. His officers murdered his son and seized power, and their first leader, Beybars, recovered Jerusalem once and for all from the Christians, halted a Mongol threat from the east, and extended his sway to the Barbary coast in the west and Nubia in the south. In this way Beybars began 300 years of rule by the Mamelukes, a military caste descended from the Turk, Mongol and Circassian slaves of the army of Salah el-Din.

Indirectly, Mameluke rule lasted much longer. Egypt was conquered in 1517 by the Ottoman Turks, a people who had their origins in another barbaric wave which rose among the Mongols of the Far East, absorbed other peoples in its advance across Asia, and swept over the Middle East. There they accepted Islam and from their capital in Constantinople they extended their empire to North Africa and the Balkans. When Egypt was absorbed in this empire it ceased to have either political or religious significance in the Eastern Mediterranean and the status of Cairo sank to that of a provincial city, where Ottoman rule was exercised through the Mamelukes. Their power in the land endured in this form into the nineteenth century.

With whatever hope the Egyptian people received their conquerors through the centuries, there was seldom any change in their condition but for the worse. As with the Ptolemies and with the Romans, so with the Arabs, the Mamelukes and the Turks: for them the relief from oppression was always short-lived and the time of neglect and despotism always long.

The Arabs brought a rich language, a sword, a simple faith and, to Egypt, where Church and State were worm-eaten with corruption, they brought chiefly a shining example. An envoy of Cyrus, the Patriarch, sent to Amr's army is reported to have said of it:

'We have witnessed a people to each and everyone of whom death is preferable to life, and humility to prominence, and to none of whom the world has the least attraction'. The Arabs had nothing, and knowing nothing of what the world had to offer them, they desired little. They burst from the mindless desert in which they had sheltered their poverty for centuries from the civilisations of Egypt, Greece, Rome, Byzantium, Persia and Mesopotamia, into a world already advanced in arts and crafts, in intellectual exercises, in methods of government and trade, and they had to learn almost from the beginning, with only the civilising vision of the one God which Mohammed had superimposed on the Arabic language to help them. But as they ate of the fruit of knowledge they were corrupted. 'Deal gently with the people,' was the injunction of the Prophet, and Amr did his best to obey. He gave back to the Copts their own patriarch, Benjamin, and respected their freedom of conscience; he did not sell them into slavery and he pledged his honour for the security of their lives, their children and their property; he did not plunder their churches; but the tolerance of Amr could only be relative to the needs of the military caste and imperial army. It was still the fate of Egypt to be the milch-cow of its conquerors, and in due course the order of the Caliph was to 'squeeze the udders until they are dry'.

The first wave of Arab conquerors in the seventh century formed a military caste and, forbidden to buy land outside the Arabian peninsula, they lived in their own camps apart from the people of the countries they occupied. The separation from the conquered peoples was for long sustained by the fact that the convert to Islam, though he might benefit by remission of taxes, could not enter into the caste. The religious communities in Egypt were accorded some autonomy in judicial and other matters under their own leaders, and the general administration of the country was broadly on the Byzantine model. Jews and Christians, as 'people of the Book', were protected at the outset, but they were still a subject people who were denied that final degree of citizenship, the right to fight alongside the Arabs in the army; they paid a special tax instead.

Ahmed Ibn Tulun, a viceroy of the Abbasids, who seized Egypt for himself, was a man with some nobility of character who patronised learning and is reputed to have behaved justly to his people; but he was ruinously extravagant, brought the condign punishment of the Caliph of Baghdad upon the country and indirectly led it to the anarchy of rule by a mad Ethiopian eunuch. When the Fatimids came, the country enjoyed once again the splendour of a royal court and, what is more, a degree of prosperity and justice which lasted until half-way through the eleventh century. There were thousands of tall buildings in Cairo, some six stories high, and the main streets were roofed and lit. Shop inspectors kept watch on prices and punished over-charging. It is probable that the farmers and peasants did not share to the full in this prosperity, since their labours still paid for the splendours of the court and the military operations, but there was evidently peace in the country and by the standards of what came before and what followed these were halcyon days.

The excellent administration established in the reign of the Fatimid Caliph, Abu Mansur Nizar al-Aziz, contributed a great deal to the general well-being by restoring the control of the Nile, on which the prosperity of the country depended; but the Fatimids were foreigners and heretics, and their empire, largely as a result of the resistance of the orthodox Sunni Moslems in Africa, Syria and Palestine, had begun to disintegrate by 1050. The Fatimids eventually drowned themselves in the blood of the caliphs and viziers who plotted and murdered for power; and this gloomy chapter was darkened further – once again – by the undisciplined behaviour of mercenary and slave troops who, brought into the country by the benevolent Caliph Abu Mansur, ran amok in the period of decline. The taxation by the extravagant caliphs and the extortions of the troops so crushed the people that thousands in despair abandoned all efforts to farm the land. For Moslem, Christian and Jew alike, the era of Arab rule ended, as it had begun, in hunger and poverty.

The enlightened Kurd, Salah el-Din, was his own vizier, treasurer and chief justice, and whenever he was in Egypt he controlled the finances of the State with strictness and its judicial system with fairness. He restored some efficiency to the management of the Nile and negotiated commercial treaties with the Mediterranean trading communities. During his reign Egypt was a secure country, and he was able to divert the trade with the East away from the disturbed Euphrates route to Egypt and the Red Sea. The Mameluke Sultan Beybars not only fought brilliantly for his empire but worked for his country, digging canals, improving harbours and creating between Cairo and Damascus a fast mail system by relays of horses. But, at best, Salah el-Din could only mitigate the effect on the people of his costly wars, for which they had to pay, and Beybars heralded an era of regal fantasy that was ruinous to the country. Nothing could make headway against the ultimate waste of wealth. The Mameluke Caliph al-Nasir dug a canal, on which 100,000 men worked, connecting Alexandria to the Nile, built an aqueduct from the river to the Citadel in Cairo, founded about thirty mosques and a number of monasteries, public drinking-fountains, baths and a number of schools; he ordered a new land survey, suppressed wine-drinking, flogged a baker for profiteering and encouraged trade with Europe; but his exorbitant taxes caused widespread misery and hastened the downfall of his own caste, the Bahri Mamelukes. His reign was followed by civil wars and famine, and plague ravaged a people unfit to resist it. The Black Death, which wasted Europe for two years, wasted Egypt for seven.

Thereafter the unhappiness of the Egyptians was seldom relieved. Under the Burji Mamelukes the whole ruling caste was corrupt. The sultans themselves debased coinage and cornered essential commodities like pepper and sugar. The condition of famine was chronic and when, from time to time, the peasants broke out in revolt they were brutally suppressed. Marauding bedawin fell on the cultivated lands, and what they left behind in the fields was devoured by the locusts. The plague returned again and again. And, as though all this were not enough, the progress of the unknown Western world added its quota. When Vasco da Gama discovered the Cape route to the East, the traffic in spices and other tropical products, one of the main sources of national income, was diverted from Egyptian ports, and Portuguese and other European ships began to close Arabian waters to Arab ships.

The Ottoman Empire in turn was organised for war, and although its conquest saved Egypt for a time from total anarchy, it brought conditions which, in the end, were as disastrous for the people as the Burji rule. When Sultan Selim departed after the first conquest he left a Turkish viceroy, but the twelve *sanjaqs* were in charge of Mameluke emirs who had been spared his vengeance. Each bey, surrounding himself with Circassian slave warriors, ruled his territory like a despotic monarch, collecting taxes and seizing foodstuffs and cattle for his troops. Mameluke beys composed the administrative council and were the last word in government, so that the pasha from Constantinople soon ceased to exert any authority. The tribute which the Mamelukes had to pay to Constantinople fell into arrears and the peasants and other workers were squeezed to make good the deficiency. There was rivalry between the pashas and the beys in which the Mamelukes, possessing the military power, usually won: in 280 years of direct Turkish rule, no less than one hundred Ottoman viceroys came to Egypt. The cultivator of the soil was relentlessly exploited: he had no security, for his labour was the property of the State, and Turk and Mameluke unashamedly sold it to the highest bidder. Canals and irrigation were neglected; there was no such thing as justice in the land; but there was, inevitably, continuous famine, and again and again pestilence.

Towards the end of the eighteenth century the relaxation of Ottoman control and outright plunder by the Mameluke beys brought the country to the verge of extinction. Bedawins pillaged what remained of the fertile territories, and everywhere along the Nile there was brigandage on the roads. Such conditions were fatal to the Egyptian economy, which depended so much on the orderly control of the river. As canals silted up for lack of labour to clear them, large stretches of once-fertile land reverted to desert or wild scrub, and along the Nile peasants fought each other for the barest subsistence. In the towns a middle class of Egyptian and foreign artisans preserved within their guilds a fanaticism which at times brought pressure to bear upon their rulers, but in general the urban conditions were little better than those in the countryside. Owing to the geographical position of Egypt, about £6 million worth of entrepot business still came to the country, but raids on caravans and canal barges, the taxation imposed by the Mamelukes and the shift of trade to the Atlantic route were all wasting this trade. In any case the heyday of Egyptian craftsmanship had gone with the end of building and decorative arts early in the fourteenth century, when the Ottoman Turks had taken the finest of the craftsmen away to Constantinople. Religion was in the hands of the *ulema*, who had progressed little, if at all, from medieval times; and for the mass of people it meant slavish adherence to tradition and the mumbled *rote* of Koranic *suras*. Education consisted of memorising the Koran, which was taught by men who knew nothing else to students who sat in the dust around their feet.

It is usual to date the start of 'modern Egypt' from the Napoleonic conquest at the end of the eighteenth century. As a result of misrule the population, which had been seven millions even in pharaonic days, had fallen to two and a half millions. While Europe was preparing for the industrial age, Egypt had advanced little since the Arab conquest. In other respects a great change had taken place. The Egyptians entered the Arab period as a nation represented by the Coptic Patriarch in opposition to the foreign Melkites of Byzantium, and when Amr restored Benjamin to them he was in effect recognising the Egyptians as a nation; for to him, as a follower of the Prophet, there was no distinction between religious and civil nationalism. But the inherent simplicity of their religion fitted them ill for resistance to the Arabs and Islam. They had turned easily to Christianity, which offered something which, in their earlier paganism, they had come to seek: a concept of life after death. The single nature of Christ was something which the Egyptian, with generations of pharaoh gods behind him, could readily conceive, whereas the intellectual refinements of Byzantine Christianity remained foreign and unintelligible.

Islam, with its simple concept of the one God, was not so far removed from the monophysite doctrines of the Egyptian Christians. Another Arab commander, Ibn el-Walid, had already found that people of similar Christian beliefs had helped him to defeat the Byzantine army in Syria. The Copts were the focal point of resistance to Byzantium in Egypt and their Bishop in Alexandria instructed them to offer no resistance to Amr's Arab army. It was a striking example of the strength of the faith that fired the Egyptian national movement.

The urban Egyptian, although he welcomed the Arabs as destroyers of a hateful foreign rule, was more resistant than the peasant to their faith. He had more consciously preserved the Coptic language, his own kind of Christianity, and his desire for national independence. Yet he, too, lost all three to the Arabs and Islam eventually, because he submitted willingly to the faith or was tempted by the material benefits which made him a client of the Arabs. He, like the peasant, became pliant to the sword and spirit of the conquerors, and this pliability cost the Egyptians their national heritage. They were resistant as a nation to Byzantium, but they submitted to the Arabs, and so by the time Napoleon arrived they had ceased to be a nation.

The process took place gradually through the centuries. The Arabs secured permission from Mecca to buy land outside the peninsula and settled in Egypt; and the Copts turned Moslem and married the Arabs. So the barriers dividing the two peoples broke down. The Copts shortly gave up the language they had stubbornly preserved for so long and which the Arabs had first allowed them to keep. The process was hastened when the Ummayads decreed in 706 that it had to be replaced by Arabic.

The converts to Arabic, whether Egyptian, Syrian, Persian, Greek or Jewish, created the great period of Arab learning, but the learning was not Arab. It was the learning of other peoples put in the Arabic language. Most of the converts themselves submitted to Islamic traditions and in Egypt little else of learning was finally left. The Greek language had disappeared and with it Hellenic idealism; Rome was forgotten and Byzantium rejected; what remained of pharaonic wisdom in Coptic tradition withered with the language in the sanctuaries of the Church. During the six centuries of Arab rule Egypt drifted outside the stream of culture and learning, and its own claim to either vanished. Even the greatness of Salah el-Din only increased Egypt's isolation, by restoring the country's Islamic orthodoxy and by driving back the Christian crusaders who might have provided a link with the Renaissance and the Reformation in Europe.

Yet the fact that the Egyptian people had no history beyond that of submission and suffering for twelve centuries after the Arab conquest should not obscure the truth that few periods are as important as these interminable 'dark ages' to the understanding of contemporary Egypt. During this period the Egyptians lost all the attributes of a nation, but they never lost their conscious- ness of 'separateness' from all others and of self-identification. There was at least the distinction between the oppressors and the oppressed. This sense of separateness from all others, the self-identification of Egyptians with each other, is the most important element in the re-emergence of the nation, for it imparted to the national struggle an underlying consistency. The Egyptians have for centuries, and directly as a result of the Dark Ages, been conscious of themselves as victims; of pasha, khedive, Mameluke or Turk, or even of Greek and Copt who identified himself with the foreigners as tax collector or money-lender; and feeling themselves victims, they were equally opposed to the French, to their own rulers and to the British. If they sided with one against the other, it was only in order to get rid of the first as soon as possible.

The centuries of suffering taught Egyptians that, in the end, all foreign rule is bad, and Napoleon was quick to discover this when he invaded Egypt in 1798. Although he proclaimed that, as a friend of the Sultan of Turkey, he had come to put an end to their sufferings and, as the friend of Islam, to sustain their religion, the Egyptians withheld their skinny arms from the embrace which he expected. He was compelled to force a landing in vile weather when the Alexandrians refused their permission, and as his 40,000 veterans marched in 'hollow square' across the desert to Cairo, the peasants, in response to the call of the imams, drove their animals and crops into the distance, leaving the bedawin to murder the forage parties which the French sent after them. The Egyptians rallied to the banner of their troublesome Mamelukes, who, after emptying the national treasury, prepared for war. Even the Pasha, viceroy of France's friend the Sultan, whose rights Napoleon said he had come to save, declared war against him and fled to Syria.

The instinct of the Egyptians was right, for Napoleon's expedition was primarily concerned with French survival in Europe and it was as such that he justified it to the Directory in Paris. France was at that time supreme in Europe, its armies stretching across the continent from Rome to Antwerp, but Britain was unconquered. Napoleon had an army massed at the English Channel for an invasion but could not make the crossing as long as the British Navy was master of the sea. Napoleon argued that Britain's strength could be sapped by cutting her communications with India.

Even without this excuse it was inevitable that at some stage in their struggle Britain and France would clash over Egypt, 'the anteroom to the throne of Asia'.* When the clash did come, the British were victorious. The French evacuated Egypt in 1801, leaving a small British army in brief occupation to restore the authority of the Sultan. The Egyptian people, downtrodden though they were, never gave Napoleon a chance and less than six months after the landing in Egypt his civilising mission had collapsed in face of their enmity. His plans to conciliate their religious prejudices, to reorganise the administration and to teach them government, were all frustrated by their implacable opposition.

* Sir George Young, *Egypt*, 1927.

*Chapter 4*

# Rebirth

---

## I

**B**RIEF THOUGH THE incursion of Napoleon was it struck a spark that warmed the dying heart of Egypt. The persistent waste of population which had been the astonishing phenomenon in the fertile Nile valley over centuries was halted shortly afterwards, but the re-emergence of the Egyptian people was a more immediate symptom of revival. It began when they sustained resistance to the French in Cairo and much of the delta while the Mamelukes warred apart. Then the work of the 120 scholars whom Napoleon brought to Egypt and the excellent *Institut Français*, which he created for research and which ultimately did much to spread knowledge of Egypt abroad, gave Egyptians a glimpse of the science and skill of the outside world. In particular, his introduction of the Arabic printing press, which he had stolen from the Vatican, and his use of the printed propaganda sheet, taught the Egyptians how to communicate and this became a vital element in their national movement.

During their brief occupation the British restored the power of the Sultan, but the Mamelukes still fought among themselves and together fought the Turkish mercenaries. The Turks were themselves divided into factions: Kurd fought Albanian and Janissaries fought them both until the country was reduced to anarchy which the Turkish governor was powerless to end. The people of Cairo, who were tired alike of pasha and Mameluke, and almost regretted the departure of the French, had not forgotten their own rising against Napoleon's army in 1799 and required only strength and leadership to revolt. In 1805, Sheikh el-Sharkawy, Rector of the Moslem University of Al-Azhar, and Omar Makram, head of the religious nobility, rallied the sheikhs, the notables and the chiefs of the city guilds in as representative an Egyptian movement as was possible at that time and, turning to the factions in conflict, chose one of their chiefs as their leader. This was Mohammed Aly, commander of the Albanian forces nominally in the service of the Turkish Pasha.

The Rector and Omar Makram led a delegation to the Chief

Judge to present a list of grievances against the Governor and when he failed to reply promptly they brought the people of Cairo out on strike and organised demonstrations against the Turks. Their two leaders then went to the house of Mohammed Aly to declare the deposition of the Sultan and invested the Albanian with the fur, the mantle and the robe of office in his stead. The Albanians and the armed populace besieged the protesting Pasha in the Cairo Citadel until at last the Sultan withdrew him and appointed Mohammed Aly governor.

This date in May 1805 on which the Egyptians reasserted their rights marks the start of the modern Egyptian national movement. Although for decades afterwards their fate seemed little better than it had been under earlier conquerors whom they accepted as leaders against oppression, the initiative of Sheikh Sharkawy and Omar Makram was never entirely lost. Their immediate gain was only a national army, but that was important enough, for the army became an integral part of the national movement and an instrument of liberation acting within a self-contained nation, administratively separate from the Ottoman Empire.

The choice of Mohammed Aly as their instrument is one of the strangest episodes in the history of the country. He was born of humble parents in Kavalla in 1769, and served the Ottoman Empire first as a tax collector, in which capacity he did extremely well for his master and therefore, one presumes, extremely ill for the people. After trading for a time in tobacco, he returned to the imperial service as a soldier. He took part in the Sultan's military expedition to Syria against Napoleon and again in the Turkish landings at Aboukir. When he secured by intrigue the command of an Albanian contingent, which was the core of the Turkish forces in Egypt, he became a person to reckon with. He was as alien and unlettered as any army commander in that quarrelsome coterie. He spoke Turkish, disliked the Arabs and despised the Copts (whom he soon plundered to replenish his empty cash-box). At no time was he concerned with the emancipation of the Egyptian people, except in so far as it could serve his ambition. Egypt was important to him; he worked unceasingly to rebuild it from the ruin of centuries; but from first to last it was, for him, the weapon he would wield in his struggle for power.

He was, nevertheless, a great man by any standards and he gave no greater evidence of his genius than in 1803 when he recognised the importance of the Egyptians to his ambition and joined cause with them to end internal strife. His judgement was justified when they turned to him two years later. Until 1803 the only difference between him and the other factional leaders was that he became the most formidable, but in that year he supported the people's protest to the Pasha against the exactions of the Turkish soldiery and so brought the people crowding at his heels.

He proceeded to use his power with skill, deceit and ruthlessness, until in the end his own Albanians were brought to heel by an army of Egyptian peasants and the rule of the Mameluke beys was ended for ever. The British Government, clearly misunderstanding the situation, supported the Mamelukes, choosing as chief among their leaders one Elfi Bey, an extravagant character who had already greatly impressed London, but by the time a British expedition landed in Egypt in 1807 the Mamelukes had already been dispersed. Six years had made a great difference; instead of marching easily on Cairo, the British force was resoundingly defeated by Egypt's chosen leader, and the heads of the British dead were paraded on pikes in Cairo. Four years later Mohammed Aly completed his domestic campaign by a massacre of the Mamelukes at the citadel. He had accomplished a great deal of what the Egyptians desired of him; and if he became in the process a ruthless dictator, it was from the Egyptian point of view a welcome replacement of many masters by one.

Mohammed Aly's purpose was primarily to secure revenues for the State, and in order to do so he restored the power of the central Government and imposed its authority everywhere. He gave the country a constitution which was in essence a reinstatement of the traditional form of government by the ruler and his *diwan*, or consultative council, and he nationalised the means of production, distribution and exchange by taking titular possession of all lands, all taxes and all foreign trade, thus securing for himself about five-sixths of the agricultural income of Egypt. He reorganised taxation, eliminating the iniquitous system by which a village was held responsible as a community for the taxes of its members, and got rid of the tax-farmers who had squeezed as much as they could for themselves out of the peasants against a fixed sum for the Government. Under Mohammed Aly's system the *omdehs* collected the entire produce of the peasants, deducted from it the rents and taxes, sold the produce through the State organisation, and then paid the peasant his share of the proceeds. There was still much for the peasants to complain of. Taxes were, as usual, flogged out of them and were, if anything, slightly higher than before; but their lot undoubtedly improved. Agricultural wages increased fourfold whereas their cost of living rose very little, and there was order and security; no longer did predatory provincial overlords, grasping officials and marauding nomads and bandits strip them bare. They got a fair price for their crops, and in time the small farmer secured the right to sell the holding that Mohammed Aly leased to him, becoming to all intents and purposes a leasehold proprietor.

All sectors of the national economy improved by the establishment of law and order. The farmers and peasants, responding to better conditions or driven by the *coubash*, cleaned ditches and canals, so that the Nile again flowed over once-neglected fields. No less than 20,000 water-wheels – as many again as existed on the Nile – were installed, and an extra million acres of land were brought into cultivation. The growth of long-staple cotton was directly encouraged by Mohammed Aly and was destined to transform the whole economy of Egypt. He promoted foreign trade by introducing a bi-metal currency, establishing a stable rate of exchange and eliminating most of the difficulties which had handicapped commerce with infidels. External trade would have developed further but for the protection he gave to his new industries. He spent £12 million on national enterprises, which began the mechanisation of old crafts such as textiles and glass-making, and he introduced the manufacture of heavy products such as armaments and machine tools.

He was intent to make Egypt a modern state on the European model and then to take from the weakening hand of the Ottoman Sultan the hereditary authority of himself and his family in Egypt, and for this purpose a powerful army was essential. He tried first to use Sudanese, but of the 30,000 he brought in chains down the Nile only 3,000 survived and this compelled him to turn to his valuable Egyptian peasants. He used French instructors to weld them into an efficient fighting force and by 1826 possessed an army of 90,000 men with an artillery train equal to the best in Europe. Under his son Ibrahim, a brilliant field commander, this force fought the Sultan's battles in Arabia and Greece and extended the frontiers of Egypt south to Gondokoro. Mohammed Aly had by this time the strongest army in the empire and when the Sultan, with more fear of the viceroy than gratitude for his services, quarrelled with him, Ibrahim marched his fighting peasants almost to the gates of Constantinople, defeating the Sultan's troops three times on the way, and was only turned back from the capital by a warning from Russia. Mohammed Aly got the *firman* to rule Syria from this exploit, but when he demanded commercial independence of the Porte in 1838, Sultan Mahmoud sent against him the able German General von Moltke with the imperial army. Mohammed Aly, who had now a quarter of a million men under arms, had no difficulty

4—ME

in defeating it and when the Turkish navy defected to Alexandria the Ottoman throne itself seemed within his grasp.

Britain frowned on the curious evolution of Egypt into an empire reaching from the Red Sea to the Persian Gulf before it had become an independent country and occupied Aden as an outpost against Mohammed Aly in 1837. The demand for commercial independence of the Porte in the following year was in direct opposition to the Anglo-Turkish Treaty which gave Britain the right to trade in the Ottoman Empire against a tariff of not more than 3 per cent. This breached Mohammed Aly's protective tariffs system and threatened to destroy his struggling industries and was the main reason for his claim to independence. When von Moltke failed to impose the Sultan's will, the British Foreign Secretary, Lord Palmerston, embarked on an energetic diplomatic effort which culminated in the Treaty of London of 1841. This treaty imposed by Britain and the Powers defined the net political gain of Mohammed Aly by giving to him and to the eldest male of his line, under international guarantee, the right to govern Egypt and establishing within certain limits Egypt's administrative independence of the Porte. As the hereditary rights of his family had been the principal aim of Mohammed Aly's policy, the Treaty was good value to him; but it left Egypt juridically subservient to the Porte and, by imposing a limit of 18,000 men on the Egyptian army, made certain that Ibrahim's peasants would never again threaten it.

The strain imposed by Mohammed Aly's policy was, in any case, too great for Egypt. Half the revenues of the State were spent on the armed forces and the countryside from which the wealth of Egypt derived was again deteriorating as the army drew more and more peasants away from the farms. The home-loving Egyptians hated the army and hid, fled or mutilated themselves to avoid service, and the entire rural community, in time-honoured fashion, sullenly restricted production so much that Mohammed Aly was compelled to whip them to work on canals and ditches and his own estates. As he strove to keep funds flowing to his forces, he profiteered in his nationalised trading concerns and squeezed the peasants for more taxes. These were difficulties that Mohammed Aly was possibly too weary to face, for at the time of the London Treaty he was seventy-two. In 1847 he transferred power to his son Ibrahim as Regent.

The Treaty removed the pressure on the economy caused by the army and the forced pace of industrialisation and the return of the peasants increased available labour force and did much to restore the happiness of the countryside. Furthermore it brought Egypt into the 3 per cent tariff area of the Anglo-Turkish Treaty of

Commerce of 1838 and this improved Egypt's trade, which had been obstructed by the protective tariffs. The reconstruction and development of the port of Alexandria strengthened the country's commercial position by making it a much more efficient link in the route to India, reducing the time necessary for the Indian mail to a month, and 15,000 travellers began to cross Egypt by land every year.

Before Mohammed Aly died the foundation stone of a barrage was laid at the bifurcation of the Nile just south of Cairo. Although the original structure proved faulty the plan was itself historic. The control of the Nile had undergone little change since ancient Egyptian times when Mohammed Aly began his reign. He ended neglect of the river by cleaning and reopening the disused canals, and this was the source of the wealth he created. State revenues rose from less than £1 million to £3 million, and the population from less than 3 million to 4 million. The barrage was more than just a renewal of old ways in the Nile: it carried controls a stage further and was prophetic of future great works which would rise along its course in Egypt and the Sudan. In the encouragement of cotton cultivation Mohammed Aly also showed a visionary sense. Egypt never again turned back. The failure of most of his industrial experiments, the delay in pursuing systems of Nile control, bankruptcy, and the predatory claims of creditors, did not completely close the door on the techniques of the modern world.

Thus Mohammed Aly laid the foundations of modern Egypt but he did not fulfil the parallel ambitions of the Egyptian leaders who called him to power because he failed to emancipate the Egyptian people. He had recognised the strength and importance of the Egyptian revolt at the turn of the century when he used it for his own purposes, but he remained to the end an alien autocrat. Sheikh Sharkawy sought – to use the phrase of a century later - to 'Egyptianise' the country; to be rid of the heretic, the infidel and the foreigner. Mohammed Aly turned more and more to foreigners to train his army, build and manage his industries, and teach his young people the ways of the Western world. Far from restoring the country to its own way of life, Mohammed Aly disrupted it. The sons of sheikhs were taken out of Koranic schools and sent to the land of foreigners to learn the crafts of infidel people, while the Egyptian craftsmen were socially and economically undermined by the new industrial processes. Long before Mohammed Aly died the new Egypt was falling more and more into the hands of foreigners, and this was neither desired nor understood by the Egyptians. He ruled as the leader of a caste of Turks and associated aliens, using

Copt, Armenian, Jewish and Greek officials. Even progress in agriculture was in part due to the creation of a class of landowners, consisting of relatives, friends and followers to whom he gave large uncultivated tracts of land. In the reclamation of this land Egypt was certainly enriched, but the landowners were enriched and strengthened and became the 'Turkish' aristocracy. At the end of his reign, Egypt consisted of a rich, alien ruling class and a bureaucracy which was also largely alien, a substantial and growing population of foreign traders and technicians, and a subservient population of Egyptian farmers and peasants, labourers, craftsmen and petty traders.

The Treaty of London provided that appointments to the senior ranks of the army must be approved by the Sultan, which ensured that the army would for decades to come be officered by foreigners and so completed the defeat of the national movement. Thereafter the struggle of the Egyptian people was directed towards the elimination of the foreigners and it was logical – however incoherent the events themselves might appear – that its first revolt forty years later should try to secure the 'Egyptianisation' of the army; and that after another seventy years its revolution should come from Egyptian officers who revolted against the King, the court, the landed aristocracy and the foreigners – in short, against those dominant groups which owed their power in no small degree to Mohammed Aly.

He left the stage set for a new occupation of Egypt which was to take place gradually, much in the fashion of the conquest of the country by the Greeks two thousand years earlier, by commercial penetration culminating in military conquest. The Ottoman Empire had already prepared the way by the capitulatory privileges, granted to foreigners for the reasonable purpose of encouraging trade by protecting them in its Moslem territories against penalties imposed on non-believers, so that firms would trade with confidence. The rights granted were: freedom to live and do business in Egypt; religious freedom; exemption from taxes normally imposed on non-Moslems; protection from civil and military authorities, who were denied the right to enter foreign quarters; and freedom from Ottoman courts, which meant that foreigners were tried in their own consular courts. As long as the Turks were strong enough, these extensive privileges served their purpose without undue hardship to the Ottoman peoples, and in Egypt in particular they did little real harm while Mohammed Aly and Ibrahim ruled the country, but their successors were unable to prevent the abuse of capitulations from increasing the subjection of the country.

The Viceroy Ibrahim died in November 1848, a few months before

his father, and the succession went to the eldest of the line, his son
Abbas. This reactionary slave of tradition turned his back on the
foreign consuls and his face to the Caliph of Islam, Sultan of Turkey.
He swept away all the foreign advisers of Mohammed Aly and
Ibrahim, closed the secular schools and eliminated French influence
which his grandfather had fostered. Europe hated him. Said, who
succeeded him five years later and had been educated in France,
turned aside equally from the ways of Abbas and the economic
experiments of his grandfather. He abolished State monopolies,
exacted taxes in money instead of kind, and restored private property
in land. Neither of these contrasting policies were intended to
benefit the Egyptians.

Most Egyptians welcomed the campaign of Abbas against
foreigners, but it was conducted for his ends, and the Turkish landed
gentry were left to oppress and flog their peasants at will. The
common people rejoiced when he was murdered by his own bodyguard. The gargantuan, amusing and sophisticated Said was less
cruel but their lot was little improved and in some respects his
reign was more harmful to the country. Private ownership of land
established the power of the Turkish aristocracy more firmly
because they invested every penny spared from extravagant living
in the purchase of land and industrial development was halted.
Taxes in cash instead of in kind and the closure of State monopolies,
which had given farmers secure marketing, left the country a prey
to the Greek moneylenders and the foreign trader. The money-
lender travelled on the heels of the tax collector, saved the peasant
from the lash by lending him money for his taxes, and the trader
bought the crop at forced prices so that the peasant could repay
the moneylender.

Said's policies were hailed as a sensible modernisation of Egypt
by foreign traders who invested their money in the country,
developed its overseas trade, and flocked into the towns and cities
where they enjoyed the privileges of the capitulations. As they could
not be taxed the goods they imported killed the infant industrial
life of the country. Said's personal extravagance set an example to
his friend and successor Ismail, and his commitment to the Suez
Canal concession compelled him to take Egypt's first loan of
£3,300,000 at the ominous rate of 7 per cent. It was estimated that
the foreign debt was already £10,000,000 at his death. In his
creation of the debt and his encouragement of foreigners he established Egypt's two most enduring difficulties and, in proportion to
his opportunities, he did as much as Ismail to hasten the British
occupation.

Abbas gave the British the Cairo–Alexandria railway concession, which Mohammed Aly had resolutely opposed, and Said allowed British troops to use the overland route from Alexandria to Cairo on their way to the Indian mutiny; but there was no more disastrous and ill-timed act for Egypt than Said's concession to his friend Ferdinand de Lesseps for the Suez Canal. It granted for ninety-nine years a lease of valuable land and mineral rights and the right to use forced labour for four-fifths of the work. It provided for construction in six years, after which the tolls were to be fixed at ten francs a passenger or ton, and profits divided as to 75 per cent for the shareholders, 10 per cent for the promoters and 15 per cent for the Egyptian Government. A loan of 200 million francs was floated in 1858 and the remainder found equally by Turkey and Egypt, and work began the following year.

The concession was impossibly generous to the concessionaires. The Canal was a European requirement and Egypt, which could not hope to get enough profits from it to compensate for the loss of transit trade on the Alexandria–Cairo railway, stood to lose. Said negotiated on the basis of assumed but illusory benefits and in the face of opposition from Britain, the most important maritime power. Its construction should have waited until traffic, multiplied by the development of the steamship, justified the cost. Further, it was inevitable that Britain should seek to control a link so vital to the communications of her empire. The Canal, wrote George Young, 'changed for the worse the relations between the British Empire and Egypt by shifting the main objective of British policy in the Near East from Constantinople to Cairo. Thereafter it would have been difficult for Egypt, even with the most diplomatic of princes and the most democratic of governments, to prevent the British Empire from guarding so vital and vulnerable a line of communication by garrisoning at least the Isthmus'.* By his domestic policy, Said set the stage for Ismail; and by his Suez Canal concession he set the stage for the British occupation.

Said died four years after the start of the work, and the Canal was in difficulties instead of nearly finished. About 20,000 Egyptians were working under the lash under conditions so bad that thousands died of exposure and under-feeding and the project had become an international scandal. One of the first acts of Ismail was to agree with the Porte and the British Government that the onerous terms of the concession should be revoked. While prepared to meet the liabilities of Said in respect of shares in the Company, he demanded a complete revision of the concession, including the retrocession of

* Sir George Young, *Egypt*.

land and mineral rights and the abandonment of the system of forced labour.

The Suez Canal Company was at this time in danger of liquidation for lack of funds. M. de Lesseps, not averse to a little pressure in these matters, secured assurances from the Emperor Napoleon III (whose wife Eugenie happened to be de Lesseps' cousin) and thus fortified, the Company resisted the demands of Ismail and the Porte. Ismail, with a surprising display of ingenuousness, referred the matter for arbitration to Napoleon, who acceded to the Egyptian claims but assessed the indemnity to be paid to the Company for the rights it sacrificed at 84 million francs. This was just short of half the original capital of the Company; and Ismail was already committed to purchase half the shares. He secured immunity from any further claims by the Company by the payment of £3 million, in settlement of which the Company agreed to take the interest on the Khedive's shares until 1895. The Company was extricated from its financial difficulties because Ismail paid for the Canal.


## II

Ismail, the grandson of Mohammed Aly by the soldier Ibrahim, succeeded Said in 1863 and began to work at once for the removal of those limitations on his country's autonomy left by the Treaty of London. He had to buy from the Porte what the smallness of his army prevented him from taking by force, but in ten years he completed the work of his grandfather by securing self-government for Egypt. The Sultan granted him a *firman* in 1873 which gave him the hereditary right to rule Egypt and the Sudan according to the law of primogeniture, to enact all laws and decrees for internal government, to negotiate and contract commercial loans with foreign countries, and to enlarge his army and navy at will.

The damage done to the American cotton trade by the civil war of 1863 and the abolition of slavery gave an auspicious start to Ismail's reign by quadrupling the value of Egyptian cotton, but it produced a period of reckless extravagance which foreign investors encouraged. World money markets regarded Egypt as one of the most promising fields, for not only did it appear to offer a promising future but it gave investors, under their capitulatory rights, greater privileges than they could get at home. They imposed ruinous conditions: for a liability of £77 million the State received only £50 million and was burdened with the charges of the greater sum. When the cotton boom collapsed, the European bankers soon realised that Egypt could not bear the burden. As early as 1873 the

revenues of the railways and the royal domains had been pledged,
the funded debt was beyond the means of the country and the
floating debt had risen dangerously, and three years later, at the
end of all expedients for raising money, Ismail postponed payments
on the debts.

British officials advocated the repudiation of the debt and financial
reconstruction, but the French would not agree and the moment
passed when, in all equity, Europe might have saved Egypt from
ruin. A Commission of the Debt consisting of French, Austrian
and Italian representatives was formed to guard the interests of
foreign creditors, and the Khedive Ismail appointed Mr. Rivers
Wilson and M. de Blignières as Financial Controllers with a degree
of executive authority. Then, when the report of the Debt Commission and the Controllers blamed him for the financial situation,
he announced that he would become a constitutional ruler and
appointed Mr. Wilson Finance Minister and his French colleague
Minister of Public Works. By divesting himself of authority, Ismail
laid the responsibility for unpopular measures on the European
Ministers, and in an outbreak of anger army officers arrested them.
They were only released on the personal intervention of the Khedive,
who thereupon demanded the restoration of his full authority. This
was refused and his son Tewfik was made President of the Council.

In 1877 Ismail turned for support to the Egyptian people. The
European Ministers, he said, were going to hand over the country to
Europeans to the detriment of the Moslem faith, and when the
Ministers protested, he announced the formation of an all-Egyptian
Government with Sherif Pasha, leader of the liberal faction, as
Prime Minister. But it was too late. If the European creditors had
treated him badly, he had treated the people abominably. He was
a Turk surrounded by Turks, and he, too, had 'squeezed the udders
until they were dry' and finally left the country a prey to foreigners
who dominated with writs and bills. Britain and France called on
him to abdicate and when he appealed for 150,000 volunteers to
save the country from infidels, the sullen, discontented army and
people did not respond. The Sultan thereupon deposed him and
Ismail sailed into exile on 30 June 1879.

The Khedive looked on Egypt as a vast estate to be farmed and
developed for himself and his family, but if he had no compunction
in squeezing the last farthing from the peasants, he was prepared to
spend a great deal on development. The country therefore benefited
to a remarkable extent during the early part of his reign. As late as
1876, on the eve of the crash, Egypt was described by the Cairo
correspondent of *The Times* as a marvellous instance of progress.

Ismail transformed the centre of Cairo in time for the opening of the Suez Canal. Cairo and Alexandria were endowed with gas through a French company, and another French company brought fresh water to the capital. During his reign, 910 miles of railway were laid, 500 bridges built, 8,400 miles of canal dug and 5,000 miles of telegraph line laid. The privately owned postal service was reorganised as a public concern which secured Egypt's admission to the Universal Postal Union in 1874. The town of Suez was developed to meet the needs of the Canal, and Alexandria was endowed with a fine modern harbour in which two miles of breakwater enclosed many acres of still and deep water. The modernisation of the lighthouses both on the Mediterranean coast and the Red Sea made the Egyptian light service equal to that of any in Europe. He created a mercantile fleet with sixteen ships plying the Mediterranean and nine the Red Sea. In terms of stone, mortar and metal, Egypt leapt forward towards the modern world.

In keeping with his modern State, he revived and enlarged the educational system of his grandfather, Mohammed Aly, but Ismail's needs, which covered industry and almost every other aspect of the State's progress, were greater. He divorced education from the War Department, revived the Higher Educational Council and restarted the educational missions abroad. In 1878 there were 5,800 schools in Egypt, as compared with 185 in 1862.

Ismail sinned and was sinned against, and neither for him nor the people who exploited him can much be said in extenuation. Whatever estimate is made of his material contribution to Egypt, it is clear that he ensured the subjection of his country to Europe and eventually to Britain. From the moment that Ismail secured Egypt's administrative independence of the Porte and his dynastic rights in Egypt, his need was so to conduct himself that he eased rather than increased the bonds which bound him to the foreign population and their countries. Instead, he tied the knots tighter than ever, and when he abdicated new agencies of international control, which were to bedevil Egypt to great or little extent for more than half a century, were already established.

The capitulations, the Mixed Courts, the Suez Canal, the very burden of too many foreigners, had their genesis in history, and Ismail, at most, played only a part in encouraging some of their worst aspects. His financial mismanagement and his gross extravagance led to organs of financial control which made the country in some degree subject to most of the countries of Europe. Although the much-publicised personal extravagance of Ismail accounted for less than £15 million of the £100 million of debt he accumulated, and

some £16 million were due to financing the Suez Canal and £2
million more the result of suppressing slavery in the Sudan in
accordance with Europe's wishes, the fact remained that his spending
was persisted in beyond any reasonable limits and he ceased to be
master in his own house six years before his abdication. The Commission of the Debt, or 'the Caisse', charged with the task of
receiving revenue set aside for the service of the debt, acquired
immense powers over the financial management of the State, and
the right to sue the Egyptian Government before Mixed Courts in
which Europeans predominated. The Dual Control of Mr. Rivers
Wilson and M. de Blignières was imposed a few months after the
Caisse. Ismail, in short, put a bankrupt Egypt into receivership, and
his son Tewfik came in fetters to succeed him.

## III

The Sultan Abdul Hamid sought to take advantage of Ismail's
abdication by repealing the *firman* establishing the succession to the
throne, but the British and the French successfully defended the
rights of Tewfik and his relations. So far the two Powers were at
one with common opinion in the country, for there were few, other
than the most conservative elements in the dominant Turkish
minority and the senior army officers, who still supported the
Sultan. But this reassertion of the *status quo* regarding the khediviate
could not halt the increasing nationalist agitation.

The Dual Control was in a difficult position. On the one hand it
was afraid of, and opposed, the popular movement stemming from
Al-Azhar and the villages and represented by the Egyptian officers;
on the other, its programme for rehabilitating the country's agriculture compelled it to defend the rights of the *fellaheen*, and this
brought it into conflict with the economic interests of the Young
Turks. Nor could the authority of the Dual Control be disguised.
The Khedive, young and inexperienced, could not impose the
personal authority of the ruler and the Dual Control ruled Egypt.
This was in keeping with the policy of Britain and France. Britain
was already concerned with the protection of its communications in
the Canal and the French were actively building an empire in
North Africa. (They seized Tunisia in 1881.) British understanding
of the situation might have been clearer if Major Baring had not
been transferred to India in 1880. Sir Auckland Colvin, another
British official from India, who replaced him, recognised the
moderation of the Constitutionalists but was only concerned to keep
them out of alliance with the Egyptian officers in whose agitation

he could see the seeds of an Indian Mutiny. The Constitutional Nationalists, under Sherif, successfully opposed the reinstatement of European Ministers or the granting to them again of any executive powers in the State, but the Egyptian Government was not allowed to dismiss the foreign officials, so that the Europeans' advisory and consultative functions in the Cabinet were as decisive as ever.

The Constitutional Nationalists submitted a constitution to Tewfik but he rejected it and Sherif Pasha thereupon resigned. A new Ministry was formed under the pro-British Turk, Riaz Pasha, with the reactionary and hated Osman Rizky as Minister of War. It contained two Constitutionalists, one of them being Mahmoud Sami Bey. The Constitutionalists, who were intent on political action, were driven closer to the Egyptian officers. When on 20 May 1880 a petition for a redress of grievances regarding pay and promotion was presented by two colonels, Ahmed Bey Arabi and Abdul Aal, Sami Bey was almost certainly behind them. The French Agent supported the colonels' claims and the Khedive cautiously toyed with them through a peasant officer who had risen to be his A.D.C. But the two colonels were not simply concerned with their own grievances, and they went in person before the enraged Riaz Pasha to demand the dismissal of Osman Rizky. Tewfik summoned the Council of Ministers, who decided to arrest the colonels. This decision precipitated an army revolt.

Arabi and Abdul Aal went boldly to Kasr el-Nil Palace where they were, as they expected, arrested. A regiment of their peasants followed hard on their heels and, before the court-martial could decide whether to execute or expel the two colonels, marched off with them in high fettle. Osman Rizky resigned and Sami Bey, who was the bridge between the Constitutionalists and the colonels, was made Minister of War in his place. Arabi became a national hero overnight and the Constitutionalists used him to press for their policy. Even the Khedive Tewfik, whose docility hid a talent for intrigue, insured his future by some back-stage support.

The Nationalists were now powerful enough in the Chamber to demand full budgetary control, but the French Government refused to compromise, and the Powers sent a joint note stating that the Chamber could not vote on the budget without infringing decrees establishing the control. The Khedive was compelled by nationalist pressure to dismiss Sherif Pasha, who had resumed high office but was now too conservative, and appoint Sami Bey Prime Minister, with Colonel Arabi as Minister of War. Colvin reported to the British Government that the financial structure erected in Egypt was now at the mercy of Arabi. The atmosphere in London had by this time changed; any desire to compromise which had been manifest earlier had given way before pressure to intervene and a violent Press campaign against Arabi (who was accused of plotting massacres of British residents in Egypt). The Nationalist movement was being driven as much by the acts of the Khedive and the European Powers as by any plan of its own into an extreme position, and the dangers which at first existed only in the imagination of the foreigners began to be real, as the Sheikh el-Islam and fiery orators preached the *jihad* against the infidels.

On 20 May British and French warships arrived off Alexandria and the Consuls ordered the dismissal of the Ministry and the deportation of the two colonels. The Government promptly resigned and denounced Tewfik, who, being afraid of an uprising in Cairo and as little inclined as the Sultan to appear at the head of a crusade against the pan-Moslems of Egypt, reinstated the Government in response to petitions from the *ulema*, the notables and leading Christians. As a result of this abortive ultimatum from the Powers, Arabi's position advanced a further stage; he became in effect the ruler of Egypt and Tewfik was powerless to oppose him.

On 10 June fifty Christians, including a British naval officer, were killed and the British Consul injured in rioting at Alexandria. Although Arabi's regulars restored order, he was considered in England to have been responsible for the tragedy. He was, as a result, forced to concede something to the Christian Powers, and, as part of his peace pact with Tewfik, Mahmoud Sami relinquished his post to an anti-militarist.

The Powers were now anxious to put an end to the whole nationalist movement. Admiral Sir Beauchamp Seymour, in command of the British naval squadron, demanded that Colonel Arabi should stop building earthworks in Alexandria. This work, first begun in May, had been halted on the orders of the Sultan and then restarted by Arabi. He had also reinforced the Alexandria garrison, and furthermore called for a *levée en masse*. The British Government ordered Admiral Seymour to destroy the earthworks and silence Alexandria batteries if they opened fire. No work was taking place at the earthworks on 9 July when the Admiral informed the Consul that he would open fire within twenty-four hours unless all the forts were surrendered. The Powers and the Porte were also informed, but despite a request from the Porte for more time, fire was opened early on 11 July. By 5 p.m. the forts had been wrecked, and the Egyptian army then withdrew from the city, leaving it to the flames and to mobs, who murdered a number of Europeans. British Marines, who landed next day, restored order.

Tewfik took shelter in Ras el-Tin Palace in Alexandria under the protection of British guns and was joined there by the notables, including Sherif Pasha and the right wing of the Constitutionalists. The popular, or Egyptian, party was now clearly on its own, and this made it much easier for Britain to represent its action, as Gladstone did, as a crusade against anti-Christian anarchical forces. Under pressure from the Opposition he held firm to the policy of intervention, whereas the French Government withdrew from it, and ordered 5,000 men from India and 15,000 from England. The first attack by a small British force was repulsed at Kafr el-Dawar, outside Alexandria, where the Egyptians had strong positions, but Colonel Arabi was no general. Strong points planned at Kafr el-Dawar, and at Tel el-Kebir between the Suez Canal and Cairo, had not been built and he delayed blocking the Canal itself until too late. General Sir Garnet Wolseley landed his forces at Ismailia and in an engagement at Kassassin the Egyptians acquitted themselves well before withdrawing; but at Tel el-Kebir Wolseley's forces surprised them as they slept and although they fought with great courage and determination, 10,000 of them were left dead on the field.

The Egyptian movement was smashed at that battle, for the only strength it could muster against the entrenched power of the Khedive and the aristocracy was the army which had been destroyed. A small unit of British dragoons took the surrender of Arabi and Cairo at the same time. On 1 September the Khedive issued the laconic decree, 'The Army is dissolved'. Arabi was exiled,* a few Nationalists were executed and some were imprisoned.

The British had entered Egypt and were not to leave until seventy-two years later, when they came to terms with a new military movement that succeeded where Arabi failed. Never in those seven decades were the British able to come to terms with the forces rejected and then crushed in 1882.

## IV

The southern boundary of Egypt had throughout history taken in more or less of the Nile valley south of Wadi Halfa, but little remained in Egypt's possession when Mohammed Aly sent his sons down the river in search of recruits for his army and the gold of Sennar. Egyptian forces ranged as far as Dar Fazokl, on the upper

---

* Arabi was later allowed to return to Egypt with a pension of £1,000 a year, on which he lived pleasantly in Cairo, and could be seen, a placid and forgotten gentleman, driving around Cairo in his carriage at the fashionable hour.

reaches of the Blue Nile, conquered Darfur and Kordofan, reached Fashoda on the White Nile, and defeated the Abyssinians on their frontier. In 1841, after Mohammed Aly himself had visited the gold mines and a rebellion had been suppressed at Kassala, the Sudan was divided into seven provinces: Khartoum, Fazokl, Sennar, Kassala, Berber, Dongola and Kordofan.

The Khedive Ismail, in his turn, determined to enlarge his Sudanese empire and at the same time to show Europe that he was an enlightened man. He sent Sir Samuel Baker in charge of an Egyptian expedition to the Upper Nile, with the triple purpose of suppressing the slave trade, setting up trading posts, and establishing a line of garrisons to secure Egyptian authority over all the territories of the Nile basin south of Gondokoro. Sir Samuel was eventually made Governor-General of the Equatorial Province and was succeeded in that post by Charles James Gordon in 1874. After an Egyptian defeat on the frontiers of Abyssinia in 1876 General Gordon was appointed Governor of the Sudan, including Harar and the Equatorial Province, and held the post for four years. He had 40,000 Egyptian troops, with the main force at Khartoum and forty-eight posts scattered widely over the territory and deeply into the south.

Corrupt administration, the depredations of the troops and the slave trade, which decimated the population of the pagan south, had reduced the indigenous peoples to utter misery. The Mahdi, Mohammed Ahmed, welded together the northern peoples with the two elements common to them all: the Moslem religion and discontent, and when he was about thirty-three he decided to raise the flag of revolt against the hated 'Turk'. The motives of the people who flocked to his side were mixed. Whereas some were angered by the corrupt and oppressive behaviour of the Egyptian officials and soldiery, others took to arms for the less laudable purpose of stopping any further interference with the slave trade by people like Sir Samuel Baker and General Gordon. The man whose torn hide bore witness to the savagery of the Turk made common cause with people just as cruel.

Mohammed Ahmed condemned the sinful luxuries of the oppressors and called for the austere purity of the true faith. The first Egyptian expedition against his base on Abba Island in the White Nile on 12 August 1881 was destroyed almost to a man while the Mahdi's followers suffered very few casualties, and as this was clear evidence to his simple followers that God was on the side of his chosen one, more Arabs joined the cause. The Mahdi at this stage had the considerable advantage of being able to promise the faithful a sure entry into paradise if killed and a share of the booty if they survived, whereas the troops of the Egyptian Government could expect no booty from the scare-crow mob that the Mahdi had around him. Two more half-hearted Egyptian operations failed and then on 7 June 1882 a major force was annihilated. The Mahdi's 6,000 were strengthened by the capture of all their equipment and armament, and the substantial Dervish force now took the offensive. They captured Sennar and in January overran El-Obeid, the capital of Kordofan, after wiping out another force sent to relieve it.

Impoverished by the Khedive Ismail and the Arab revolt, Egypt lacked the funds to mount a campaign adequate to defeat the forces which had risen from the rock and sand of the Sudan, and by the time El-Obeid fell the British were in occupation of Egypt and obsessed by its financial problems. They declared their indifference to the Sudan's fate but the Egyptian Government fumblingly assembled at Khartoum under General Hicks an army intended to retake El-Obeid and destroy the Mahdi's movement. This force, formed in part of prisoners dragged from the gaols, consisted of 15,000 men and was, as Hicks gloomily implied in his despatches, doomed from the start. It struck westwards from the Nile towards the Kordofan capital and vanished for ever. Britain then gave orders to evacuate the Sudan, for it was obvious that she could not collect Europe's debts in Egypt and at the same time recover a million square miles of Africa.

General Gordon was sent to Khartoum to arrange for the evacuation of the remaining garrisons, a task which seemed hardly more possible than that of the ill-fated Hicks but less hazardous if not pursued beyond the limits of commonsense. He remitted taxes, released prisoners, reorganised the administration wherever there was administration to reorganise and, in an attempt to wean the fighting tribesmen of the slave traders from the Mahdi and perhaps mobilise them against him, undertook to leave slave trading alone. He then stayed firm in the passion and courage of his faith, pledging himself not to leave until everyone was brought down to safety or, at least, had had his chance. He was cut off. The British Government could not leave to his fate this man whose romantic courage swayed the emotions of the nation, and sent General Sir Garnet Wolseley at the head of a relieving force to the gates of Khartoum, which it reached in October 1884, only one day after Gordon had died at the hands of the Dervishes. There was now nothing to be done but evacuate. By June 1885 British and Egyptian troops had withdrawn to a line across the river at Wadi Halfa.

The Mahdi died in that year and his place was taken by Abdullah el-Taishi, his principal Khalifa, under whose abominable rule the Sudan descended into anarchy and was lost to the knowledge of the outside world. As the century drew to a close the great Powers became involved in a struggle for East Africa, and Britain, France and Italy established by agreement among themselves a series of protectorates which limited the territories of the Sudan to the south and on the Red Sea. General Kitchener, the Sirdar of Egypt, then built a railway southwards into the Province of Dongola, and using this and the river he moved the Egyptian troops under their British officers to the front. They inflicted their first defeat on the Khalifa's forces at Firkah in June of 1896 and pushed on to Hafir and Dongola. The railway crept forward into the Nubian Desert until it came within striking distance of the Dervish stronghold at Abu Hamed, which the river column, after a forced march through difficult country, stormed in August 1897. The railway was then hastily built to a point close to Berber, which the defeated Dervish army had evacuated in its retreat, and reinforcements, including British troops, were there retrained for the next phase. Two of the Khalifa's Emirs, Mahmoud and the redoubtable Osman Digna, coming north to retake Berber, entrenched their 19,000 men in a stockade at the confluence of the Nile and the Atbara rivers, and there they were punished by artillery fire and stormed by the 13,000 men of Kitchener's army. Two-thirds of the Dervishes were killed for the loss of only 500 men of the Anglo-Egyptian force. This broke the strength of the Khalifa for offensive action and he therefore massed his remaining 40,000 troops outside his capital at Omdurman. The Sirdar, with an army reinforced by some of the best British troops to a total of 53,000 men, moved steadily upon them and launched his attack on 2 September 1898. The Dervishes were routed, leaving 11,000 dead and 16,000 wounded on the battlefield. The British lost fourteen officers and 122 men and the Egyptians nine officers and 241 men – less than were lost at the battle of Atbara. Colonel Wingate later overtook and killed the Khalifa and most of his Emirs. Osman Digna surrendered in 1900.

The British and Egyptian flags were hoisted over Khartoum as soon as the Anglo-Egyptian forces entered it on the night of the battle of Omdurman. This plainly showed that the Sudan was not restored to its former condition as an Egyptian possession, and when Lord Cromer visited Khartoum in January 1899 he told an assembly of the sheikhs that in future they would be governed by the Queen of England and the Khedive of Egypt. He gave effect to this principle in a condominium agreement which was signed that same month by the Egyptian Foreign Minister, and which remained the basic document governing the Sudan's status until 1953. It laid down that Sovereign rights were to be exercised by the Monarch of Britain and the Khedive of Egypt, in order to give effect to the rights accruing to Britain by conquest, and provided that supreme military and civil command should be vested in a Governor-General appointed by Khedivial decree on the recommendation of the British Government. It did not refer to Turkish suzerainty but clearly dispensed with it and so abolished from the Sudan all the privileges enjoyed by the Powers in Egypt; indeed it laid down that no foreign Consuls could reside in the Sudan without the consent of the British Government. Egypt bowed before the facts unwillingly but, in truth, the prospect of the Sudan was too dreary to inspire immediate ambition. It was a wasted land; the population which was estimated at 8,000,000 before the Mahdi rebellion had fallen to about 2,000,000 as a result of war, tribal strife, famine and disease.

If the Condominium ingeniously preserved the Egyptian connection and a share in the sovereignty, it also preserved Egypt's responsibility for the deficits on the Sudan budget. While British administrators and troops pacified the region and built a new country on the debris of the old they charged it to Egypt from which Sudan was administratively separated, and when the railway from Khartoum to Port Sudan, on the Red Sea, was opened in 1906, it also acquired economic independence.

## V

Lord Cromer, who returned to Egypt as Consul-General, ruled for a quarter of a century and managed the anomalies of his own position and foreign interference in the financial affairs of the country with consummate skill. His first task for many years was to provide for the debt and to balance the budget, and in devoting funds to rebuilding the country, he contributed caution and good husbandry rather than innovation. He spent his surpluses where they could most easily make money: on agriculture, railways and public works generally. He neglected those services which were a straight charge on the Exchequer and which offered no immediate return and those industrial experiments which were a risk to the economy. Egypt was made solvent and then prosperous; but the Egyptian people complained that the neglect of industry went further than the national interest justified.

The three phases of Egypt's recovery were outlined by Lord

Cromer in his report for 1898. The first extended from 1883 to 1887, when the whole effort of the Government was directed to the maintenance of financial equilibrium. The danger of insolvency was over in 1887, and the reforms and developments, notably in agriculture, were creating surpluses. 'It was then decided', wrote Lord Cromer, 'that fiscal relief should take precedence over additional expenditure. The corvée, which was, in reality, a very heavy and objectionable tax, was therefore abolished at a cost of £400,000 a year. The land tax was reduced by £430,000. . . . In all, a reduction of direct taxation to the extent of £1·1 million was accorded. In addition, a number of indirect taxes were substantially reduced.' The period of fiscal relief came to an end in 1894, after which money was devoted to remunerative objects such as drainage, railways, hospitals and, to some extent, to education; but constructive spending was limited again by a decision to launch a campaign for the recovery of the Sudan from the Dervishes.

The annual value of Egyptian imports increased between 1881 and 1897 by £2·6 million a year. The cotton crop increased in the same period from 3 million to 5 million cantars, but a steady decline in the price of cotton – and of sugar – prevented an increase in the value of exports. The stage was nevertheless set for a boom period at the turn of the century, when Egypt, which twenty years earlier had been foundering in a sea of debt, was prosperous and Europe and America were suffering an economic depression. The Ministry of Public Works could not develop the port of Alexandria fast enough to keep pace with the growth of trade. This prosperity came from the Nile and the soil. British engineers from India scientifically remodelled the irrigation system after 1882 in a manner which steadily expanded production.

Lord Cromer's last year in Egypt was darkened by the ugly shadow of Denshawi. In June 1906 some British officers were shooting pigeons in the village at the invitation of the local sheikh when they were surrounded by the inhabitants and disarmed, and in the struggle a village woman and several men were wounded. The angry crowd mauled the officers, who fled back to their unit to give the alarm. British soldiers returning to the village found one officer, Captain Bull, dead in the track from head wounds and sunstroke, and clubbed to death a villager who was beside the body. This miserable tragedy, the outcome of accident and anger, provoked a state of panic among the foreign communities of Egypt and their newspapers and the Press of Britain unleashed a violent campaign calling for exemplary punishment of the guilty villagers. Of the fifty-two arrested, four were executed, three were given fifty lashes each, and others were sentenced to long terms of imprisonment with hard labour.

To the British officials and most other foreigners, who refused to believe there was a real disaffection among the peasants of Egypt, the trouble seemed due to an outbreak of fanaticism which demanded repression. The severity of the verdicts and the ultimatum to the Turkish Sultan which followed it were therefore considered a demonstration of proper firmness against Islamic excesses. What would have happened if Lord Cromer had not been away in England on holiday at the time it is impossible to say, but as he acquiesced in the sentences when he knew of them he was blamed by the Egyptians for their viciousness. A quarter of a century of rule, wise by most standards of judgement then available, beneficent in its intention and its material results, and patient in face of doubts and difficulties created alike by the penury of the State, the interference of outside powers and the unsure hand of the British Government, was forgotten. For the remaining year of his service in Egypt, Lord Cromer moved under the protection of British bayonets through silent, angry streets. Denshawi, the scene of a tragic accident and a revengeful punishment, has never been forgotten in Egypt.

There was no policy open to Lord Cromer that could have made Britain popular in Egypt. Material well-being, which he had done so much to provide, although it is a subject for criticising a foreign ruler who fails to provide it, will not for ever win hearts in an occupied country. Britain had no intention of handing the country back to its people, which was their greatest desire; Lord Cromer himself was soon convinced that early evacuation, whatever the promises given, was impossible. He secured co-operation from some moderate political elements which derived in the main from the old Constitutional Nationalists, but they were no longer leaders of opinion. On the one hand, their retreat from the Arabi movement at its climax had earned them the reputation of collaborators; on the other, their ideas of constitutional advance under the British had made no progress. For, as time passed, the cadre of British officials settled down into an established service offering permanent employment and pension rights in which there was less interest than ever in training Egyptians to run their own country; instead there was an increasing tendency to fill the higher ranks of the service with British officials.

Even the fiction of Khedivial authority was dispensed with by Lord Cromer when Tewfik was succeeded in 1892 by his eighteen-year-old son, Abbas Hilmi, who had been educated in Vienna and had acquired at the court of the Hapsburgs the manners of an autocratic prince. His relations with Lord Cromer began well, largely because Britain had resisted an alteration of the *firman* governing the succession which would have deprived him of his Khedivial throne, but he belonged at heart to the generation of Young Turks and had contact with their movement. 'The Khedive is going to be very Egyptian,' wrote Lord Cromer to the Foreign Office, and, in the sense that Abbas Hilmi wanted to rule his Egypt in the manner of his grandfather, Lord Cromer was right. He protested against the lack of respect shown him and then dismissed the Prime Minister and several other Ministers. Lord Cromer forced him to take them back and when he insulted the British army, he compelled him to publish a humiliating recantation in the *Official Gazette*. Lord Cromer thereafter paid him scant attention; he was left frustrated and embittered in back-stage conspiracies with the Pan-Islamic Movement, the nationalists and the Sultan of Turkey.

Lord Cromer claimed at the end of his career in Egypt that he had always been a friend of the peasants. There was justice in the claim, for the peasants were spared the whip and the burden of forced labour, gained by the good order of the countryside and by the water they were given, and they shared in the general prosperity which came to agriculture. But there could be little alleviation of overwhelming poverty. 'More than anything else, Egypt is a land of contrasts,' remarked M. de Guerville. 'Here a palace where reigns unbridled luxury, there a hovel swarming with people scarcely human.'* Egypt would doubtless have been immeasurably worse off under its own rulers who had not at that time, and could not have acquired in the short space of twenty years, the capacity or moral fibre to govern well; but the fact remained that under the relatively beneficent rule of the British the social divisions of Egypt were widened and the country was left in the hands of foreigners and their indigenous satellites.

The British were punctilious in preserving the *status quo* in every-thing, even in their tolerance of domestic slavery, conforming to the orthodox concepts and customs of the country to a degree greater than many Egyptians desired. On the one hand, they imposed an administration whose methods and standards were unnatural to the people; on the other, they avoided conflict with Islam and made it difficult for the Moslem Egyptian to modernise and reform the social practices. They gave little opportunity to the Egyptians them-

* A. B. de Guerville, *New Egypt*.

selves; they ruled through the Turkish and Armenian Pasha, the Turkish and Levantine Bey, and the Christian bureaucracy associated with them. Commerce, industry and banking were also in foreign hands. M. de Guerville described the upper class of Alexandria as consisting of Egyptians, Greeks, Levantines, Italians, French, English and Germans, and in this context the Egyptians were of Turkish origin.

The Egyptian people further complained that the neglect of industry went further than financial stringency justified and that education was deliberately neglected to keep them subservient to the British. Lord Cromer's report for 1902 shows that for the whole period from 1882 to 1901 only £2,000,000, or 1½ per cent of the total State expenditure, was spent on education and health. In 1890, when the financial pressure was greatly eased, only £81,000 was spent on education, and even in 1906, at the end of Lord Cromer's rule, it was represented as a new forward policy in education when £374,000 was set aside for it.

The prosperity that Lord Cromer brought to Egypt encouraged the maintenance of British rule and a resistance to the national movement. The foreign superstructure of Egyptian society was strengthened, and it resisted stubbornly any changes which might affect its privilege and new wealth. International controls still existed; financial stability had eased relations with the Commission of the Debt, but the British, however much they condemned capitulatory privileges, had been unable to remove them. Bondholders and traders, and in time the Powers, became content with British control. Eventually, in 1904 when the French Government were facing troubles in north-west Africa and wanted a free hand in Morocco, they agreed not to obstruct Britain in Egypt by asking for a time limit to the occupation. The governments of Germany, Austria and Italy agreed. It was recognised that Britain intended to stay in Egypt indefinitely.

As old age approached, the habit of rule engendered in Lord Cromer an autocratic temper. His benevolence towards the Egyptians was corroded by the hardening conviction of the fitness of his rule and the limitations of the Egyptian mind and character. He saw no bridges to build, emotional or otherwise. Egypt had providentially acquired the blessings of British rule and in the slow slip of time might learn to govern itself. It was his impression that Lord Dufferin, on whose proposals the liberal Egyptian had based his hope of eventual emancipation, 'had no very great confidence in the results of the experiment he had initiated'. As Lord Cromer believed that Britain's mission in Egypt could not be ended in the foreseeable future and had come to the conclusion that there never had been much hope that Egyptians could be trained to govern themselves, he saw no reason to conduct policies which assumed a change. On the one hand he pushed Abbas Hilmi to one side, thus depriving himself of the authority that the Khedive might have exerted, under his advice, for the country's good; on the other, he treated with contempt the entire national movement. Thus 'Cromerism' had spent itself long before its creator retired from Egypt. Whatever gratitude had been felt for material progress and orderly administration had disappeared before the turn of the century; the attempt to run Egypt by British officials to the exclusion of Egyptians was a failure; and after twenty-five years of British rule Egypt was less fit to govern itself than at the start.

The valedictory address of Lord Cromer at the Khedivial Opera House on 4 May 1907 revealed his complete satisfaction with the policy he had pursued but, more important, it broadly reflected the British Government's attitude. 'Whatever influence I can exert will be exercised in the direction of steady progress on the lines already laid down,' he said. 'I shall deprecate any brisk change and any violent new departure. More especially, should it be necessary, I shall urge that this wholly spurious and manufactured movement in favour of a rapid development of parliamentary institutions should be treated for what it is worth; and, gentlemen, let me add that it is worth very little.' He expressed the continuing belief that the *fellaheen* were content with British rule: 'I who claim to have always been their true friend', he said, 'warn them against allowing themselves to be duped and misled by their pseudo-representatives, who, without a shadow of real authority, credit them with ideas which they neither entertain nor fully comprehend. . .'. Finally, and despite the fact that Lord Cromer recognised that the Arabi rebellion had been against the Turkish aristocracy, he failed to see that the Egyptian movement was directed against all foreigners. All those interested in the introduction of true civilisation into Egypt should hold together, he advised; and he added, 'I do not mean merely that the Englishman, the Frenchman, the German and other Europeans should lay aside their petty rivalries and combine together in a common interest, but also that all who are in favour of rational government and of steady progress – be they Moslem or Christian, European, African or Asiatic – should unite in resisting those forces which are in reality, whether from ignorance or intention, advocating the course of retrogression'. In other words,

Egyptians should co-operate with all foreign elements to secure that kind of progress Europe considered right for Egypt, and against those forces which, in ignorance or wisdom, constituted their national movement. The ingratitude of which the Egyptians have since been so often accused consists in their inability, by the very nature of their history and condition, to take the advice.

## Chapter 5

# The National Movement in Action

## I

WHEN LORD CROMER left Egypt, Egyptian nationalism had strength and influence which it was never entirely to lose again. The movement which in 1805 had taken the form of a revolt of the notables against the Pasha of the Porte and which survived in antagonism to the powerful foreign elements in the State, underwent a significant change in the reign of the Khedive Ismail, when it reached down to the common people and turned against the Turkish ruling class.

This change was largely the work of Jemal el-din al-Afghani, an Islamic preacher who came to Cairo from Constantinople, whence he had been exiled for his opinions. He inspired Islamic nationalism by teaching that all progress could be reconciled with and was revealed in Islam, which should be united under a Caliph whose nationality was unimportant as long as he could rule and defend his territories. He had great influence everywhere in the Moslem world and particularly in Egypt, where his powerful personality played on the pupils and teachers of Al-Azhar, who went out to the towns and villages of Egypt spreading his message of an Islamic revival. The simple people of the Nile valley identified Islam as 'of them', that is, not of the Copts, of the Greeks, the Circassians or the other Christian foreigners, who were allied as friends or servants to the oppressive ruling class.

His message had direct impact on the army, where subservience of the Egyptian was most obvious; the *fellaheen* provided the rank and file and a large number of the regimental officers, but the higher ranks were drawn from the Turks, Circassians and Albanians, and the language used in the service was Turkish. The lower ranks, therefore, expressed the feelings of the villages and united those feelings in action. Just as industrial areas pool the discontent of workers, so in the socially backward conditions of Egypt the army of peasants with its native officers gave Egyptian national sentiment its chance of self-expression.

Colonel Arabi recognised that the Egyptian regiments alone

possessed the power to demand the removal of their grievances. He was neither a pettifogging mutineer nor, as the British Press came to represent him, a fanatic out to slit the throat of the foreign infidel. His protest, reflecting the feelings if not always the articulate ideas of the Egyptian people, was directed against the Turkish pashas who occupied every civil, social and military position of importance and were ruining the country by their corruption and despotism. He was, naturally, opposed also to domination by foreigners; but this opposition came second to the revolt against the ruling caste, and for that reason the European states might have been able to find a new relationship with Egypt through the Arabi movement. When they broke with it they broke with Egypt; and for Britain this spelled decades of struggle against the national movement.

Ahmed Bey Arabi, the son of a village sheikh, had been educated at Al-Azhar and had at one time been A.D.C. to the Viceroy Said. Even Sir Auckland Colvin, not the most sympathetic of observers, said he was a man who 'spoke with great moderation, calmness and caution, is sincere and resolute, but not a practical man'. He is described as a big, simple and slow man and he was impressive as a speaker in the manner of the religious teachers who so pleased the unsophisticated mass of Egyptians.

He was the first of his type in the history of modern Egypt to raise his voice against authority, and because he set an example his short-comings and failure were and are forgiven by nationalists. Ever after, any man who came from the peasantry – like the great Zaghloul later – could rely on the support of towns and villages of Egypt. With the emergence of Arabi the Egyptian people became, for the first time, in halting fashion, articulate.

The Turkish ruling class consisted of families who had been settled in Egypt for centuries and of yet more families who had come to Egypt during the nineteenth century, but they were people of several races drawn from all parts of the Ottoman Empire: Kurds, Levantines and Circassians, Turks of mixed descent from north-west Africa and the Mediterranean islands, and the true Turk of Constantinople. They identified themselves with Egypt but not with the Egyptians, whom they tended to despise and from whom they kept themselves apart, using the Turkish language and leaning towards the European in their social behaviour. They sent their sons to Europe to be educated, paid lip-service to European customs and ideas, and were proud of their ability to speak French. They had become, in the main, morally degenerate through self-indulgence and corruption, and their power bore no relation to their will or capacity to serve the country of their adoption. 'The curse was,' wrote Lord Milner, 'that the men who had the power to govern were devoid of the morality which was essential to governing well; for centuries the idea of power has been dissociated from the performance of duty.'*

The lower ranks of the bureaucracy and in commerce consisted to a large extent of foreign groups, mainly Syrians, Armenians and Jews, who had lived in Egypt for generations but held any nationality except Egyptian in order to benefit from the capitulatory privileges; and because they were born and bred in the country, they were regarded by Europeans as a specially useful kind of native. The Copts, being Christian and established for centuries as the clerical class of the country, tended to associate with the Turks and foreigners in the towns, although in the countryside, and particularly in Upper Egypt, village life drew them close to the Moslems in the common need for Nile water, the sharing of labour in the fields, and the social occasions which now and then enlivened their existence.

Moslem Egyptians were farmers, peasants, craftsmen and the hewers of wood and drawers of water in town and country, and their aristocracy consisted of sheikhs who lived in their villages off the proceeds of their land. By custom and inclination they kept apart from the Turkish ruling class and its bureaucracy; and from an inherited fear of authority they were inclined to servility towards the meanest functionary in tarbush and frock-coat. Most of them were educated in the mosque school and knew no language except Arabic, but they were not otherwise inferior to their rulers or to the educated effendi of the government offices. Lord Milner considered them, on the contrary, as vastly superior to the class above them. They were avaricious and narrow-minded, in peasant fashion, but they also had dignity and were endowed with shrewdness, energy and commonsense, qualities which they used with some success in the limited field of provincial and village government. Below the sheikhs, and often allied to them by family ties until whole groups of villages were like clans, were the peasants and small farmers, a docile mass of hard-working men, women and children who, with great fortitude of spirit, had preserved through centuries of suffering an innate cheerfulness. They were usually very poor, but they were cushioned against the worst blows of fate by the benevolence of the sheikhs or, when that was lacking, the corporate self-help of the villagers themselves. They were devout in a superstitious way rather than fanatical, but their gusty, short-lived passions could easily be excited. Seventy per cent of the entire population lived on the land;

* Lord Milner, *England in Egypt*.

and the Egyptians in the cities and towns were peasants just one step removed from it and with family roots still firmly set in the Nile mud. They were certainly closer to the country people than to the motley urban assembly whose life they shared.

The peasants and small farmers – those people from whom the Arabi movement received its support – were at first well pleased with British rule, for they were weary of disorder and content with good management which ensured them justice and sufficient Nile water for their land. They had many benefits, such as the replacement of the *corvée* by paid labour and the pittance that came to them in wages for public works. But material benefits do not forever satisfy a people ruled, if only because the younger generation does not know the evils of the past and the older soon forgets them. The Egyptians – and when they thought of themselves they did not include Turkish pashas or Syrian, Armenian and Jewish underlings – began again to want control of their own country. They were swayed in part by al-Afghani's Islamic revival, which protested against the rule of the infidel, and in part influenced by the very benefits that British administration brought to them.

Towards the end of the nineteenth century those Egyptians who could afford to do so began to send their sons to school. The first effect was to alienate the educated from their parents and their villages as they sought to make their lives in Cairo or some other big town, but they soon saw the privileged position of foreigners and were fired by patriotism and plain envy to a fervent and often ill-balanced resentment. They resented above all the barriers which stood between them and employment or advance in the government service, almost the only career open to the half-educated Egyptian. It was no consolation that Jew and Christian, Levantine and Armenian, were more efficient; all he saw was that government service was almost closed to him. At the top were the British and some other Europeans, next to them were the families of the Turkish landowners, who had been brought up in the belief that they had a pre-emptive right to preferment, and in the lower echelons were the Copts, the Levantines, the Jews and the poor Armenians. The Copts, most numerous of the clerical class, were, it is true, Egyptian; but as a non-Moslem minority they had lived so long in the protecting shadow of foreign rulers that they were identified with them.

The Turkish aristocracy had their own particular form of opposition to foreign domination. All the groups welded by Mohammed Aly into a homogeneous and rich landowning class identified themselves with Egypt; it was, in their opinion, their Egypt. By the time

Ismail had brought the country to bankruptcy the younger generation of Turks had begun to develop their own concept of nationalism.
Born to the conviction of their right to rule and having acquired at
school in Europe some rudimentary political ideas, they expected
that constitutional development under the British would re-establish
the dominant position of their class. When they saw that the British
Consul-General and his administrators had no intention of trans-
ferring power the Young Turks agitated for self-government and
constitutional reform.

Because they were able to use European liberal ideas more readily
than the native Egyptian they were able to formulate national
demands and to canalise much of the resentment of the Moslem
Egyptian into their movement, with the result that the Egyptian
national movement revived in alliance with these younger Turks.
This contact between two sections of national revival drawn from
different sources was one means by which Western thought was
injected into Middle Eastern nationalism, but the contact was
superficial in Egypt. No real integration could take place between
the Young Turks who were the progressive wing of the ruling class,
whose social privileges they were out to strengthen, and the non-
Turks who were concerned to secure changes that would
'Egyptianise' the State at the expense of the Turks.

The underlying conflict between the Young Turks and the
Egyptian nationalists was evident in the alliance they made during
the early years of the British occupation. The Constitutional
Nationalist Party, under Sherif Pasha, argued for a constitution,
opposed the reinstatement of European Ministers, and demanded
control of the budget by the Chamber of Deputies, all of which was
clearly in conflict with the European intention to control the
government in order to recover the debts, but the constitutionalists'
true aim was to re-establish their control over the State and to this
end they were willing to compromise with the British if they could
get enough independence for their purpose. This was the converse
of Arabi's aim, and as his movement gained strength in the country
and the Khedive Tewfik was unable to control it, the gulf between
Arabi and Sherif Pasha widened. The main demand of Arabi was
the removal of non-Egyptian officers in the army, but that would
have destroyed the power of the Turks, including the liberal Young
Turks. All the other trappings of the Arabi policy were prepared by
Sami Bey, a constitutionalist who tried to turn the result to his
purpose but failed. In the last resort the constitutionalists turned to
the British and when the revolt broke into open rebellion, Sherif
Pasha and his party took shelter with the Khedive Tewfik in Ras

el-Tin Palace in Alexandria under the protection of British guns. The native Egyptian rebellion was then clearly aligned against the Turkish ruling class as well as the British and other foreign elements.

It was a significant development for the future of the national struggle although with the defeat of the Arabi revolt the native movement was for a time destroyed as an effective force and the ruling class again led resistance against the British. With the accession of Abbas Hilmi, after the death of the Khedive Tewfik, this national force believed it had found a powerful leader. It rallied strongly to his support when he dismissed the European Ministers from his Government, regarding in this case Lord Cromer's insult to his dignity as an insult to Egypt, but when he recanted his insult to the British army the nationalists realised that he would not risk his position and lost all hope that he would lead the struggle for liberation.

The nationalist leaders, for the most part lawyers and journalists who had been educated abroad or in the foreign schools of Egypt, were themselves incapable of successful rebellion, for they had no contact with the Egyptian army which alone could have made revolt possible. Their weapon was the spoken and written word, and in respecting their freedom of speech Lord Cromer showed a fine contempt for it. Their propaganda, inaccurate and untruthful and often scurrilous, consisted principally of attacks on the British and a demand for their evacuation and was devoid of practical plans for the government of the country or the social advancement of the people.

The movement was led at this time by Mustapha Kamal, who was born in 1874, and although he died when he was thirty-four, he ranks in Egypt as one of the great nationalists and is commemorated by a statue in one of the main squares of Central Cairo. He was educated in France, where he acquired the charm and fine manners of the Paris salons and was petted by Anglophobe deputies such as M. Deloncle and writers such as Madame Adam and Pierre Loti. French bitterness against Britain in Egypt was still acute in the late 'nineties, and the charming, witty young nationalist from Cairo found a ready audience for his anti-British sentiments. He was at times a friend of the Khedive, who made him a Bey, and of the Sultan Abdul Hamid, who made him a Pasha, but his reputation rests principally on his eloquence as a writer and speaker, and as the founder of the National Party. Even his sternest critics among the foreign population were prepared to admit that he had the magnetism of a born leader of men, and there were many who thought

Lord Cromer was wrong to treat him with such neglect that he had no part to play in the country's development.

Mustapha Kamal demanded a constitutional government, independence, more education and a literary revival, but apart from one reference in his writings to industrialisation, he showed no interest in economic questions. He has been described as 'not only conservative, but reactionary'.* His movement co-operated with the *ulema*, the most traditional and conservative group in society, and worked as far as possible with the Khedive and the French against the British. Even so, largely through his newspaper *Al-Lewa*, which he published in both English and French, he became the most powerful influence among the literate Egyptians, and through *Al-Lewa* he raised enough money to start a number of independent national schools which became hot-beds of schoolboy extremism. He represented the educated 'Young Turk' element in the national movement and was far removed from the spirit of the Arabi revolt, but his influence reached out to the native Egyptian and his National Party revived a truly Egyptian movement.

## II

As far as the Egyptians were concerned, once Lord Cromer had saved their country in the material sense there was nothing more he could do for them except to restore the country progressively to them and get out. The difference between the aspirations of the moderate reformers and the extreme nationalists was in the manner in which they were prepared to achieve them. The moderates accepted the backwardness of the country as a fact and therefore stressed immediate needs, such as free education, more Arabic language classes, the rapid replacement of foreigners by Egyptians in the government service and the application of the Mixed Courts' jurisdiction to criminal cases. There were also those who were moderate because they believed that only by conciliation could they persuade the British Government to make concessions and the privileged powers to permit them. Men like Mustapha Kamal, on the other hand, demanded all that the moderates asked for and exploited the refusal as reason to agitate against the British. The proposals for constitutional and social progress were advanced by moderates who assumed the continuation of British rule, but the real national demands were: firstly, the removal of the capitulatory privileges; second, the evacuation of the British; third, the possession of the Sudan; and, fourth, possession of the Suez Canal Company.

* C. C. Adams, *Islam and Modernism in Egypt*.

No British government was ready to concede anything but the first, and that – the removal of the capitulatory privileges – depended on the consent of Powers which were not prepared to give it.

Resistance to Britain extended in its different ways through all strata of society. The Denshawi incident showed clearly how strongly the peasants were in revolt. Lord Lloyd said a quarter of a century later that the result of this incident 'was to arouse at length the spirit of discontent among the *fellaheen* for which Mustapha Kamal and his fellow agitators had long been seeking in vain';* but, in fact, Denshawi was itself the result of unrest which had been growing in Egypt ever since 1895, the year in which special tribunals were established to try offences against the occupation troops. (The Denshawi villagers were sentenced by one of these tribunals.) In the towns the unrest expressed itself in virulent political agitation against the occupying power; in the countryside, where political concepts were hardly known, it was expressed in religious agitation against the infidel. Contemporary observers report that the security of foreigners and Christians was much less in the late period of Cromer's rule, despite British efficiency at the Ministry of Interior and the presence of British troops, than it had been in the time of the Khedive Ismail. The common belief that the Egyptian was still happy collecting his cotton and his cash under the British had little substance in fact, and the decree establishing the special tribunals was itself an indication to the contrary. The British army held manoeuvres and exercises to remind the Egyptian who was master in his house. There were riots in 1906, apart from Denshawi, and those in Alexandria were followed by a warning parade of British troops.

Islam itself was in a state of ferment at the end of the century and there were anti-Christian movements in Morocco and Macedonia. The Sultan of Turkey occupied part of Sinai and there was danger of war with Britain until he capitulated before an ultimatum and a demonstration by the British Fleet in Turkish waters. Mr. Edward Dicey, Cairo correspondent of the *Daily Telegraph*, estimated that 90 per cent of the people of Egypt would have risen for the Sultan if that war had broken out. Lord Cromer put the case the wrong way round when he said in his final report that the national movement was 'deeply tinged' with Pan-Islamic ideas, for 'Egyptianism' was revealed in the countryside through Islamic sentiment.

There is evidence in the appointment of Saad Zaghloul as Minister of Education in 1906 that Lord Cromer had come to believe that it

* Lord Lloyd, *Egypt after Cromer.*

was time to encourage the more reasonable nationalists; he commended Zaghloul as an intelligent patriot, and members of the foreign community hailed him as 'genuinely progressive' and a true patriot, and his appointment as Minister as one of the most opportune events of the year; but some years later Zaghloul donned the mantle of national leadership and became the most relentless opponent of the British in Egypt. As a true patriot – and whatever the foreign communities said about him later, he was certainly that – he rejected submissive collaboration, and as the British offered him only this, there was eventually no other course open to him than outright opposition.

Egypt's concern about the Sudan was understandable. Its very existence depended on the waters of the Nile which came to it from the Sudan, and no Egyptian could contemplate with equanimity a hostile power controlling the river from Khartoum. There was no guarantee that the British would always be friendly, whereas sovereignty over the Sudan would assure Egypt's economic future. The Condominium which Lord Cromer imposed put the ultimate status of the Sudan in doubt and thus fostered at once anxiety and nationalist agitation in Egypt, for it seemed to be a disguised form of British annexation, a view which was reinforced by the dominant role of the British in the Sudan, the imperialist mood of Britain at the end of the century, and the grandiose schemes mooted in London for a railway from the Cape to Cairo. When, in 1906, the railway from Khartoum to Port Sudan gave the Sudan an outlet for trade independent of Egypt, the opening date was described in the vernacular Press of Cairo as 'the day of Egypt's funeral'. Mustapha Kamal claimed sovereignty over the Sudan in the early years of the century, and ever afterwards the claim has held pride of place with the demand for British evacuation in the national aspirations.

### III

Sir Eldon Gorst, who succeeded Lord Cromer in 1907, fully agreed with Lord Cromer's view that any advance towards democracy must be taken slowly and cautiously, and as he had no admiration for the nationalists there was no fundamental alteration in British policy. The change under Sir Eldon Gorst lay in the tactical handling of the country. The new Consul-General was given the thankless task of ending the anxiety of foreign communities and the general insecurity in the country without conceding any of the essential demands of the Egyptians, for he took office at a time when no section of British opinion was prepared to conciliate the national-ists. His task was made more difficult by the fact that years of prosperity had given way to economic depression and that the administration was weakened by the departure of many experienced British officials after Lord Cromer retired.

Sir Eldon was a disappointment to the foreign communities. They desired a change from the policy of Lord Cromer in the direc-tion of more autocratic rule by Khedive and the upper-caste Turks; they did not want to see any weakening of authority in face of the national Press and the growing threat to security in the country. Instead, Sir Eldon seemed to be yielding to nationalist pressures. He established friendly relations with the Khedive in order to end his obstruction to British policies, not give him more power; but he allowed him greater freedom in the choice of Ministers and relaxed the tight rein in which the British advisers held them. He resuscitated the Legislative Council and arranged for the respected and dignified Hussein Pasha Kamel, son of the Khedive Ismail, to become its President; he cut back the British civil service in Egypt; and wherever possible he had the Syrian functionaries replaced by Copts.

Sir Eldon was not a weak man of liberal temper toying with the problem of Egypt. He sought to create a body of moderate opinion standing behind a co-operative Khedive and powerful enough to rule wisely in accordance with the broad intentions of British policy. He succeeded in breaking the homogeneity of the national move-ment by drawing the Copts away from it, with the result that the Coptic newspapers were consistently friendly to Britain during his service and the National Party was consequently weakened by the quarrel between Moslem and Coptic members. No less than five moderate parties came into existence, and although they all claimed the independence of Egypt and sovereignty over the Sudan, they mirrored the willingness of some educated people to seek their ends in co-operation with the British. When Mustapha Kamal died suddenly in 1908 the sapping effect of Gorst's policy became obvious. Once his powerful influence was removed from the movement the native Egyptian section – the hard core of nationalism – broke into bitter denunciation of all back-sliders in the cause and their war-cry became Egypt for the Egyptians. The young Turkish intellectuals, once again recognising that the movement was not seeking a con-stitution that would restore their power, then turned against the National Party and formed their Party of Nobles.

Sir Eldon Gorst's policy had only demonstrated that all might work together except the Moslem Egyptians, who turned in upon themselves and out against all others, including the collaborating Khedive and the Egyptian Christians. The result, however, was not what he expected. There arose a dangerous fanaticism which made a peaceful and progressive government impossible. The façade of unity built by Mustapha Kamal crumbled but nothing that the British could use was built in its place. Sir Eldon Gorst could not even point to any improvement in security as a result of his policy, for prison records for 1908 show an increase of 11,000 prisoners over the previous year, and foreigner and Copt regarded with alarm the decline of British authority.

After twenty-five years of British occupation the first Egyptian Prime Minister was appointed in November 1908; but he was a Copt, Boutros Pasha Ghali, the most able and prominent of all the Copts, whose loyal co-operation with the British had earned him the K.C.M.G. Moderate sections of opinion and the foreign Press welcomed his appointment because he was known as a man of intelligence and of firm and upright character, but he had antagonised the nationalists by signing the Condominium Agreement and presiding over the judges at the notorious Denshawi trial. He personified Coptic collaboration with the occupying power. His appointment, therefore, seemed deliberate provocation to the National Party and further embittered the relations between Egyptian Moslems and Copts.

The success at this time of the Young Turk revolution in Constantinople gave new heart to the national movement. Turkey was still nominally suzerain and the Egyptian believed that this was now the time for its Government, purged of the reactionary Sultan, to exert its rights in Egypt and demand the application of those reforms which it promised for Turkey. In the event the Young Turks of Constantinople scorned the Egyptian movement, but before their scorn became obvious their revolution threw into even greater relief the collaboration of men like Boutros Pasha. At this inopportune moment the British Government encouraged the Suez Canal Company to submit a draft convention, the main object of which was to extend the existing concession for forty years beyond its terminal date in 1968, in exchange for some minor financial benefits in the interim. The Government was prepared to accept this convention with only minor amendments, but this provoked a public outcry and new furies of agitation which culminated in the murder of Boutros Pasha on 20 February.

The appointment of Mohammed Pasha Said as Prime Minister in place of Boutros Pasha was received as a victory for the national movement, for he had been a follower of Mustapha Kamal and was reputed to have had many differences of opinion with Boutros Pasha while serving as a Minister in his Government. Said Pasha, who was by no means an extremist, seemed to give his support to the proposed Suez Canal Convention, but he announced that on this matter the Government would abide by the decision of the National Assembly. The assembly duly rejected the draft Convention and was thereupon criticised by the foreign communities for its lack of sense which, they said, showed how ill-fitted the country was for self-government, a view in which Sir Eldon Gorst concurred. The nationalists, undismayed by criticism and encouraged by the defeat inflicted on the Government and on the Khedive (who had advocated acceptance of the draft Convention), called with greater confidence than ever for a new constitution.

A contemporary account of the condition of Egypt in 1910 given by an English resident* described it as so 'exuberantly disorderly' in the capital and the provinces that the lives of European residents were in danger. He stated that there was public knowledge of the spread of sedition in the army, that disorganisation prevailed in the Ministry of the Interior, that arrangements were known to exist for a general massacre by an organisation known as the Society of Mutual Brotherhood, and that there were 'disgraceful outrages, assaults and thefts' which were condoned if not encouraged by public functionaries, who were known to be fomenting religious animosities. The responsibility for this state of affairs was firmly placed by opinion in England and foreigners in Egypt on Sir Eldon Gorst, who was accused of permitting so many concessions that British authority had collapsed.

Sir Eldon was already fatally stricken with cancer when the British Government decided on a policy of greater firmness and sent Lord Kitchener to replace him in 1911. (The Khedive went in sorrow to the bedside of the dying Gorst, who had for a few years given him the respect he had always wanted.) Once again the Consul-General went forth in splendour, a monarch without a throne, and many Egyptians, wearied of the ever-present threat of disorder, welcomed a firm hand on the country. He enforced a new Criminal Conspiracy Act, a Press Censorship Act, and a School Discipline Act with unflinching severity. When Italy declared war on Turkey, and Egypt should have gone to the aid of its suzerain in Tripolitania, Kitchener used every administrative expedient to prevent it. His hand fell with equal severity on the Khedive and the national movement, which was cowed.

* J. Alexander, *The Truth about Egypt.*

Nevertheless, Lord Kitchener soon realised that coercion was not the complete answer to the problem, and in 1913 he gave Egypt a new constitution with representative institutions as a step towards self-government. It allowed provincial and municipal councils effective powers of local government, the Legislative Council a more real say in the government of the country, and the General Assembly, which was consultative, the right to suspend and initiate legislation and to debate in public. It did not satisfy extreme national opinion but it won over that substantial section of moderates which had been drifting away from the British administration steadily since the beginning of the century. Saad Zaghloul was a typical example. He had continued to collaborate with the British and had spoken in favour of the draft Suez Canal Convention, but he had gone into open opposition when Lord Kitchener arrived. Under the new constitution he accepted the post of Vice-President of the Legislative Council.

The relations between Britain and Egypt were better in 1914 than they were at any time since the middle 'nineties of the previous century, and had Lord Kitchener been able to remain for some years to guide the Egyptian people towards responsible government and educate the British to accept it, rational evolution towards Anglo-Egyptian co-operation might have been possible. This would, however, have required the British Government to prepare to return Egypt to the Egyptians, for the constitution had been accepted as one step towards independent government and, in the manner of all semi-representative institutions, the Legislative Council would undoubtedly have become the spearhead of a movement for more rights. The matter was never put to the test. In 1914 the First World War began and Lord Kitchener was called to take supreme command of the British Forces.

## IV

On 5 November 1914 Turkey joined the war on Germany's side and within twenty-four hours the Prime Minister of Egypt instructed the country to co-operate fully with the British. Quite apart from the fact that Egyptian Moslems were being asked to co-operate with the infidel against the faithful, the position of Egypt was anomalous, for although it was to all intents and purposes governed by Britain it still nominally acknowledged Turkey as suzerain. The British Government, compelled to impose some logic on the situation, declared Egypt to be a Protectorate in December 1914. Abbas Hilmi was deposed and replaced by Hussein Kamel, the eldest of the

Mohammed Aly line, who was given the title of Sultan.* Sir Henry McMahon replaced Lord Kitchener as Consul-General, but effective power was wielded by Sir John Maxwell, who was sent to direct the British war effort and issued his war regulations without much regard to customs of government or Egyptian susceptibilities.

The hopes raised by the Kitchener constitution were dashed; the very word *himaya* to express Protectorate had hateful connotations for the Egyptian people, who used it to express 'protection' of foreign peoples and therefore related it to all the worst abuses of the capitulatory system. Although Hussein Kamel was popular with the nationalists, whereas Abbas Hilmi had been hated and feared, the title of Sultan was an offence to national sentiment, which had consistently opposed any aggrandisement of the princely house that had oppressed the people and survived under British protection. The declaration of the Protectorate and the war-time regulations ruined whatever chance there had been of an understanding between the British and the national movement, but war-time conditions did not allow the movement any opportunity to express itself or to act. There were two unsuccessful attempts on the life of Sultan Hussein Kamel in 1915, after which the nationalists, driven into direct connection with former terrorist groups, bided their time in silence and studied the problem of revolt.

The British drove a combined German and Turkish force from the eastern frontiers of Egypt late in 1916. By that time the position of the Turks in the Arab region had deteriorated. The underground Arab national movement, which sought autonomous rule within the Turkish Empire, had come at last to believe it should throw in its lot with the Christian allies in order to secure Arab independence when the war ended, and the Shereef of Mecca was also in touch with the British to secure an Arab kingdom as reward for military collaboration. The combination of the Shereef's leadership and national co-operation produced the Arab Revolt of 1917, associated with the name of T. E. Lawrence, in which the Arabs finally rejected the Turkish call to a Holy War against the infidel and took the field on the British side. General Allenby led his forces into Jerusalem in December and moved triumphantly north with the Arab guerrillas to enter Damascus on 1 October 1918.

The Egyptians made no effort to rise in support of the Turks during the war years, partly because the towns and cities were armed camps in which the people were compelled to be hewers of wood and drawers of water. Nevertheless, while Indian regiments were

* The Khedive Abbas Hilmi was in Constantinople at the time and was told not to return.

disturbed by Pan-Islamic propaganda, the Egyptian army of 30,000 men loyally policed the Sudan, and the Egyptian labour corps, consisting of volunteers attracted by short-term contracts and high pay, contributed 8,500 men to the campaign in Mesopotamia and 10,000 men to France. Army reservists were called up for railway construction in 1916 and more Egyptians were recruited for camel transport work in Palestine and Syria. There were eventually 135,000 Egyptians taking part in the Syrian campaign, and official records, including General Allenby's despatches, bear witness to their reliability. Of the 21,000 Egyptians in the camel transport service in 1917, 220 were killed, 1,400 wounded and 4,000 died in hospital.

The situation inside Egypt in 1917 was unhappy. The Government was compelled by the heavy demands of the Syrian front to conscript recruits, commandeer donkeys and camels, and requisition the country's corn, and there was no time for nice study of the manner in which these acts of compulsion should be committed. Inevitably the poor suffered. Village *omdehs* paid off old scores as they shepherded their enemies into the arms of recruiting agents or swept animals into the insatiable Syrian caravan. The unjust way in which corn was collected fed a sense of grievance everywhere. By the end of the year the poor could hardly get enough food to support life and had lost what little faith remained in British justice. This, the culminating point of discontent, had grown under the heavy hand of military rule. The Legislative Council had been suspended and the national Press suppressed or brought under control by a censorship which the Cairo Correspondent of *The Times* described as 'incompetent, inept and savage'. The prisons were full of political suspects and no more than five people were allowed to meet together without incurring arrest. The Government, aware of the threatening undercurrents, imposed the Disarmament Act in an attempt to strip the country of private weapons, but it incensed popular feeling more than ever by the violation of Moslem homes that the search for arms entailed.

The National Party emerged stronger than ever from the war. It had drawn to itself wiser leaders, notably Saad Zaghloul, whose career before the war had been a matter of controversy in the national movement. Zaghloul, who was of peasant stock, had started life as a lawyer and came under the influence of Princess Nazli, on whose advice he learned French and moved in the circle of the Turkish ruling class. He married the daughter of Mustapha Pasha Fehmy, who was for a long time Prime Minister and a friend of Lord Cromer, and at the turn of the century his co-operation with the British was taken for granted by Cromer and the country. He was shrewd in the peasant manner, but a friendly and amusing man whose taste for gambling and good food evidently led him in the early years of his career to accept the comfortable fruits of office which came by moderation in politics and co-operation with his rulers. After Lord Cromer made him Minister of Education in 1906 he continued to serve in successive Ministries despite the enmity of Abbas Hilmi; and the national movement, seeing in him the true Egyptian of the type which they desired to lead the country, were disillusioned by his political behaviour, notably when he joined the Cabinet of Boutros Pasha Ghali and supported the draft Convention for the Suez Canal Company. He had, however, his native sympathy with the Egyptian movement. When the hope engendered by the Kitchener constitution was shattered by the declaration of the Protectorate, he turned finally to the nationalists, and was then set on a course which made him leader of a rebellion and a political Arabi, prepared to exploit fanaticism and violence to achieve the end he sought.

The Egyptian movement at Zaghloul's disposal had been strengthened by the war-time affluence which had come to Egyptian landowners, both large and small. The country's wealth was doubled during the war and although much of it went to the Turkish upper class and the Egyptian peasant was impoverished by inflation, it improved the position of the upper-class Egyptian in relation to both Turk and foreigner, for he gained from the greatly increased value of his land and the boom in cotton prices. The small industries which grew up to meet war needs also enlarged the small Egyptian middle class. There were more lawyers, doctors and journalists, and there were more youths at schools and universities, which were hot-beds of political agitation; there were, in short, more money and more men for the movement, and they converged for the time being on the old National Party because the schismatic minor political parties had withered away during the enforced idleness of the war period. Nor could there now be any challenge from the Turkish ruling class, which had lost for ever its homogeneity and dominant position.

The Sultan Hussein Kamel died in 1917 and his place was taken by his brother, Ahmed Fuad, who was almost a stranger to his country and spoke Italian better than he spoke Arabic. He kept himself apart at this stage from both the British and the nationalists, nursing himself for a more favourable occasion to exert his influence while the British shouldered the responsibility for post-war evils. He had good reason to be careful, for there was a plain assumption

of permanence and a clear disregard for Egyptian national sentiment in almost every act of Britain in Egypt at that time. The
Army Council approved a permanent air base at Aboukir, the first
buildings of which were erected in 1917 on land requisitioned at
prices fixed by the British against bitter protests from the landowners. It was an indication of British attitudes that General Clayton
and Sir Reginald Wingate proposed in 1917 that Britain should
annex Egypt. At the same time the quality of the British administration was deteriorating, for it was impossible under war conditions
to hand-pick the British officials as Cromer and Kitchener had done,
with the result that the British element in the Civil Service was not
only larger but of poorer quality. The employment of British officials
in Egypt was no longer justified by any expert knowledge they
brought to the country. Nevertheless the number of Egyptians in
executive positions in the Service, which had been 27 per cent in
1905, was only 23 per cent at the end of the war; there were 1,700
British officials in 1920 as compared with a few hundred in Lord
Cromer's day. In place of the relatively small body of well-disciplined
troops of the pre-war period there was a large army, recruited willy-
nilly for the purposes of war and usually insensitive to the political
importance of good or bad behaviour.

Egypt was burning with a feeling of injustice. Far from profiting
from those acts of liberation which the Allies had preached as their
purpose in the war, she was emerging in great subjection. Britain
and France announced in November 1918 that the Allies contemplated the enfranchisement of all peoples oppressed by Turkey,
which meant that the Arabs who had fought a small campaign in
the desert, when victory was almost in sight, would get their
independence, while Egypt, which had been thrown into the Allied
effort from the beginning would remain a Protectorate. Even the
Press censorship had encouraged the Egyptians' anger by publicising
to the limit the Allies' contention that they were fighting the war
to preserve the liberties of small nations. Were President Wilson's
Fourteen Points, a charter of international morality, to be applied
to all nations except Egypt?

As soon as the Armistice was signed, Saad Zaghloul asked permission to present the Egyptian case in London, but the request
was refused and a similar request from the Prime Minister was also
rejected. This uncompromising stand rendered the position of every
moderate in Egypt impossible. When Zaghloul took the leadership
of the national campaign in January 1919 he demanded on its
behalf complete independence, and the war-time planning at once
became obvious in a flood of propaganda which poured from secret

printing presses all over the country. The first objective of the campaign was the right to send a delegation to the Peace Conference in preparation for which lists of delegates were circulated everywhere for an election, and although the authorities seized many of the lists sufficient were signed to establish the credentials of the delegates. The utmost that the British would concede was for the Prime Minister to go to London, but the 'election' had rendered Rushdi Pasha's position untenable beside that of Zaghloul and he asked that Zaghloul should go with him. When this was refused on 1 March 1919 he resigned. Sir Reginald Wingate, who had a lifetime of experience in Egypt and the Sudan behind him, fruitlessly advised the British Government to receive Zaghloul, and when recalled to London to report was not allowed to return to his post.

The bitterness in Egypt was intense when the Peace Conference assembled in Paris with the Hedjaz Government of Arabia represented. Zaghloul sent notes arguing the case for Egypt's admission to Mr. Lloyd George, M. Clemenceau, President Wilson and Sr. Orlando. General Watson, in command of the Forces in Egypt, warned Zaghloul and his supporters against continuing agitation, and when they responded by publishing next day a lively protest against the warning, Zaghloul, Ismail Sidki, Mohammed Mahmoud, and Hamid Pasha el-Bassal, a leader of the bedawin, were promptly shipped to Malta. The University students streamed into the streets and rioting broke out in Cairo, spread to Alexandria and then to the provinces. Although the British troops were called out to restore order and several rioters were shot, the country was at a standstill by 11 March. Trains, telegraphs and railways were sabotaged and the bedawin besieged British residents in Assuit. Egyptian attacks were directed against the British troops and some officials in uniform, and at Deirut a mob murdered two British officers, an official and five soldiers.

There were evident signs of prior organisation in the way in which the attacks were directed to public buildings, communications and the army, and in fact the movement was led by a Committee of Independence in Cairo, which formed Committees of National Safety to direct the rebellion and appointed provincial 'governments'. The British army overcame the revolt by force, first reasserting its authority in the delta and then moving up the Nile in armoured cars and trains, with aircraft in support. Suspicious gatherings were dispersed by gun-fire and bombs. On 9 April thirty people were executed for the Deirut murders.

Lord Allenby was sent to Egypt on 25 March as High Commissioner with special powers to deal with the situation and, after consultations with all sections of opinion in Cairo, including the Committee of Independence, he proclaimed that Zaghloul and the other detainees would be released from Malta and were free to go to Paris. There was a brief moment of goodwill in which British soldiers and even the Sultan Fuad – whose failure to lift a finger in support of the Egyptian people in their struggle against the British had made him the most unpopular man in Egypt – were cheered in the streets. Rushdi Pasha agreed to resume the Premiership. But the goodwill was fleeting. The national movement, which had not in any way amended its demands for the abrogation of the Protectorate, had learned that violence on a sufficient scale could wring concessions from the British Government. Rioting began again; but the Committee of Independence, realising that this time violence in Cairo was unlikely to help Zaghloul in Paris, restrained where before it had encouraged and substituted passive resistance. It called for a strike in Cairo and Alexandria and, by coercing the reluctant and the timid, made it for a short time effective. They sent a committee of government officials to Rushdi Pasha to demand that he formally recognise the mandate of the *Wafd* (that is, the 'delegation' of Saad Zaghloul), refuse to recognise the British Protectorate, and demand the replacement of British sentries everywhere by Egyptians. Thus was born the great post-war political party of Egypt with Zaghloul as leader; it was ever after known as the Wafd. For a while the nationalist campaign was kept within bounds by the optimistic reports which Zaghloul was groundlessly sending from Paris, for the British Government and its closest allies had agreed that the Protectorate should continue, and Article 147 of the Versailles Treaty confirmed it. On 20 April Lord Allenby reaffirmed it in Egypt by proclamation, and on the same day the United States Consul-General gave it formal recognition.

Britain believed that the rebellion in Egypt had spent itself against the rock of Lord Allenby's determination and that now it only remained to give the country a constitutional form within the Protectorate. Nationalist resistance seemed to have subsided. The tractable Mohammed Said Pasha had accepted the premiership; with his co-operation and the tacit agreement of the Sultan the British Government felt it could now prepare to stabilise the position.

Some consideration had been given in Britain to proposals to annex Egypt to the British Empire and grant something like Commonwealth status, or, alternatively, to abandon the Protectorate and preserve essential British interests in the form of a treaty, but it would have been impossible to secure Egyptian agreement to either policy. The national movement was more united than it had ever been, and men like Zaghloul would not have accepted the restrictions on Egyptian sovereignty desired by Britain, whether by treaty or as a semi-autonomous state inside the Empire; they were probably neither more nor less opposed to the Protectorate. British interests and Egyptian aspirations were in such fundamental conflict that agreement was impossible as long as the Egyptian national movement remained united.

The High Commissioner* announced on 10 November 1919 that his Government had decided to despatch a mission under Lord Milner in order to work out the details of a constitution and start preliminary work on it, but the announcement made it clear that the intention was 'to preserve autonomy under British protection'. Zaghloul immediately gave orders to boycott the mission and the High Commissioner received protests from every section of society. There were more riots, in one of which, in the square outside Abdin Palace, many people were killed. Mohammed Pasha Said resigned and Lord Milner's mission arrived in Egypt only to find that the boycott ordered by Zaghloul was 'for all practical purposes complete'.†

The British Lord President, Mr. Balfour, told the House of Commons that 'British supremacy exists in Egypt; British supremacy is going to be maintained', but when the Milner mission report was published in Britain it surprised opinion by recognising the principle that relations between Egypt and the Empire must be established by agreement, and suggesting that if Egypt was recognised as an independent nation, and Egypt accepted the Empire as mandatory for European affairs in Egypt, a negotiated settlement could be reached. Before the report was published, Zaghloul Pasha was invited to London from Paris and Lord Milner tried to secure the Wafd's acceptance of his proposals that the Protectorate should be abandoned in favour of a Treaty of Alliance by which Britain would undertake to defend Egypt's independence and integrity, that Egypt would undertake to be guided in its foreign relations by Britain and confer on Britain certain rights inside Egypt, and that in return for recognising the constitutional monarchy, with democratic institutions and diplomatic representation, the British Empire would be allowed to station a force in Egypt 'which was not to constitute a military occupation or prejudice the rights of the government in Egypt'. One of the internal rights was that Britain should retain a

---

* Under the Protectorate the Consul-General had become the High Commissioner.

† Lord Lloyd, *Egypt after Cromer*. Lord Lloyd accompanied the mission.

number of advisers and a measure of control over Egyptian legislation and administration in so far as they affected foreigners. All
reference to the Sudan was excluded.

The Milner proposals admirably met Britain's needs by stripping
the British Government of any responsibility for the domestic affairs
of the Egyptian people (that onerous task was handed back to the
Egyptian Government) while retaining the officials to direct, and
the army to enforce, the suitable conduct of relations with foreign
powers and peoples. The Egyptian Government would have the
direct contact with other powers which Ismail had sought from the
Sultan of Turkey forty years earlier, but by no stretch of imagination
could it be said that the Milner Commission offered Egypt independence. Zaghloul Pasha demanded the immediate abolition of
the Protectorate, a strict limit to the number of British troops in
Egypt and their confinement to a region adjoining the Suez Canal,
an end to Britain's claim to responsibility for foreigners when
capitulations ended, and equal share with Britain in the administration of the Sudan.

These demands touched the very substance of the British position,
and Lord Milner, being unable to accept the reservations, published
the mission's report as it stood on 20 December. The British
Government then sought to negotiate a settlement in London with
Adly Pasha Yeghen, the independent Prime Minister and opponent
of the Wafd, but Adly Pasha dared not depart from the terms
demanded by Zaghloul who was so powerful in Egypt that a settlement could only come by agreement with him. Adly Pasha resigned
on his return to Cairo and the agitation fostered by the Wafd made
it impossible to find anyone to replace him. When the Wafd leaders
refused to desist from political activity they were again deported.
Lord Allenby was this time prepared for the rioting and sabotage
which followed and quickly cowed the country, but by this time he
was privately pressing the British Government to terminate the
Protectorate unconditionally. He was firmly opposed by the Foreign
Office, but his hand had been strengthened in dealing with his own
Government by Egyptian intransigence; he had obeyed its orders,
maintained security and was holding firm, but it was obviously a
condition of total deadlock which could not be allowed to last for
ever. He was called to report to his Government and when he
returned with a declaration which ended the Protectorate he was
swept on a wave of popular enthusiasm from the station to the
Residency. On 28 February 1922 it was decreed that the Protectorate
was terminated and that martial law, which had existed ever since
2 November 1914, would be ended as soon as an Act of Indemnity

for all inhabitants of Egypt was passed. It reserved to Britain the security of communications, the defence of Egypt and of foreign nationals in Egypt and the Sudan, pending the conclusion of the agreements covering these points.

Although the declaration stated that Egypt was to have independence it had not granted it. Lord Lloyd, who later as High Commissioner based his entire policy on it, pointed out that it had given Egypt 'a qualified independence, an independence which was subjected to certain definite reservations', and that these reservations 'were an absolutely vital part of that declaration'.* It was no more acceptable to the Egyptian nationalists than had been the report of the Milner mission on which it was based, but it was a unilateral statement of policy by Britain and those moderates prepared to accept the end of the Protectorate as a useful forward step were not called on to persuade the country to accept it. Sultan Fuad became King Fuad and Sarwat Pasha formed a Government which established a commission to prepare the constitution. The first draft declared that Fuad was King of Egypt and the Sudan, but the clauses were withdrawn when it seemed likely that this would lead to the annexation of the Sudan by Britain. The constitution was enacted on 19 April 1923, just over a year after the Commission's work had begun, and martial law came to an end after the promulgation of the Act of Indemnity in July. Two months later a General Election was ordered by royal rescript.

The leaders of the Wafd were still in exile. The party would have nothing to do with the Declaration of Independence and were bitterly critical of the King and those people who were co-operating with the British. Claiming to speak for the Egyptian people, it objected strongly to a constitution which enhanced the power of the King and would be difficult to change. Secret terrorist organisations, which always lurked in the shadow of the national movement, again became active and more British officials were murdered. Only when Zaghloul Pasha and his party returned to the country in March 1923 did terrorism cease. Zaghloul took the field at the head of the Wafd as a political party claiming power; he had accepted nothing and could enter the elections with a free hand.

The constitution declared Egypt a sovereign, free and independent state with Islam its religion and Arabic its official language. It guaranteed personal liberty, but the liberty of the Press was limited 'for the protection of social order'. All public and military employment was restricted to natives of the country except where otherwise provided by law – a reservation required to cover the continuing

* Lord Lloyd, op. cit.

employment of British officials. Legislative power was vested in the
King, ruling with a Senate and a Chamber of Deputies, the Cham-
ber to be elected and the Senate to be two-fifths appointed by the
King and three-fifths elected. The constitution applied only to
Egypt but without prejudice to Egypt's rights in the Sudan, and the
King's title was left in abeyance until 'authorised delegations fixed
the final status of the Sudan'.


## IV

The elections were an overwhelming victory for the Wafd, which
got 90 per cent of the votes and 188 seats to the twenty-seven of
all other parties, and Zaghloul Pasha became Prime Minister on
27 January 1924. He had not in any way modified his view that the
continued presence of British troops was incompatible with Egyptian independence and that the Sudan was part of Egypt, but he
hoped that the Labour Party, which had come to power in Britain
and had promised independence to Egypt, would be more accom-
modating. When, in May, he asked for a promise of independence
from Mr. Ramsay MacDonald's Government as prior condition of
negotiations, the Labour Government's reply made it clear that the
declaration of 1922 had given Egypt all the independence it needed,
and although Zaghloul pressed his case in London in September,
the Labour Government remained firm. He returned to Egypt and
promptly gave Ministerial posts to two noted extremists, Abdul
Rahman Fahmy, who had been condemned to death, and Mahmoud Fahmy el-Nokrashy Pasha, who had been imprisoned, for
their connection with the terrorist outbreaks and whom he had
only a little earlier released.

Mutinies among Egyptian troops stationed in the Sudan in
August focused attention on one man who symbolised for Egypt its
continuing subservience: Sir Lee Stack, Sirdar of the Sudan and
Commander-in-Chief of the Egyptian forces, a dual position which
it might have been wise to modify in 1922. On 19 November he was
going from the War Office to his house in Cairo when he received a
volley of shots from seven men dressed as students who were lined
up on the sidewalk. He died the following day. Zaghloul hurried to
the Residency to express his profound regret and the Egyptian
Government put a price of £10,000 on the murderers' heads. This
availed nothing with Lord Allenby, who was personally deeply
moved by the death of this distinguished officer. After attending the
funeral and without waiting for final instructions from London, he
drove with military escort to the Council and delivered a sweeping

ultimatum. He demanded an apology, the punishment of the criminals, the prohibition of political demonstrations, the withdrawal within twenty-four hours of Egyptian troops in the Sudan, the immediate removal of all restrictions on irrigation in the Sudan Gezira, and the withdrawal of all objections to the assumption by Britain of responsibility for foreigners in Egypt. When the Egyptian Government accepted all except those relating to the Sudan, Lord Allenby, who had by this time received the support of the British Government, announced that the instructions regarding the Sudan would be enforced in any case, and that meanwhile the Alexandria customs would be occupied. Another mutiny of Egyptian troops in the Sudan was joined by Sudanese battalions and was put down only after severe fighting. Zaghloul Pasha resigned and Ziwar Pasha, who took his place, accepted all the demands. The King dissolved parliament on 24 December.

The murder of Sir Lee Stack and the actions taken by the British and King Fuad after it brought to an end the revolutionary period which began in 1919. The Wafd Party was cleared of any complicity by the arrest of eight men, one of whom confessed and so brought about the execution of the other seven.

The drift towards violence had begun before the formation of the Wafd; it was there in the days when Saad Zaghloul himself was collaborating with the British, and towards the end of his career – he died in 1927 – even his intransigence was not enough for the extremists of Egypt and there was an attempt to assassinate him in July of 1924. The mood of the people, which he had himself engendered by years of uncompromising eloquence, made it impossible for any man to lead Egypt for long while co-operating with the British. The country's temper was determined by the mass of Egyptian town dwellers, and often of the country people as well, by whom politicians like Zaghloul were made great and without whom a politician or a king could rule Egypt only by force.

The Wafd was an amalgam of nationalist groups, all of which were to some extent republican in inclination and were certainly opposed to any extension of royal power, but, despite the fact that the whole nation had followed the party blindly into rebellion, its leadership represented an upper class which had taken the place of the former Turkish aristocracy. Zaghloul had no sympathy with popular agitation for social ends. When, in 1923, there were disturbances among urban factory workers, whose condition was depressed by post-war inflation, Zaghloul preferred repression to reform and used troops to throw hundreds of workers into gaol. The Wafd's opposition to the King, however, was an inherent reflex against the power of foreigners in Egypt and emotionally in direct line with the rebellion of Arabi and the cry of 'Egypt for the Egyptians' in Gorst's time.

King Fuad, son of the exiled Ismail and practically unknown in Egypt when he came to the throne, was to them a foreigner who had given no support to the national cause in the immediate post-war period except to demand that he should be King of the Sudan. The declaration of 1922 brought to his side those groups, small in number but with important interests at stake, which wanted a negotiated settlement with Britain, and at the same time it weakened the national movement by drawing away those people – among them Ismail Sidki and Mohammed Mahmoud who had been exiled with Zaghloul in 1919 – who believed that the constitution was a useful advance towards independence. When it became apparent that King Fuad had acquired new and real power in the country, a great part of Wafdist energy was diverted into the struggle against him and his party, the Union Party, and the moderate Liberal Constitutionalists who sometimes worked with him.

The declaration of 1922 had broken the unity of the national movement by turning a powerless Sultan into an influential King around whom could rally all elements opposed to the Wafd and to other radical minorities. Because the constitution of 1923 gave the King the right to dissolve or suspend parliament and to appoint Ministers, the British High Commissioner ceased to be solely responsible for the satisfaction or denial of private political ambitions and the King not only acquired the power to satisfy them but also to foster his own through the ambitions of others. Lord Lloyd, who succeeded Lord Allenby as High Commissioner in October 1925, believed that the conflict between the national movement and the King was so strong that the nationalists were concentrating their efforts to free the army from British control in order to overthrow his dynasty. 'There is no doubt that if once the Wafd had become satisfied with their control of the army they would not have hesitated to launch these combined forces in an assault on the Monarchy,' wrote Lord Lloyd of an attempt by the Minister of War in 1926 to override the supreme powers of the British Inspector-General of the Forces.

These changes in the domestic balance of power brought about by the declaration of 1922 made Egyptian politics a triangle of forces, the British, the King and the Wafd, within which Egypt lived politically for the next twenty years. During those years the power of Britain remained paramount in the triangle and was exerted against the King or the Wafd as the case required; Britain could intervene to an undefined extent because she had reserved to herself the security of the Canal, upon which imperial communications depended, the defence of Egypt, which meant the continuance of the occupation, and the protection of foreign interests, which meant the retention of the post of High Commissioner and the authority of the judicial and financial advisers and the Director of Security. As the need to protect foreigners required the capitulations to continue until the British Government got the settlement it wanted, Britain failed to fulfil the Lausanne treaty pledge of 1923 to end them for another thirteen years in Egypt.

Lord Lloyd conducted British affairs in Egypt with logic rooted in the 1922 declaration and, determined 'to make the policy of 1922 a real policy',* he interfered as little as possible except when the reserved points were affected. Unfortunately the reserved points touched many aspects of Egyptian life and if in the end the Labour Government became dissatisfied with its Pro-Consul in Egypt, the defect in reason lay with it and not with him. Lord Lloyd recognised that it would be ideal to secure British interests by agreement but did not think it possible, seeing much better than his Government that real power rested with Saad Zaghloul, no matter what the composition of the Government, and that as early as 1917 it had already been too late to satisfy the Egyptians and at the same time to retain the control over Egyptian territory which the British Government considered essential. 'The authorities,' he said, 'appeared to have no idea of what was happening in Egypt, of the state of political feeling there, or of the grievances which are burning in the hearts of the *fellaheen*.'† It was not his fault that the British Government failed to understand how impossible it was to get their kind of settlement from anyone. His belief that the British should stay in control of the Ministries of Finance, War, Justice, Education and Communications for a decade was logical if the British Government considered control of Egypt essential to imperial security, and when it tried in 1927 to get an agreement on the reserved points Lord Lloyd advised against it on the grounds that no constitutional government dared accept.

The Government of 1927 was in office by consent of Saad Zaghloul. The King had tried to prevent this by restricting the franchise in 1926, but the resulting uproar forced him to hold elections under the existing electoral law. They were, as usual, won by Zaghloul with 200 seats against fourteen, but the British Government was committed in advance against Zaghloul taking

* Lord Lloyd, op cit.
† Ibid.

7—ME

office. At that particular moment, Judge Kershaw, who had presided at the trial which acquitted Ahmed Maher Pasha and Nokrashy Pasha, two leading Wafdists, of complicity in the murder of Sir Lee Stack, resigned his judgeship in protest against the verdict and the British Government refused to accept it. The atmosphere was so unpropitious for the return of Zaghloul to office that he himself advised that Adly Pasha Yeghen be given the premiership. This was done, but the resulting Government was a Wafdist coalition led by Adly Pasha and containing Sarwat Pasha and Mohammed Pasha Mahmoud, all three of whom were at that time Liberal Constitutionalists in alliance with the Wafd, and the parliament was almost entirely Wafdist with Zaghloul as its president. Zaghloul, nevertheless, used his influence to quieten anti-British agitation and this Government was essentially unchanged for nearly two years.

An Anglo-Egyptian settlement was again sought with Sarwat Pasha, who succeeded Adly Yeghen as Prime Minister, but whatever prospects of agreement existed they evaporated when Saad Zaghloul died on 23 August 1927. Mustapha Nahas Pasha, another man of peasant background, who was Zaghloul's first lieutenant and had shared his second term of exile, had no taste for compromise, and he told Lord Lloyd that he would not agree to a single British soldier remaining in Egypt. The negotiations with Sarwat dragged on until 1 March 1928, but collapsed when Britain insisted on Egyptian assent to the reserved points of 1922 at a time when the Chamber of Deputies, deprived of Saad Zaghloul's leadership, was in an extreme mood. Sarwat Pasha resigned and Nahas Pasha formed his first Ministry on 15 March. It was short-lived; King Fuad was no lover of the Wafd and, when scandal blew up about alleged financial corruption on the part of Nahas Pasha and two others, he dismissed him.

Mohammed Pasha Mahmoud, who became Prime Minister, got the King to dismiss the Chamber of Deputies and it remained dismissed until the end of 1929. The Labour Party was now back in office in Britain and when it became apparent that the Foreign Secretary, Mr. Arthur Henderson, disagreed with the pro-consular tendencies of Lord Lloyd, the latter resigned and was replaced by Sir Percy Loraine. Mahmoud Pasha negotiated a new draft agreement of sixteen points with Mr. Henderson but the Wafd refused to discuss it until a new parliament had been formed by general election. Adly Pasha then formed a Government to hold elections which took place in December 1929 and were, once more, an overwhelming victory for the Wafd. Nahas took office and the new Chamber gave him a mandate to negotiate. The talks with Mr.

Henderson went smoothly for thirteen of the sixteen points of the Mahmoud draft, and so far provided for the withdrawal of British troops to the Canal Zone, which Zaghloul had advocated in 1920, but was less than Nahas himself had demanded in 1927, but when Nahas's alternative draft regarding the Sudan proposed that there should be unrestricted immigration and that each side should have the right to raise the question of the 1899 Condominium within a year, this was so unacceptable to Britain that negotiations again broke down.

The British inability to reach any understanding with the Wafd enabled the King to resist Nahas Pasha because he knew that the British could be relied on at least to stay neutral between them. At the same time, the increasing threat from Italy in North Africa made it abundantly clear to all Egyptian leaders that without British protection their country would be unable to resist aggression. Nahas Pasha, who was, in the words of Lord Lloyd, 'devoid of Zaghloul's peculiar gifts of mind and character which had made Zaghloul so powerful a leader',* chose this inappropriate moment to plunge straight from his 'patriotic' rejection of British terms into a claim for power to prevent the King suspending parliament. When two bills which he submitted in May 1930 were refused by King Fuad, Nahas resigned and appealed direct to the streets, first by attempting to hold meetings of the parliament which the King had suspended and then by riots and sabotage.

King Fuad turned to the strongest and ablest man in the country, Ismail Sidki Pasha, who, after arresting some Wafd leaders and suppressing their newspapers, proceeded to amend the electoral law. Neither Wafdist nor Liberal Constitutionalists liked this, but Britain and the King were on his side, and the Wafd fruitlessly complained to the Residency against Sidki's use of British troops to prevent demonstrations. The elections in May 1931 ensured the defeat of the Wafd, and for the next three years the formidable Sidki maintained a brooding calm in Egypt, two sides of the political triangle holding the third in place.

It was high time that Egypt had a period of convalescence. The Wafd Party's concentration on the campaign against Britain and the King had encouraged in Ministers and officials alike a neglect of day-to-day administration at a time when Egypt was badly in need of attention to its domestic affairs, for it was suffering an acute economic depression in common with most of its European cotton customers. Sidki Pasha devoted his attention to home problems with manifest advantage to the country until his health broke down in

* Lord Lloyd, op. cit.

September 1933, and then his influence continued to prevail through two more governments.

In May 1935, King Fuad himself asked for the restoration of the 1923 constitution. The dangers to Egypt inherent in the Italian invasion of Tripolitania and Abyssinia caused his change of front, for it was evident that good relations with Britain could be achieved only with Wafdist co-operation and this was denied to his Government. The Egyptian Prime Minister, Tewfik Nessim Pasha, announced that the 1923 constitution would be restored after the election of a new parliament, and King Fuad persuaded the politicians to combine in a national front, which included Nahas Pasha, Sidki Pasha and Mohammed Pasha Mahmoud, all of whom, greatly perturbed by the Abyssinian crisis, expressed their readiness to sign a treaty along the lines of the 1930 draft and to discuss outstanding differences in a friendly spirit. The Wafd won the 1936 elections, and Nahas Pasha, as Prime Minister, headed a delegation of seven Wafdists and six prominent politicians from other parties who quickly reached agreement with Britain in August.

King Fuad, who had restored the influence of the Mohammed Aly line in Egypt and led the nation's politicians to this timely agreement, did not live to see it. He died on 25 April, leaving the difficult inheritance of kingship in Egypt to his young son Farouk who was at school in England.

The Anglo-Egyptian Treaty was only possible at that time because the world situation had convinced both Britain and Egypt of the need to resolve their difficulties, but it went far to meet Egyptian claims, and it was unfortunate for future relations that the fears which generated it were justified by a war which withheld its benefits. Britain undertook to sponsor Egypt's membership of the League of Nations, and on 26 May 1937 Egypt was admitted; the fundamental question of sovereignty over the Sudan was postponed, but the position of Egypt prior to the murder of Sir Lee Stack was restored by an undertaking that there would be no discrimination against Egyptians in matters of commerce, irrigation or the possession of property, and that the selection of officials would be made from Egyptians as well as British when qualified Sudanese were not available. There was an undertaking to end the capitulations; it was a gross injustice that restrictions of judicial sovereignty, originating in the weakness of the Ottoman Empire in the eighteenth century, should be applied to Egypt alone in the 1930's, and that the General Assembly of the Mixed Courts, a body largely consisting of foreign Judges, should still have authority over a wide field of Egyptian legislation. The annexe to the 1936 Treaty undertook to end these limitations and, in the meanwhile, the Mixed Courts took over all jurisdiction remaining to consular courts. The end of capitulation could only be achieved by agreement with the capitulatory powers, but the Montreux conference took less than a month in April and May of 1937 to discuss and sign a convention which ended the authority of the General Assembly of the Mixed Courts over Egyptian legislation and all jurisdiction of consular courts, and provided that Mixed Courts should hand over their jurisdiction to National Courts in 1949.

Although the 1936 Treaty declared the British military occupation at an end, Britain retained the right to station troops in a zone along the Suez Canal, with the duty of defending the Canal until both sides acknowledged that the Egyptian army was strong enough to do so. The British Royal Air Force was given permission to fly over Egypt for training purposes and areas for army training were demarcated. Britain undertook to defend Egypt against aggression. Both countries agreed to renew the alliance after 1956, but Egypt was given the right then to ask a third party to decide whether it was still necessary to have British troops in the country.

The vast majority of Egyptians welcomed the Treaty for the degree of independence it gave them and the security it offered against Italian ambitions, but, as Gamal Abdel Nasser later pointed out, the officers' movement was opposed to it, and so were most radical groups including the extreme wing of the Wafd itself. These groups were for the most part unorganised and met in the army mess, the café or the mosque, criticising the decision to allow British troops to remain anywhere in Egypt. The most organised body of opposition was in the Moslem Brotherhood, which was already strong, well led, and destined to have influence on the country and the Arab world beyond.

## Chapter 6

# War and Its Legacy

---

## I

POLITICAL LEADERSHIP IN Egypt continued to decline very
sharply after the signing of the Treaty, partly because the
King, a boy in his teens, could not exert the dominant
influence of his father, and each group of politicians sought to
bring him under its influence. King Farouk was extremely popular
in the country, which had never looked with much favour on the
throne, and there were members of the Wafd, among them Mahmoud Fahmy el-Nokrashy Pasha and Ahmed Maher Pasha (the
two acquitted in the Lee Stack murder trial), who believed that the
time had come to drop opposition and lead him towards constitutional monarchy. This was not the view of Nahas Pasha who continued to challenge the prerogatives of the King on the assumption
that the boy would not be able to resist, with the result that he
perpetuated antagonism between the Wafd and the Palace and
drove Farouk steadily into the arms of a palace clique.

The conditions within the Wafd were by no means happy. Apart
from the radical wing which had never agreed with the signing of
the Treaty, there was the group seeking to come to terms with the
Palace, leading Wafdists angered by the subservience of Nahas
Pasha to his young wife and her family, whom they accused not only
of clandestine influence on political matters but of financial corruption as well, and opposition to Makram Ebeid Pasha, a Copt, who
was Nahas Pasha's Minister of Finance, whom they accused of too
much power in party affairs. Both Nokrashy and Ahmed Maher
were expelled from the Wafd Party and formed a new party, called
the Saad Wafd to show that they represented a true succession to
Saad Zaghloul. The struggle inside the Wafd, the struggle between
the Wafd and the Palace, the struggle between the Wafd and the
other parties, paralysed the Egyptian Government. Finally there
were Wafdist blue-shirts and Royal green-shirts parading and
occasionally battling in the streets.*

---

* In 1937 Nahas was shot by a green-shirt. He survived, and in 1939 both these
troublesome youth movements, modelled on Mussolini's, were dissolved by decree.

Nahas Pasha was dismissed from office in December 1937 and in the spring of 1938 the Wafd were beaten in 'rigged' elections held under the 1923 constitution, winning only twelve seats against the Saadists' 84 and the Liberal Constitutionalists' 99. A Government was formed consisting of Saadists, Liberals and two small parties, the People's Party and the Union Party (a palace group), with Mohammed Pasha Mahmoud as Prime Minister.

The disintegration of the national movement which had begun with the 1923 constitution was then practically complete. What remained of the Zaghloul struggle was a complex of competing personal ambitions reflected in parties which were equal only in lacking any programme of domestic reform. They had evolved in resistance to the British and because little of this was left after the signing of the Anglo-Egyptian Treaty they had little to offer the country. The Moslem Brotherhood looked on the political leadership with increasing contempt, and the seeds of a clandestine movement began to germinate in the army.

During the Second World War Egypt remained neutral on British advice, but, as the correspondent of *The Times* subsequently noted, contributed more to the Allied effort than was required by the Anglo-Egyptian Treaty. Article 8 of the Treaty was immediately put into effect on the outbreak of war so that all Egyptian facilities were at Britain's disposal, and the Prime Minister, Aly Maher Pasha, declared a state of siege and became Military Governor. There were those, such as Ahmed Maher Pasha, who thought that Egypt should immediately declare war in order that it should demand its reward at the end, but this required confidence in the Allied victory which all Egyptians did not possess.

King Farouk, deeply impressed by the strength of Germany, felt that if Italy came into the war it might be better for Egypt to be tied as little as possible to the British, a view shared by Aly Maher, who thought that Egypt should walk the tight-rope, offering to the British Government its strict rights under the Treaty without going too far out of its way to antagonise any other country. He had taken action promptly against Germans in Egypt, but he continued to be carefully friendly towards the Italians, from whom he received an assurance that Egypt's neutrality would be respected. This made him very popular, for the mass of Egyptians believed it was not their war and were against a whole-hearted effort on behalf of the Allies. Sheikh Hassan el-Banna, leader of the Moslem Brotherhood, was against co-operation and the clandestine movement in the army talked of using its arms against the British and making contact with the Germans. General Aziz al-Misri, then Military Inspector-General, was in touch with the clandestine movement and after he was deprived of his post attempted to fly to Rommel and was arrested.

The British Ambassador, Lord Killearn, pro-consular by temperament and little inclined to put up with the whims of the young King, watched with impatience while Aly Maher dragged his careful feet during the early quiet months of war, and when he showed reluctance to expel or intern Italians and confiscate Italian firms as enemy property after Mussolini's declaration of war in June 1940, he ordered the King to dismiss him.*

Under Hassan Sabry Pasha, who succeeded Aly Maher and died in November, and Hussein Sirry Pasha, who succeeded him, the Allied cause was well cared for.

Unfortunately for Sirry Pasha there was discontent in the country over food shortages, notably wheat, for which the people blamed the appetite of the British troops, and doubts about an Allied victory increased with tales of Axis victories. In September the Italians were deep in Egyptian territory and Alexandria was bombarded. Some relief came in February 1941 when the British forces drove the Italians back 500 miles, but British troops were then diverted to Greece, and Rashid Ali el-Gailani created unrest in Egypt by seizing power by *coup d'état* in Iraq. In the summer 650 people were killed in and around Alexandria by Axis air-raids, and the Italians, again well inside Egypt, isolated the fortress of Tobruk; but the Government, far from withholding its support, allowed the Egyptian army to take over guard duties on the Suez Canal.

When Axis air-raids on Egypt ended in September public feeling against the war eased slightly, but it was still a gloomy matter and doubts about the prospects of an Allied victory remained. At the Palace, people inspired by Aly Maher Pasha still sought to create a government less committed to the Allied cause in order to preserve a friendly link with the Axis. It was a reasonable precaution for Egypt but not one which Mr. Churchill or Lord Killearn could contemplate at a time when student demonstrators were crying in the streets 'We are Rommel's soldiers'. The conflict between the Palace and the Government came to a head on 6 January 1942 when the Government broke relations with Vichy France and expelled the popular French Minister, Jean Pozzi. The King, who had not been consulted because he was away at the time, demanded

* Lord Killearn, as Sir Miles Lampson, succeeded Sir Percy Loraine as High Commissioner and had remained in Egypt as the first British Ambassador after the signing of the 1936 Treaty.

It was unfortunate that the young Lady Killearn was Italian, the daughter of the Chief Surgeon in the Italian army. The palace clique grumbled that if 'their' Italians should go, so should Lord Killearn's.

the resignation of the Foreign Minister. Sirry Pasha supported his Minister but resigned on 2 February because he had lost palace support.

The situation in the western desert was critical; Rommel captured Benghazi on 9 February. Lord Killearn informed King Farouk that only a government led by Nahas Pasha would command the confidence of the country. When King Farouk temporised, Lord Killearn issued an ultimatum; when the King rejected the ultimatum, Lord Killearn arrived at the Palace at nine o'clock at night on 4 February accompanied by the G.O.C. of British troops in Egypt and an armoured escort, and Farouk capitulated. Nahas Pasha, enemy of Britain but never averse to office, formed a Government, and in March he held elections in which the Wafd won with 223 seats in the Chamber of Deputies. The problem of government in Egypt was solved for the next two years, for the Wafd had still considerable support, and where it did not get it – as from the Moslem Brotherhood – Nahas cajoled or threatened the opposition into silence.

The Wafd faithfully repaid its debt to the British Ambassador, and it is to the credit of Nahas Pasha that when the Axis forces reached Alamein, sixty miles from Alexandria, he set an example of firmness to the frightened public, foreigners and Egyptians alike, by arresting fifth-columnists and closing the Royal Automobile Club which was a fashionable centre for pro-Axis sentiment. With the defeat of Rommel at Alamein the war began to recede from Egypt and in May 1943 the Axis forces were no longer on the continent of Africa.

The absence of danger produced new difficulties as the benefits of the Anglo-Egyptian Treaty were forgotten. The large garrison in Egypt was still an important element in the Allied strategy, but the presence of scores of thousands of British and Commonwealth troops revived antagonism, largely because the troops were often insensitive to Egyptian susceptibilities and were exasperated by the worst elements in Egypt who battened on them. But there was an undoubted upsurge of genuine nationalist feeling. The important official class and the army had never fully accepted the policy of the Government, many people had by this time joined the Moslem Brotherhood, and the instinct of Egyptians generally was to restrict the power and influence of foreigners. This had been evident at the time of Alamein when the Nahas Government compensated for its support to the British Army by putting through parliament a law to make the Arabic language compulsory for commercial accountancy and all official correspondence.

The foreign communities did not encourage conciliation, for the outbreak of war so soon after the signing of the 1936 Treaty and the strength of Lord Killearn prevented them from realising that their position in Egypt was already radically changed. The British Chamber of Commerce, for example, protested to the Government against the growth of nationalist tendencies, citing the Arabic language law and new difficulties in getting visas, and warned that it might be necessary for the British Government to intervene if Egypt persisted in favouring home firms, such as the Misr group in which foreign capital was forbidden, to the detriment of foreign interests. The British-owned *Egyptian Gazette* told the Egyptians to give up the vote-catching cry of nationalism. Although by the 1936 Treaty the British had relinquished the power of intervention in peace time, the British and other foreigners and most of the British Press continued to behave as though Egypt were a subject country, and this disregard of the changed relationship antagonised Egyptians in all walks of life.

## II

Egyptians firmly believed that Britain should concede total evacuation and the union of Egypt and the Sudan in return for the services which Egypt had rendered during the war. In the debate on the Speech from the Throne in November 1943 speakers of all parties insisted that immediately the hostilities were over the Government should demand both its 'rights'; and Nahas Pasha and the Wafd, though in power and co-operating fully with the British, could only agree and emphasise the sincere goodwill of leading British statesmen, for the Wafd leader himself had presented the same demands to the British Ambassador while in opposition. The stage was set for a new round of Egyptian demands, although the twenty-year Treaty had barely run seven years.

The reputation of the Wafd Government steadily deteriorated. It had already been in office longer than any previous Wafdist Ministry, and therefore its talent for corruption and its lack of talent for efficient administration were unusually obvious. Its term of office had started well enough when the danger of famine was quickly removed, in part by its own efforts but more particularly by the operation of the British Middle East Supply Centre, which began to take effect in 1942. The autocratic methods of Nahas himself and the influence of Madame Nahas and her family led to a quarrel with Makram Ebeid Pasha, his ambitious Minister of Finance, which terminated first in Makram's dismissal from the

Government and then in his expulsion from the party with fifteen Wafdist deputies and four senators. Makram Pasha had been Secretary-General of the party for fifteen years and his dismissal almost completed the eradication of the old-guard Wafdists whom Nahas had taken over from Saad Zaghloul. Makram compiled a 'black book' setting forth the corruption of prominent Wafdists and in particular the Wakils, the family of Madame Nahas, and sent one copy to the King and others to public circulation. There was so much truth in the case which Makram Ebeid presented that the King could have dismissed Nahas if Lord Killearn had not intervened, 'to the embarrassment of the army commanders', to prevent his doing so.*

King Farouk, whose long-standing enmity towards Nahas Pasha was reinforced by the ultimatum by which Lord Killearn had put him in power, was determined to get rid of the Government. He had a powerful ally in Sheikh Mustapha Maraghy, the Rector of Al-Azhar, who taught his volatile students to recognise the gross insults which the Wafd had inflicted on the King. More and more, Nahas was compelled to use his authority as Military Governor to suppress criticism from all sides, and in 1944 he interned Makram Ebeid for continuing to distribute pamphlets which endangered public security. The Government's position was further undermined by a terrible epidemic of malignant malaria which persisted in Upper Egypt from 1942 until 1944 and wiped out whole villages, and was in part due to malnutrition caused by corrupt and uneven distribution of food supplies. King Farouk was once more prevented from dismissing Nahas by Lord Killearn, but did so on 8 October 1944 when Killearn was out of the country. Ahmed Maher Pasha became Prime Minister of a coalition of Liberals, his own Saadists, Makram's new Kotla Party and the leader of the now small National Party.

Lord Killearn had wrecked the triangle of forces within which the political life of Egypt was evolving by creating an implacable enmity between Britain and the King, partly by imposing policy on him and also by his high-handed personal behaviour. Secondly, he widened the gulf between King Farouk and the people, for just as the nationalists lost faith in Abbas Hilmi when he recanted his insults to the British Army, so they were affronted when the King accepted the gross insult of 4 February 1942. Thirdly, he undermined the Wafd Party, which, being accused of coming to power under British bayonets, lost its militant nationalist wing, which slid away into the Moslem Brotherhood and other small extreme groups,

* *Great Britain and Egypt, 1914-1951*—Royal Institute of International Affairs.

and into the clandestine army movement, thereby making it doubly certain that the Wafd out of office would be more extreme than ever in order to eradicate the belief that it had been bought by the British. This was immediately obvious when the Wafd moved into opposition, for Nahas Pasha embarked upon a virulent anti-British campaign and the King, who enjoyed the spectacle of Nahas biting the tail of the British lion, did nothing to stop it. These conditions made it extremely difficult to regularise Britain's post-war relations with Egypt, if indeed they could be regularised at all. The organised movement of revolt against both the political leadership and the King was so far advanced in the Moslem Brotherhood and the army movement when the war ended that the post-Wafd Government felt compelled to release from prison such people as Colonel Anwar Sadat, who had plotted to contact the Germans in the desert.

Ahmed Maher Pasha, the Prime Minister, was the first of a number of victims of the extreme and militant nationalism which had grown during the war. He had tried from the outbreak to ensure that Egypt should not be excluded from the peace conference, as it had been from the Versailles Conference, by committing it to the Allied cause. When the Yalta Conference decided that only those states which had declared war on Germany and Japan by 1 March would have the right to take part in the San Francisco Conference and become founder members of the United Nations, Ahmed Maher prepared to declare war, a policy which Britain encouraged; Egypt had acquired genuine rights because the Egyptian people, despite doubts and antagonism, had fulfilled their duty under the Treaty and, at Britain's most vulnerable moment during the build-up for the Battle of Alamein, had not committed a single act of sabotage. The Wafd, which was concerned as usual only with returning to power, contended that the declaration of war could be made only by agreement of the whole people, that is, by an election that returned the Wafd to power, and it spread rumours that Egypt would be expected to send a labour force to the Far East – an evocative reference to the hated labour corps of the First World War. Ahmed Maher denied the story on the authority of the British Ambassador but it was still widely believed, and when he went before parliament with the declaration of war he was shot down as he left the Chamber of Deputies to put the case to the Senate. Egypt nevertheless declared war.

The assassin was said to belong to a small extremist group known as the *Misr el-Fattat*, but Ahmed Maher's friend, Mahmoud Fahmy el-Nokrashy Pasha, who succeeded to the premiership, believed to the end of his days that the Moslem Brotherhood instigated the murder. He had Sheikh Hassan el-Banna and some of his followers arrested, and although they were released for lack of evidence, it was probable that this was the first of many assassinations by the Brotherhood's terrorist wing, for it had penetrated every other movement, including the Wafd and the clandestine army group. The murder of Ahmed Maher was significant because it marked the beginning of a campaign against Egyptian 'traitors'. The rebellion of 1919 was against the British; the rebellion of 1945, which began thus spectacularly in the courtyard of parliament, was against those people in Egypt who were considered to be responsible for the subjection of their country.

When Sheikh Hassan el-Banna was released he hastened to Nokrashy Pasha to offer condolences on the death of his friend, Ahmed, but Nokrashy was not deceived. He imposed restrictions on Brotherhood activities and kept the principal members under police surveillance. He did, however, allow them to hold general meetings and at the conference of the movement on 8 September 1945 the Supreme Guide told his followers: 'In the time when ye will have – O ye moslem brothers – three hundred phalanxes, each one of them equipped spiritually with faith and principle, mentally with science and culture and physically with training and exercise; at that time ask me to plunge with you into the depth of the sea, to rend the skies with you, and to attack with you every stubborn tyrant, then, god willing, I will do it'.* He further told them that the brethren were not considering revolution but that they made it clear to every Egyptian government, 'that if conditions remained as they were and there were no immediate reforms and everything remained as it was, then revolution would inevitably ensue'.† From that time onwards the Brotherhood were almost continuously in conflict with the Government.

The Egypt which emerged from the war was devoid of people who could lead the country, for there was neither the Zaghloul of the 'twenties nor King Fuad's cautious manipulation of political life of the 'thirties. The Wafd, still with support derived from the mystique of Zaghloul, had a political machine which could ensure that it won any freely held election, but, unfortunately for the country, the struggle for power within the party had led to the withdrawal of many of its best members, the autocratic temper of Nahas and the corrupting influence of people close to him deprived it of moral authority, and it was as reactionary as and less efficient than any possible government. (Opposition politicians contended

---

* Quoted by Dr. Ishak Musa Husseini, *The Moslem Brethren*.
† Ibid. The words in this case are Dr. Husseini's.

that the Wafd was always dismissed too soon for its real iniquities to be recognised because the Wafd was always able to claim that its downfall was due to the machinations of the British Embassy or of the King.) Out of office it supported the most extreme currents of Egyptian national opinion and opposed the Palace, a policy which served it well in the struggle for power, because the desire for total evacuation of the British troops was deeply rooted in public opinion.

The King was rapidly wasting the fund of goodwill he had when he came to the throne. He had gathered round him at the Palace two groups, one largely foreign and corrupt, the other of Egyptians who genuinely believed in Egypt's need for a throne and sought to direct the King towards policies that would sustain it. Time was to show that this honest faction, Mortada el-Maraghy (the son of the influential Sheikh of Al-Azhar), Abdul Fattah Amr, Egyptian Ambassador in London, and Hassan Youssef, who became deputy chief of the Royal Cabinet, lost ground to the others in the Palace and became convinced that King Farouk was ruining the nation. The constitution required a steady-minded king and Royal Cabinet, for in the factional strife that passed for party politics in Egypt, only the King could be the balancing factor. King Farouk did not provide this, for he was governed by his hatred of the British (only partially modified by the tact of the new British Ambassador, Sir Ronald Campbell), his hatred of the Wafd, and his love of pleasure and the society of bad people. He was intelligent enough to be cynical about the political life of the country and lacked the intellectual and moral stamina to be interested in its improvement, but the political leaders depended on him for their opportunities to rule and were compelled to be sycophants.

For the majority of Egyptians in town and village, life had become more difficult. There was unemployment caused by the reduction of the number of troops in Egypt and price inflation caused by the war and the politicians were blamed for both. The people were therefore susceptible to extreme nationalist groups outside the parties, of which the most powerful was the Moslem Brotherhood. It had developed an ambitious leadership, an extensive organisation, and a terrorist wing. The mass of simple and sincere Moslems followed the Supreme Guide with touching faith while in secret the fanatical *élite* swore oaths of entry into the armed phalanxes.

Sheikh Hassan el-Banna, who had complete command of the secret forces, almost certainly had had them in mind from an early day in his self-appointed mission. He drew the members of his Islamic army from the many branches of the movement and after careful selection he passed them through various degrees of training – which included reciting the Koran and learning to use guns, revolvers and hand-grenades – until they became members of secret cells in which the terrorist swore by Allah: 'to be guardian of Brotherhood principles, a fighter in the cause of Allah, to listen and obey and to fight as best I can'.* At this stage he was committed to unquestioning obedience to his cell leader and, beyond the cell, to the high command led by the Supreme Guide himself.

Sheikh Hassan believed at the end of the war that he was approaching the time of action. He started a daily newspaper, *Ilkwan el-Muslimeen* (The Moslem Brotherhood), which had for a time the largest circulation of any daily in the country and was rich from the piastres subscribed by the members. As early as 1942 the movement had had more than half a million followers, and its doctrines, by sermons, lessons and pamphlets, had since extended far beyond the limits of the movement proper and become more powerful in the universities than the Wafd. It spread the standard ideas of Egyptian nationalism: the King was unfaithful to Islam, the Government pandered to foreigners and to foreign countries, nothing was being done for the poor and, above all, Egypt's leaders were afraid of the *jihad* – the holy war.

The clandestine movement inside the army had much narrower range although it was allied to the Brotherhood by some of its leading members and was to some extent aware of Brotherhood plans, and for a time it also conducted propaganda outside the army and tentatively formed a civilian wing, but its importance lay in the army and, therefore, for the first time since Arabi, it brought the Egyptians close to the point where they could revolt against their rulers.

The secular left-wing movement also emerged much stronger from the war period. Organised communism had its beginning in Egypt in the 1920's, but was split into several rival factions and was never numerically strong. After the Second World War the international communist movement had some contacts with groups of intellectuals and with the trade unions. The National Committee of Workers and Students was formed by a prominent deputy, Mustapha Musa, who almost certainly had contacts with the Soviet Embassy. In September 1945 a delegation from Egypt attended a conference in Paris of the World Federation of Trade Unions, which was already under communist control, and in October of that year a Workers' Committee of National Liberation was formed under communist influence in the Cairo industrial suburb

* Quoted by Dr. Husseini, op. cit.

of Shubra el-Khaima, where there was a large and poor working population – mainly textile operatives. The extremist *Misr el-Fattat* group professed to be socialist.

The trade union movement had had a tenuous existence in Egypt since the first union was formed in Cairo in 1902, and in 1922 there were thirty-eight trade unions in Cairo, thirty-three in Alexandria, eighteen in the Canal Zone towns and six in the rest of the country, all of which were recognised by the Conciliation Board but had no other legal status. They were dissolved in 1931, revived in 1934 and again dissolved in 1936, but during their periods of dissolution they continued to function in a limited way. In 1942 the unions were recognised but the law reflected official suspicion of all union movements by forbidding the unions to form a national organisation, banning political activities and giving the police the right to attend their meetings. In 1948 the trade unions registered with the Labour Department numbered 478 and claimed 124,000 members, few of whom were communists, but in the towns of Egypt there was widespread, if vague, awareness of socialist ideas which had largely replaced the internationalism of the League of Nations and democratic ideology of the 1920's. Capitalism and Western imperialism were both indistinct concepts in Egypt but were felt to be the real enemies.

The characteristic of all these extreme movements, whether right-radical or left-radical, was that they considered the struggle against imperialism as represented by the presence of British troops to be the same thing as the struggle against the Egyptian ruling class. The Brotherhood warned its members to beware of 'the nobles', and the officers of the clandestine army movement were in the main drawn from the middle class of farmers and professional men, and were approximately the same – allowing for the social changes that had taken place in sixty years – as those from whom Arabi drew his support. The unions were composed of urban workers who desired to elevate the Egyptian workers at the expense of foreigners in the country. Despite the fact that the Turkish elements had long since been absorbed the ruling class was never completely accepted by these essentially Egyptian movements; it had only appeared to be accepted as long as Saad Zaghloul and Nahas Pasha gave effective leadership to the Egyptian people. When Nahas Pasha during the war lost his hold on the minds of the Egyptian movement, the Wafd lost its dynamism and its leadership and became just one more party competing for office and part of the post-war struggle between the radicals and the ruling class.

The statement that the Egyptian politicians exploited the Anglo-

Egyptian question for popularity and to gain office was broadly true, but it obscured the more fundamental fact that it was the only point on which the radicals and their rulers could find common ground; beyond it they could only fight each other. When Nokrashy Pasha took office he hoped that pressure on him by the Wafd and the Brotherhood would be eased by the British Government volunteering to withdraw its troops from Cairo and Alexandria, and Sir Edward Grigg, who was British Minister Resident in the Middle East until August 1945, advised his Government to do so. When Makram Ebeid presented the budget in July he said that no allocation would be made for building barracks for British troops in the Canal Zone, thus challenging the 1936 Treaty which laid down that British troops would evacuate the cities and towns on the Nile only when the Egyptian Government had made the zone ready to receive them. That same month the Wafd presented a memorandum to the British Ambassador demanding evacuation and the unity of the Nile Valley under the Egyptian crown, and Nokrashy Pasha was compelled to endorse it as Egyptian policy. His own Cabinet was disintegrating about him, and under pressure from his colleagues, notably Makram Ebeid, he delivered a note on 20 December requesting that negotiations for revision of the Treaty should open in London at an early date. The British Government, which was concerned at the time about the Soviet puppet government set up in Persian Azerbaijan and was not in the mood to consider weakening its Middle East position, took five weeks to reply to Nokrashy and then expressed the view that the Second World War had proved the essential soundness of the principles underlying the Treaty. This was rightly interpreted in Egypt to mean that Britain had no intention of abandoning it.

In January 1946 Amin Osman Pasha, who had been knighted by Britain for his services during the war and was a close associate of Nahas Pasha, was assassinated for his pro-British sentiments. At the reopening of Fuad I University in Cairo on 9 February 1946 there was a demonstration of 1,500 students and it was followed by riots of workers and students in Alexandria and other towns in which a number of people lost their lives. The British Ambassador informed King Farouk that the British Government was not satisfied with Nokrashy Pasha's ability to keep order, whereupon Nokrashy resigned and was replaced by the strong man of the 'thirties, Ismail Sidki Pasha, who was now seventy-one and in poor health. A few days after he took office the National Committee of Workers and Students called a general strike as a peaceful demonstration, but during it there was considerable looting of British property in Cairo and two weeks later, during demonstrations to commemorate Egypt's martyrs in the national struggle, the mob burnt down a military post and stoned to death two of its occupants. Disorders then continued and there were bomb attacks on British troops and civilians.

All the political movements active in Egypt, including the Wafd, took part in these attacks and disorders, but the inspiration almost certainly came from radical movements such as the Brotherhood and the Workers' Committee of Mustapha Musa; the Soviet Embassy, associating itself for the first time with the internal struggle, expressed its sympathy with the Committee. The opportunist Wafd leaders, sensitive to pressures from the left, were extremely friendly towards the Soviet Union, to which they gave credit for Egypt's membership of the Security Council, and for the first time threatened to turn to Russia if Britain did not concede evacuation and the unity of the Nile Valley. All the old parties were conscious of the pressures but none more than the King, who wrote to Sidki Pasha, newly in office for the purpose of suppressing trouble-makers, describing the desire for demonstration as 'a healthy manifestation of the people's ambition to realise their just claims'.

In spite of these unpromising and even dangerous conditions Sidki Pasha agreed to resume negotiations. He tried to form a national front but finally excluded the Wafd when it demanded, as in 1936, that it should have a majority on the delegation with Nahas as its president. After lulling some of the politicians' fears by arresting the leaders and some of the members of the terrorist *Misr el-Fattat* and by closing down three of the most virulent pro-Wafdist newspapers, he was able to form a delegation of prominent politicians representing all parties except the Wafd. The British Government offered the withdrawal of all British troops in stages, the timetable to be negotiated alongside Egyptian proposals for mutual assistance in war or imminent threat of war, but the entire Press, except the Saadist organ, was against it. Sidki resigned when members of his own delegation rejected it, but four days later he resumed office because no one else could or would take it. This time Sidki Pasha went to London accompanied only by his Foreign Minister, Ibrahim Abdel Hadi Pasha, and after only five meetings he initialled a new draft treaty – known as the Sidki-Bevin agreement – in which it was agreed that all British forces would be withdrawn from Cairo, Alexandria and the rest of the delta by 31 March 1947, that the final evacuation of Egypt would be completed by September 1949, and that in the event of attack on Egypt, or of Britain being involved in a war as a result of an attack on countries adjacent to Egypt, the two governments would co-operate through a joint Board of Defence.

The most difficult matter under discussion had been the Sudan and this was covered by a carefully drafted clause which read: 'The policy which the High Contracting Parties undertake to follow in the Sudan within the framework of the unity between Sudan and Egypt under the common crown of Egypt, will have for its essential objective to assure the well-being of the Sudanese, the development of their interests and their active preparation for self-government, and therefore of their right to choose the future status of the Sudan. Until the High Contracting Parties can, in full common agreement, reach the latter objective after consultation with the Sudanese, the agreement of 1899 will continue. . .'. The draft was a great advance on anything Egypt had yet been offered but it broke down on this clause. Sidki Pasha was reported to have said on his return to Cairo that he had achieved agreement on the unity of Egypt and the Sudan under the Egyptian crown. This caused disorders in Omdurman which the British administration exaggerated in its reports to London, and in the subsequent exchange of explanations and notes between London and Cairo it became perfectly clear that Britain did not by any means intend the masterly ambiguity of the clause to mean that Egypt had a right to sovereignty over the Sudan. Sidki Pasha thereupon resigned again and Nokrashy Pasha resumed office.

Sidki Pasha had fought on two fronts at once, in negotiation with the British and against what the London *Daily Worker* called the 'fighting front in Egypt'. Sidki himself partly blamed Soviet incitement for his failure, for the whole period of the negotiations was marked by disturbances which made it difficult for the public to understand what had been gained. The conditions favoured disorder, for there were a quarter of a million workless and a much larger number under-employed. The Moslem Brotherhood was attacking Sidki and demanding a *jihad* and the severance of all relations with Britain; the Workers' Congress, formed from the communist-inspired Workers' Committee of National Liberation, called for strikes of government employees and teachers; the Wafd and the Kotla leaders, driven by their own extremist elements, supported the 'fighting front' and also called for strikes. Sidki Pasha raided the premises of both parties, imposed a law which decreed heavy penalties against government employees who downed tools, closed down eleven quasi-communist organisations, including those of the leftist intellectuals, and arrested about 220 people. There remained the Moslem Brotherhood, and in October, when Sheikh Hassan el-Banna and some of his chief associates were away on the Mecca pilgrimage, he arrested a number of its leaders, searched their houses, deported foreign members, dispersed officials who were members of the movement, and promised the Brotherhood worse than this if they did not moderate their tone and behaviour. In short, Sidki attacked all extreme elements except for the clandestine movement in the army whose activities were presumably unknown.

Even so it was not possible for the Liberal-Saadist coalition led by Nokrashy Pasha to negotiate with Britain. The Sidki-Bevin agreement had put the Sudan issue further than ever from settlement by concentrating on it, and Nokrashy began his new term of office with a statement that he meant permanent unity when he spoke of unity of Egypt and the Sudan under the Egyptian crown. The issue was a live one, for the majority of urban Egyptians believed that the British administrators in the Sudan were deliberately pursuing a policy intended to separate it from Egypt, if not bring it into the British Empire. The administrators opposed any form of Egyptian encroachment and did nothing to dispel the fear. Their behaviour was understandable enough, for by their work the Sudan had risen from the ashes of the Mahdi rebellion and they did not want to see it spoiled by Egyptian politicians whose irresponsible behaviour did not justify possession of it. Nor had Egypt any reason to complain over the division of the Nile waters – the matter of fundamental importance – for the existing agreement more than met Egyptian needs and it was the Sudanese who seemed likely to lack water for the extension of their agriculture. All this said, some British officials behaved as though they were fighting a private war, if need be against the British Foreign Office if it inclined towards concessions to Egypt, and certainly against Egypt and those elements in the Sudan who favoured the connection with Egypt.

It was in this light that the Egyptians viewed the Advisory Council for the northern Sudan which had been established in 1944. The Council had been consistently boycotted by the pro-Egyptian party but had functioned because of the co-operation of the Umma Party and other groups in the Independence Front, which believed that independence could be achieved by co-operation with the British. Later, in response to their requests, the Governor-General formed an Administrative Conference, in which the Sudanese had a majority over the British, to consider what further constitutional progress was desirable. On 29 July 1947 this conference recommended the replacement of the Advisory Council by a Legislative Assembly representing the whole country, including the non-Moslem, non-Arabic-speaking south, and that from this conference six Sudanese under-secretaries should be appointed to serve on the Governor-General's Council.

The Governor-General, Sir Robert Howe, endorsed the conference's recommendations just one week before Nokrashy Pasha, unwilling or unable to negotiate with the British on Anglo-Egyptian relations, referred the matter to the Security Council. The British were in a strong position before the United Nations because their troops had evacuated the delta despite the collapse of the Sidki-Bevin agreement and Egypt's non-fulfilment of the condition about barracks, and were now confined within the limits laid down by the 1936 Treaty, although numerically more than the Treaty required. Nokrashy's case, which came before the Security Council on 7 August, was that British troops should evacuate both Egypt and the Sudan. The Security Council, whose members had themselves numerous treaty rights in various parts of the world, proved unwilling to commit themselves – even Russia would not support Egypt's claim to the Sudan – and the Anglo-Egyptian question was therefore left 'on the agenda' of the Council.

## III

Now another matter of more immediate danger to the Arab world was commanding attention. A United Nations Commission had studied the Palestine question and, even as the Egyptian case was before the Council, presented its report recommending the partition of Palestine between the Arabs and the Jews.

Egypt had acquired during and after the war a leading role in the Palestine affair, largely through her position in the Arab League, the formation of which had been encouraged by the British Government. A preparatory commission had drafted the charter of the League in Alexandria in October 1944, and it was formed in March 1945, but between the commission and the formation drafting changes took place in the charter which were designed to impede any effort by Iraq or Jordan to bring about union with Syria, and which strengthened the influence of Egypt, Saudi Arabia and Syria. The Secretary-General of the League was an Egyptian, Abdel Rahman Azzam Pasha, a man of sincerity and devoted pan-Arab convictions, who nevertheless believed that the unity of the Arab world could be achieved only under the aegis of Egypt. Egypt had therefore considerable influence in 1947 when the Palestine crisis approached. No country in the Middle East was less ready for the role.

Egypt's policy on Palestine was at the mercy of Haj Amin el-Husseini, who, having returned from exile and set up house in

Cairo, had re-established through his Higher Committee complete ascendancy over Palestine policy in the League.* Public opinion everywhere in Egypt and the Arab world was mobilised behind his policy, and those who opposed it (as Sami Taha, the able young trade union leader of Palestine, fatally discovered for himself) had an unfortunate tendency to die at the hands of an assassin. For Haj Amin there could be no compromise. When the recommendations of the U.N. commission became known on 1 September 1947 the League decided to resist the partition plan, if necessary by force. The General Assembly nevertheless voted for the partition of Palestine and on 15 May 1948 the British terminated their mandate, the Jews declared an independent State of Israel, and the Arab states sent their armies over the frontier into Palestine. Nokrashy Pasha and some of the high officers of the army doubted the wisdom of the action because they knew the condition of the Egyptian forces, but they yielded to public opinion and the King.

The Arab campaign depended mainly on the Egyptian army and the Arab Legion of Transjordan. In the first advance the Egyptian army reached Bethlehem, where it made contact with the Jordanian forces, and came within twenty miles of Jaffa and Tel Aviv on the coastal plain, but its advance was not consolidated anywhere. Israeli forces were behind its front, Egyptian supplies were defective and badly organised, and there was no co-ordination of the various Arab armies. The Egyptians were soon compelled to pull back their forward units. The Security Council arranged a truce during which Israel received arms from Czechoslovakia despite a ban placed on supplies to both belligerents by the Council, and, when the fighting was resumed on 8 July, the Israeli army was fully geared to the effort and had supplies to sustain it. The Egyptian army was driven steadily back until, early in 1949, the Israeli forces crossed for a brief time into Egyptian territory on the Sinai front. All that remained of the Egyptian advance was a small pocket at Faluja, where a young officer called Gamal Abdel Nasser was among the men who clung bravely, but meaninglessly, to a piece of sand with their backs to the sea. The Arab assault on Israel had broken down everywhere. On 7 January 1949 Egypt and Israel agreed to cease fire and on 24 February they signed an armistice agreement by which southern Palestine, including the town of Beersheba, was left in Israeli hands and Egypt retained an arid coastal strip at Gaza which was packed with Palestinian Arab refugees.

---

* Haj Amin el-Husseini, Mufti of Jerusalem, had taken refuge in Germany during the war when sought by the British for his anti-Allied activities in the Middle East.

The Palestine disaster had a profound effect on Egypt and the entire Arab Middle East. No amount of propaganda could disguise the humiliating defeat suffered by the Arabs and the Egyptians, numerically superior to the Israelis by eighty to one. It confirmed the Egyptian radicals' opinion that the rulers of their country must be overthrown; and the army returned from the front with an intense feeling of shame and a firm conviction that it had been treacherously let down by its own leaders. The clandestine movement was provided with an almost unlimited field for growth inside the forces. The lamentations of the Moslem Brotherhood were tinged with a sense of triumph, for some of its phalanxes had been sent to the front as volunteers and had so distinguished themselves by their fighting spirit that in this period, darkened by inefficiency, treachery and defeat, they shone like a beacon light of pan-Arab patriotism. Thousands of people flocked to join the movement, until it was able to boast of 2,000,000 members.

The anger of the people combined with the *élan* and propaganda of the Brotherhood led to disturbances directed mainly against Jews and foreigners in Cairo, and a judge who had sentenced a Moslem Brother was assassinated. Everywhere there was a feeling of unrest, a sense of insecurity which derived directly from the resurgence of the movement. Nokrashy, conscious of the source of trouble and always opposed to the Brotherhood, ordered its suppression in November 1948, but very soon afterwards he was himself assassinated in his own Ministry of Interior while surrounded by his own police.

Ibrahim Pasha Abdel Hadi, next in line in the Saadist succession, moved from Chief of the Royal Cabinet to become Prime Minister. By this time it was recognised that the Brotherhood was intent on seizing power and probably on removing the King; and the manner in which Nokrashy had been murdered was ample evidence of its efficient terrorist organisation. Abdel Hadi, with great personal courage, struck with firmness and force, taking care of the terrorists by the wholesale arrest of members until thousands of them were crowded in detention camps. On 13 February 1949 Sheikh Hassan el-Banna was also assassinated. There can be little doubt, on evidence subsequently produced, that this was a 'State' murder, the deliberate removal of a man it was difficult otherwise to control, but probably the Palace's counter-terrorist movement was responsible. Abdel Hadi also suppressed other radical groups and imprisoned communists, but not on the same scale.

The destruction of the Brotherhood organisation ended disorders in Egypt for three years, a fact which justified the view that they were behind most of the troubles in the post-war period. In the calm he won by repression, Abdel Hadi Pasha conducted the government with some success, reaching an agreement with the Suez Canal Company on terms favourable to Egypt and completing an agreement with Britain, which had been under discussion for a long time, for a twenty-year Nile development plan estimated to cost £250 million. But Egypt was in a bad state. The King and the minority Government were hated alike by all the radical movements, the Wafd, the Brotherhood, and the army. What shreds of reputation were left to the King were lost when he divorced the popular Queen Farida in 1948, at the height of the Palestine crisis; extravagant stories of his shameful treatment of her and his private life were common gossip. Egypt consisted of a hated King, a hated Government, and a sullen people plotting in secret. The end was near. It only required the folly of Farouk and a new period of Wafd misrule to bring it about.

The King and Abdel Hadi Pasha did not like each other. The Prime Minister was a dour, honest man who looked with disfavour on the royal manners, mistresses and mockery, and, having purged the country of the King's enemies at the risk of his own life, was inclined to touch some powerful interests at the Palace. At this moment there was secret contact between the palace clique and the Wafd by which the idea was elaborated that if the party abandoned its enmity for the King, the two could come together and govern the country, the King with his prerogatives supporting the popular force of the Wafd. This was not the British Government's idea, but people with some importance in the British Embassy and community gave the impression that it would be a highly satisfactory arrangement. In July 1949 King Farouk brusquely demanded the resignation of Ibrahim Abdel Hadi and appointed Hussein Sirry Pasha to form a Government that would hold elections. Hussein Sirry Pasha was a close associate of Ahmed Abboud Pasha, the millionaire industrialist who was known to support the Wafd, and from this small fact the politically sensitive Egyptian people divined that the Wafd was intended to return. And so it did, with 228 seats out of 319 in elections in January 1950.

*Chapter 7*

# Revolution

---

THE COLLABORATION OF the King and Nahas might have worked admirably for the country's good, but instead it removed the brakes on corruption in both the Palace and the party, which held hands in isolation, opposed alike by conservatives and radicals in the country; and the efforts of the conservative politicians to focus attention on abuses in the Palace only gave more ammunition to those very revolutionary movements which they had themselves done their utmost to suppress.

The Wafd Government attempted at the outset to improve the lot of the common people, for there were within the leadership many who genuinely believed that the party should embark on a programme of social reform. Nahas Pasha brought into his Government as Minister of Social Affairs an independent of Wafdist sympathies, Ahmed Hussein, who had been advocating a social programme for some time.* One of the first acts of the Government was to grant higher cost-of-living bonuses to the vast but underpaid civil service and then to impose similar bonuses on private industry and commerce, but prices of essential commodities immediately rose until they more than absorbed the wage increments. It introduced in 1950 a non-contributory social security scheme whereby pensions were to be provided for widows with children, orphans, disabled people and the aged, starting as a pilot project in one province and expanding stage by stage through the entire country, but the cost of the scheme was limited to £6 million which, even so, was more than the country could afford at the time; and Ahmed Hussein resigned when he returned from a mission to Europe to find it had become another field of party corruption. The distribution of government and royal lands to needy peasants was pilloried in the anti-Wafdist Press on the grounds that many of the so-called needy were relatives of Madame Nahas and other prominent Wafdists.

The Wafd remained popular in the countryside because the boom in cotton caused by the Korean War brought prosperity to farmers

---

* Later Ambassador to the United States and not to be confused with the Ahmed Hussein of *Misr el-Fattat*, and later of the so-called Socialist Party.

and peasants, but the Government's corrupt handling of cotton seriously impoverished the country. It interfered in the Alexandria futures market to support the policy of large cotton houses which for two successive years attempted to 'corner' the cotton market, and this had disastrous results when cotton demand began to level out and then fall, for the King and other powerful people who were supporting the cotton policy then tried to keep prices at an artificially high level in order to extricate the firms. As a result, the 1951–52 crop was practically unsold. Finance Minister Zaki Abdel Motaal was dismissed because he refused to co-operate any longer, and Fuad Serag el-Din Pasha, Secretary-General of the Wafd and the most powerful man in the Government, took the portfolio of Finance in conjunction with that of the Interior.

In the Speech from the Throne in November 1950 Nahas Pasha again contended that the 1936 Treaty had lost its validity and demanded the total evacuation of British troops and the unconditional unity of Egypt and the Sudan. Nevertheless, British and Egyptian troops and naval forces held joint manoeuvres at the turn of the year, and in this improved atmosphere the British Ambassador, Sir Ralph Stevenson, presented fresh proposals for a settlement in January and negotiated a new agreement for the progressive release of Egypt's blocked sterling in March. There was little depth to this mood of conciliation, however, for the apparent success of Moussadek in Iran was encouraging intransigence and the Foreign Minister, publicly espousing the policy of neutrality between East and West blocs, refused to send an Egyptian contingent to the U.N. forces in Korea unless the U.N. ensured that justice was done to Egyptian and Arab claims. The talks collapsed in June and on the anniversary of the Treaty in August rioting mobs attacked the British and American embassies. On 8 October Nahas tabled decrees in the Chamber of Deputies for the unilateral abrogation of the Treaty, the abolition of the Condominium, and the proclamation of Farouk as King of Egypt and the Sudan.

The Wafd Government was in difficulties itself and the King, becoming increasingly anxious about his unusual liaison, was on such bad terms with Serag el-Din that there were rumours that he intended to dismiss it. Its economic policy had brought the country close to collapse and seemed bound to force it soon to reduce cotton prices and thus add the impoverishment of the peasants to that of urban people who were already hit by rising prices. In an attempt to secure some co-operation from the Moslem Brotherhood, the Government freed the members imprisoned by Ibrahim Abdel Hadi and allowed the movement freedom of action under the new

Supreme Guide, Hassan el-Hudeiby, but the Brotherhood and left-wing groups all maintained pressure for national struggle against the British.

It was because of its own difficulties and under pressure from extremists that the Wafd plunged into a conflict with Britain for which it had made no preparation,* but it was at this moment, five days after Nahas tabled his decrees and as though no insuperable obstacle to an Anglo-Egyptian settlement existed, that the British, French, Turkish and United States governments jointly presented a plan for a Middle East Defence Organisation. Any faint hope that the Government might consider it was destroyed by an accompanying British note which made evacuation of the Canal Zone conditional on Egypt's acceptance of the plan. It flatly and immediately rejected the proposals and on 16 October the Chamber approved the Nahas decrees, putting on the Statute Book at the same time the broad lines of a constitution for the Sudan with Egypt sovereign. Nahas declared a State of Emergency, and Britain, after formally replying that there was no provision for unilateral abrogation, began to strengthen her forces in the Canal Zone.

As Nahas Pasha had no intention of declaring war on Britain or even of breaking diplomatic relations, Fuad Serag el-Din, who directed the national struggle, was compelled to rely on and rearm the Brotherhood, university students and left-wing extremists for a guerrilla campaign against British troops, only allowing the *Boulac el-Nizam*, the auxiliary police, to co-operate with them. His main weapon, apart from the guerrillas, was to deny supplies of fresh food to the British troops and to withdraw almost the entire labour force serving the base, about 35,000 directly employed and nearly as many employed by civilian contractors, first by appealing to the workers' patriotism and later by intimidation. Although the Egyptian army took no overt part, the clandestine movement helped to train the guerrillas and supplied them with weapons and ammunition from the arsenals.

Sabotage and murder could not have forced British capitulations and the Wafd would have done better to let the boycott of the base take effect, for its value rested mainly on its geographical position, the north and south access provided by Port Said and Suez, the availability of a large labour force, and supplies of fresh food and water. By depriving the base of labour and food the Government

* An opposition journalist, Mohammed Hassanein Heykal, acidly reported at the time from Khartoum that the only people who knew nothing about this constitution were the Sudanese and the Egyptians in the Sudan. Heykal later became the unofficial spokesman and confidant of President Nasser.

went far towards extinction of its value and forced Britain to maintain a military establishment too costly for the purpose it served.
The guerrilla campaign contributed to this end by making every
movement in the zone extremely expensive: to send a truck with a
radio set from one point to another meant the despatch of three
trucks, two of which, one fore and one aft, were manned with armed
men. The need to expand the base to accommodate coloured forces
brought in as labourers, and Egyptian attacks on water supplies to
the base, forced an extension of military action by Britain and precipitated the final crisis.

The British troops in the zone were committed simply to defend
themselves and the installations, and were forbidden to embark on
aggressive counter-action, yet they could not put an end to the
Egyptian campaign unless they moved outside the treaty area to
suppress it. The British Ambassador had orders to stand-by to
renew negotiations and the army was not expected to make his
task impossible. The army could not win unless it prejudiced the
position of the Ambassador; the Ambassador could not win unless
the army submitted to conditions that made its own position intoler-
able. Thus the action of the Wafd Government, ill-conceived though
it was, made clear the fact – which should have been obvious – that
the strategic value of the zone depended on the goodwill of the
Egyptians, and that when challenged by them Britain could only
impose her will by reoccupying the country, a policy that neither
Mr. Churchill's Government nor the Imperial General Staff was
prepared to adopt.

Diplomatic activity between Britain and Egypt was reduced to
notes of protest and replies, and the British community continued
to do business in an increasingly unpleasant atmosphere. In the
Canal Zone the British troops were forced to widen their interpretation of defence to mean limited offence and to bring the towns in
the zone and their communications under British control. In
December they destroyed the village of Kafr Abdu, near Suez, from
which attacks had been made against their water supplies, and the
Egyptian Government thereupon recalled its ambassador from
London. In January 1952 the British troops took prisoner the
Egyptian auxiliary police force at Tel el-Kebir, and Fuad Serag
el-Din publicly warned that next time the British did that sort of
thing the Egyptians would fight back. On 25 January a strong
British force, which included some tanks and armoured cars, surrounded the auxiliary police headquarters in Ismailia and gave the
occupants one hour to surrender their arms. This ultimatum was
unjust, for at that hour in the morning it hardly allowed enough time

to get Serag el-Din out of bed, and the troops could easily have sat tight for a day while the British Ambassador worked in Cairo to save lives. When the ultimatum expired the *Boulac el-Nizam* fought with pathetic courage until forty-three were dead and many others wounded, and then capitulated.*

The effect of this event was threefold. The whole of Egypt was incensed at the British action; the police were furious with their own Government for throwing their men into a battle they could not win, and the extremist movement became convinced that the Wafd was conducting the struggle frivolously. Early on 26 January auxiliary police from the Cairo suburb of Abbassia mutinied and marched on the royal palace, and there was evident dissatisfaction among the ordinary police. Towards noon small groups of people equipped for arson began setting fire to buildings in the centre of the city, directing their attention to British firms and institutions. The exclusively British Turf Club was burnt down and nine people lost their lives, and several others were badly injured. The attacks then became more widespread against foreign and Jewish shops, bars and licensed restaurants, cinemas and hotels, and Shepheard's Hotel, which had stood 'at the gate' for more than a century, was gutted. By the late afternoon Cairo seemed to be burning in its entirety and a great pall of smoke was suspended over the city, in the streets of which people were milling round bonfires made of the stock and effects of looted buildings. The police either made no effort to stop the burning and looting or joined the mob, and the fire brigades, with their hoses cut by the rioters, gave up trying to fight the flames. First relays of half-trained troops from the city barracks could do nothing and it was not until regular units were called in from the Ismailia road, where they were stationed to guard Cairo against a possible advance of British troops from the zone, that order was restored to the city.

These disastrous riots started with an organised, punitive expedition against British establishments. The Minister of Interior and most of his senior officials were slow to show any alarm and the King was entertaining most of the senior police officers to lunch. Subsequently the King blamed the Minister, and the Minister the King, for the delay in taking action to restore order, but the only reasonable conclusion from the course of events was that both knew that fires would be started by the first small parties of incendiaries, armed with their crowbars to force shutters, their cans of petrol to feed the flames, and their rods capped with inflammable wick.

* See the correspondent of *The Times* for a moving report on 20 January 1952 of this tragic affair.

Official alarm developed only when the situation got out of hand as the Moslem Brotherhood extended the disorders to cinemas, restaurants and bars – those places where the sinful pasha and alien foregathered; almost every cinema and bar in the centre of Cairo was gutted. Finally the mob, simply out for loot, joined in. Had the army not stood firm there would have been both revolution and much more bloodshed, and the steadiness of the soldiers was partly due to the fact that disaffection in the ranks had already been canalised into the clandestine movement which did not favour mob action.*

On the night of the fires martial law was proclaimed by Nahas Pasha, who declared himself military governor, but next day King Farouk dismissed the Wafd and called his war-time helpmate, Aly Maher Pasha, out of retirement. There could have been few people less suitable for a revolutionary situation; Aly Maher was essentially a political manipulator, better fitted to play Barmecide at the court of Haroun el-Rashid than popular leader at a moment of crisis. He tried to walk the tight-rope, preserving the Wafdist parliament, proposing to form a national front, and offering to create a territorial army of youths to achieve Egypt's national aspirations. This opportunist mixture was not liked by Mortada Pasha el-Maraghy or Zaki Abdel Motaal, the two strong men of the Cabinet, and with the King's approval they forced a crisis which led Aly Maher to resign on 2 March.

His place was taken by Neguib el-Hillali, one of the country's foremost lawyers and a man of known integrity, who after refusing office in the Wafdist Government had been dismissed from the party in 1951. (Who of importance in the political life of Egypt had not resigned or been dismissed from the Wafd?) Hillali suspended the Wafdist parliament, promised to reform the electoral system and hold elections before the end of the year, announced a political purge and an investigation into corruption, and sent Fuad Serag el-Din and another ex-Minister into exile at their country homes. The British Government eased the country's financial plight by releasing £10 million from Egypt's blocked sterling on 5 April and withdrew the outposts of British troops back to their base.

Hillali Pasha hoped that the British would further improve his position by a statement of principle on Anglo-Egyptian relations which would enable him to lower the tension created by the recent

---

* The explanation of these events will probably never be known in its entirety: the Socialist Party of Ahmed Hussein seems to have been behind the first fire-raising but with official connivance. Who in particular connived at it, however, is still a mystery. The explanation given here is based on witnessing the events and an interpretation of evidence rising from inquiries about 'Black Saturday'.

Canal Zone troubles; but the British Government felt it impossible to do so on the Sudan question, which was in essence a question of principle, whether or not the Sudanese had the right to self-determination. Hillali then turned to the independence parties of the Sudan, in the hope that by discussion with them he might find a *modus vivendi*, only to discover that they would make no concessions as long as Farouk was on the throne. The Government's anti-graft campaign also brought it into conflict with powerful interests inside and outside the Palace, and its efforts to rally the public were nullified by their connection with the King, whose reputation was at its lowest ebb; he was implicated in many evils of the Wafd and his palace cronies earned him the ill-repute of the people. Everything connected with him at that time was considered evil and for this he could only blame himself, for he had shown a cynical disregard for Moslem sensibilities in 1951 when he had taken his new queen, Narriman, on honeymoon during the Ramadan fast, and again when he secured from the *ulema* a *fatwa* purporting to prove, what was manifestly untrue, that he was descended from the Prophet Mohammed. Above all, it was not forgotten that his influence had been used to burke inquiries about defective arms sent to the troops during the Palestine War.

Farouk was in conflict with his Minister of War and Marine, Mortada Pasha el-Maraghy, over army policy. Both knew that the clandestine movement inside the army was highly developed, but whereas Mortada believed that the answer was to reform the army and the country, the King wanted to suppress the movement out of hand. Royal enmity was focused on General Mohammed Neguib, a respected officer, who by the influence of the clandestine movement was elected to be president of the Officers' Club in opposition to the King's nominees, and Mortada Pasha had the greatest difficulty in preventing the King from exiling Neguib to the frontier. When he learnt in June that Farouk was planning to dismiss the Hillali Government at the behest of those interested in halting its investigations the Government resigned.*

It proved difficult to form another Government. There was a general sense of impending disaster, particularly among the politicians in Alexandria where the Government was in summer residence; many of them believed that the King was so unstable that it was useless to attempt to govern. At last Hussein Sirry Pasha succeeded in forming an administration, which included, for the first time in any Ministry, Karim Pasha Thabet, an important

---

* It was widely believed that Farouk had received large sums in his account in Switzerland in return for getting rid of the Government.

palace official who had returned from abroad in an attempt to save Farouk. But Sirry Pasha quickly came into conflict with the King over army policy and resigned after only eighteen days in office. Hillali Pasha returned but had great difficulty in persuading Farouk to accept Mortada Pasha as Minister of War and Marine as well as Minister of Interior, and on 22 July, when this point seemed settled and the Ministers went to the Palace to take the oath, they found waiting for them Colonel Ismail Sherine, the King's brother-in-law, who was presented to them as the new Minister of War and Marine. The issue was clear enough to the clandestine movement in the army: the King was seeking an obedient Minister who would be willing to use his faction in the army to root out mutinous officers. On the night of 22 July the army High Command did, in fact, meet in Cairo to consider what action should be taken against them.

Two plans for revolt had been ready since 20 July. The first, providing for the seizure of power, was prepared by Gamal Abdel Nasser in outline and by Major Abdel Hakim Amer and Major Kemal el-Din Hussein in detail, and the second, to be put into operation if the first failed, had been voted by the executive of the movement in spite of Nasser's opposition, and provided for the assassination of many leading people. When the news of the meeting of the High Command reached the movement on 22 July they rapidly advanced the hour of revolt. The drama of that evening lies in the clear knowledge each side had of the other's plans at the final stage, for, as Nasser gave orders to attack G.H.Q., the generals sent a force to surround the quarters of the rebellious officers. Yet there remained until the penultimate minute an underlying contempt for the revolt in the minds of the high officers, so much so that they sent a force commanded only by a captain to arrest the ringleaders. The captain joined the revolt and marched with Major Abdel Hakim Amer on G.H.Q.; the generals surrendered; at midnight army units moved smoothly from the barracks to occupy the tele-graph offices, the radio station, police stations and government offices; and by 1 a.m. Cairo was in their hands. The operation was just as successful in Alexandria where the King and the Government were spending the summer.

A force was sent from Cairo to guard the approaches from the Canal Zone in case the British troops marched to the King's rescue, and in the early hours of the morning the British Embassy was informed that the revolt was an internal matter which did not justify intervention. General Neguib was called from his home to take the post of Commander-in-Chief and, smiling and smoking contentedly, congratulated Nasser and his men. At seven o'clock on the morning of 23 July, Colonel Anwar Sadat broadcast from the Cairo station, in the name of General Neguib. He told the country that the army had seized power and would be responsible for law and order. He warned against violence and assured the foreigners in Egypt that the army would protect their persons and their property. The people received the news with delight, for the average Egyptian was wearied of 'the old order', which vaguely embraced everything from the Palace downwards that had gone to make his disillusionment.

Power in the country had been seized by the clandestine movement in the army, known as the Free Officers. Their executive committee told the King to dismiss the Hillali Government on the morning of 23 July and sent an emissary to Aly Maher to offer him the premiership. King Farouk, unaware that the committee were discussing at that moment whether to kill or exile him, 'invited' the committee to form a government, but was instructed to appoint Aly Maher. Wing Commander Gamal Salem and his brother Major Saleh Salem reported from Sinai that they had control of the forces there. Victory was everywhere complete by the night of the 24th.

Aly Maher was then sent to the Palace with a demand for the resignation of Farouk's entire entourage and he humbly submitted. The executive, having voted in favour of his exile, gave orders that 'the king must go by the 26th at the latest'. On the morning of the 26th Zacharia Mohieddin deployed his forces around the Ras el-Tin and Montazeh palaces in Alexandria while the troops in Cairo surrounded the Abdin and Koubbeh palaces, but the only resistance occurred at Ras el-Tin where the palace guards fired a few half-hearted shots.

The Prime Minister was again sent to the King, this time with an ultimatum that he must abdicate in favour of the infant Heir Apparent, Prince Ahmed Fuad, and be out of the country before 6 p.m. The Royal yacht *Mahroussa* was got ready and King Farouk spent his last minutes packing the maximum of valuables into numerous trunks and packing cases. With his Queen and Prince Ahmed Fuad he departed by the side door of the palace which gave access to the landing stage, from which a launch took them to the yacht, and there he was received by General Neguib, Wing Commander Gamal Salem and Colonel Hussein, with whom he exchanged formal but polite farewells. The officers disembarked and the *Mahroussa* headed for the open sea. His entourage scattered but most of them were caught and imprisoned.

The military junta told the Egyptian people that it was merely 'raising again the standard of the constitution' and appointed a

Council of Regency on 2 August as a basis of constitutional government. The function of the council, however, was only to give royal
assent to decisions of the executive of the young officers meeting at
army headquarters, who for some months more played with the
monarchy, preserving the fiction in the name of the tiny infant whom
Farouk was jealously guarding as the key to Egypt. But the monarchy
was already doomed. The officers gave themselves time to breathe
on 26 July 1952, but they had no doubt in their own minds that the
Mohammed Aly dynasty, which had ruled Egypt for nearly a
century and a half, was finished.

Aly Maher got together a radical but not revolutionary Government. His most urgent problem was the financial and economic
plight of the country, and most people, Egyptian and foreign, were
glad to see Abdel Gelil el-Emary, a capable Under-Secretary at the
Ministry of Finance, appointed Minister. It was nevertheless the
beginning of a period of conflict on many fronts. The pashas and
beys shrugged their shoulders wryly when General Neguib abolished
their titles on 30 July – *maalish*, one knew who was Pasha in Egypt
– but the talk of reform and the promise of a new and a better life
for the mass of the people was much more serious. In the industrial
areas of the main towns the workers believed their day had dawned,
and at Kafr el-Dawar, near Alexandria, the workers seized their
employer's textile factory on 13 August, and for a brief space of
about one day it seemed likely that Egypt would witness another
popular rising. Given the mood of the people it was possible that
others would follow the example of Kafr el-Dawar, believing that
they were joining the vanguard of a revolution which the army had
started for them. The military junta, who could not afford to see
the workers launch out on a revolt of their own, reacted promptly
to crush the workers at the textile factory and the two ring-leaders
were summarily tried, sentenced and hanged. The first victims of
the revolution to save the common people of Egypt were two
workers: no pashas, no beys, but no recalcitrant workers either.

The Free Officers chose at first to co-operate with people who were
not corrupt, irrespective of their political ideas; General Neguib
was at heart a conservative; Aly Maher had once drafted a national
charter but was typical of the old politician and best known for
political manoeuvring; Bahaeddine Barakat Pasha, one of the
Regents, was a forthright, honest man but far from radical. Both
the officers and the politicians were briefly deceived by these
arrangements, the officers because they thought they were getting
sober-minded and experienced men to help them to govern the
country, and the politicians because they believed they could send

the officers back to their barracks in due time. Neguib thought he was leading the revolution; Aly Maher had an underlying contempt for the young officers, and thought he could 'handle' them; Nahas Pasha and Fuad Serag el-Din, who were in Europe at the time of the *coup d'état*, flew back home in the firm belief that the revolt was intended to restore the Wafd Government. All were quickly disillusioned, but so were the Free Officers. Nasser, describing later how they turned to people of experience, wrote, 'every man we questioned had nothing to recommend except to kill someone else. Every idea we listened to was nothing but an attack on some other idea'.*

The Government ordered the political parties to publish their programmes and purge themselves of corrupt elements, and the parties, anticipating the tendencies of the military committee, proclaimed themselves radical, even revolutionary, with very little to choose between them, except for the Moslem Brotherhood which advocated an Islamic State. None purged itself, and General Neguib, choosing for attack the only party capable of resistance, pointed out on 8 August that evil elements remained in the leadership of the Wafd. He formed seven committees with almost unlimited powers to carry out purges that the parties had refused to do for themselves and ordered the democratic election of party officials, and he blocked their bank accounts pending authorisation by the Ministry of the Interior of the reformed organisations. From that moment until the middle of October the struggle between the Government and the politicians was open and acute, for the politicians realised with consternation and fear that they were now at the mercy of the army and that the game of palace politics, the only one they knew, was over.

Relations with the Moslem Brotherhood were strained but not broken, partly because there were sufficient Brethren in the army to make an open break tactically difficult and partly because the Supreme Guidance Council had not yet relinquished hope of controlling the officers. With the Wafd it was different. Nahas Pasha and Serag el-Din believed that the mystique of the Wafd was still powerful enough to secure for it a dominant position in the army and Nahas was convinced that he had almost messianic hold on the minds of the people; but the blocking of funds was a serious matter because it restricted patronage which sustained the machine when the party was out of office. It declared that it would neither comply with the new decree nor accept any reorganisation except under the leadership of Nahas Pasha; 'the Wafd is the people', he

* *Philosophy of the Revolution.*

said; anyone wanting to rule through and for the people must rule through it.

Faced with this resistance, the Free Officers, moving into the streets again in the early morning, took into custody sixty leading people, politicians and others, including Fuad Serag el-Din, two former Prime Ministers, and Prince Abbas Halim, a politically minded member of the royal family. Under pressure the Wafd suspended Serag el-Din from the position of Secretary-General and when the Supreme Court upheld the Government's decision to freeze its funds, which amounted to nearly £100,000, the party submitted by electing Saleh Fahmi Gomaa, a leading Wafdist whose record was less distasteful to the junta, in Nahas's place. This did not destroy the influence of Nahas, for he led as successor to the great Zaghloul, but the imprisonment of Fuad Serag el-Din and the freezing of the funds were effective and, by humiliating the Wafd, the officers demonstrated its weakness and, at the same time, the inability of the ageing Nahas to oppose them.

The successful outcome of the struggle made the abolition of the parties inevitable. The Saadist and Liberal Constitutionalist parties had crumbled at the first onslaught because there was neither widespread popular support nor an effective organisation to sustain them; many of the younger adherents drifted into co-operation with the new régime, while older groups settled back in grumbling protest. The Saadist Party leader, Ibrahim Abdel Hadi, who had courageously fought the terrorism of the Moslem Brotherhood in 1948, could have no future in a country run by a government which still retained relations with the Brethren. The National Party had been weakened by a split before the *coup d'état* and collapsed, the right wing under Hafez Ramadan fading away while the left wing under Fathy Radwan co-operated with the army.

The junta now moved consciously and deliberately towards the consolidation of its authority. In December General Neguib abolished the constitution, whose standard the revolution had promised to raise, and dissolved the political parties, confiscating all their funds and announcing at the same time a three-year transitional period to prepare the way for the restoration of parliamentary government. On 23 January, exactly six months after the *coup*, he told the people that he would have supreme authority for the next three years in accordance with the February constitution, which provided for a congress with executive power ruling on his behalf, while legislative authority would be vested in the Cabinet. He also announced the formation of a Liberation Rally which suggested that the ultimate aim was one-party government. It amounted to dictatorship by the junta, for the congress consisted of the thirteen members of the military committee, to be known as the Revolutionary Command Council, and the Cabinet was only partly civilian and controlled by officers who emerged as Ministers. The now threadbare mantle of secrecy was shed and General Neguib, whose supreme authority was proclaimed, was no longer supreme in the eyes of the people because at his side stood the Revolutionary Command Council and, above all, the somewhat forbidding figure of Colonel Gamal Abdel Nasser.

On 18 June 1953 the Government proclaimed the end of the monarchy and the inauguration of the Egyptian Republic, with General Neguib as President and Prime Minister, and Colonel Gamal Abdel Nasser as Deputy Prime Minister and Minister of the Interior. Colonel Nasser's closest confidant, Major Abdel Hakim Amer, was promoted Major-General and Commander-in-Chief of the Armed Forces in place of Neguib, and Wing Commander Abdel Latif Baghdadi was appointed Minister of War and Marine, and Major Saleh Salem Minister of National Guidance. Thus ended the Mohammed Aly dynasty, which had reigned for nearly a century and a half.

The change was significant as the overt consolidation of Nasser's power. He controlled security through the Ministry of Interior, his personal friend commanded the armed forces, another of the faithful controlled the Ministry of War and Marine, and Major Saleh Salem, a man of unbounded enthusiasm for the revolution, was its mouthpiece. The chain of direct control was complete: from the Free Officers inside the armed forces through the security Ministries, to the words that would express his purpose.

Many people in the ruling class were not unduly upset by the end of the monarchy and the political parties, for neither the King nor the parties had much reputation left, but when the Free Officers turned to agrarian reform they were being genuinely revolutionary and had the whole ruling class against them. Their economic ideas were nevertheless not extreme. They recognised, as everyone else recognised, that the country's fundamental problem was that people increased faster than land could be reclaimed to feed them. At the end of the nineteenth century there were less than ten million people, but in 1952 there were about 22 million, and, during this half-century in which the population more than doubled, the cropped area was only extended from 6·8 to 9·9 million acres or 50 per cent. The Egyptians were getting poorer. Nor was it easy to see what could be done about it, for there were limits to the possible expansion of cultivated area, and the growth of population, at the rate of a million in less than three years, absorbed the output of new land before reclamation or development could be completed. The Free Officers believed that there should be more equitable division of land, and that any agrarian reform should be supported by faster industrial and agricultural development.

Although the disastrous economic effect of Wafd misrule had been partly corrected by the Finance Minister of the Hillali Government, who had averted an outright collapse and restored order to the cotton market, there was almost nothing in the working sterling account through which nearly 70 per cent of Egypt's foreign trade was done. The able Dr. Abdel Gelil el-Emary, whom the Free Officers were fortunate to secure as Finance Minister, persuaded the British Government to release £5,000,000 from the blocked sterling account and overcame immediate difficulties, and by currency and import restrictions, encouraging the sale of cotton by more rational pricing, and other methods of careful husbandry, he was able to balance Egypt's foreign payments during the next twelve months.

Emary pointed out, however, that if plans for industrialisation were to succeed, Egypt must have about £500,000,000 of foreign capital, which could only be secured if the new Government restored international confidence. The first few months of the military régime were, therefore, marked by unusual moderation in foreign relations, and attempts were made to revise legislation which discouraged foreign firms. The Companies' Law, which laid down that foreign companies in Egypt must have 51 per cent Egyptian capital, used in conjunction with the Mining Law, had brought all exploration for oil to a halt in 1948, so the Companies' Law was changed to allow foreigners to retain control and the Mining Law revised in a manner acceptable, if not satisfactory, to the oil companies. The Labour Laws were also discouraging; they laid down that every firm must have a high percentage of Egyptian workers and, even more important, pay them a high percentage of total salaries, and the application of the laws made it increasingly difficult for foreign firms to maintain their expert staff or get them visas, almost impossible to discharge unsatisfactory workers without paying excessive indemnities and often damages for wrongful dismissal, or to close unprofitable workshops or factories without being compelled to pay the workers for months while the Labour Department studied the case. The principle behind this legislation was not in itself wrong, for the Government needed to protect workers in a country where there was no unemployment insurance and firms often employed too many foreigners, but the Department's application of these laws was xenophobic in the extreme and the Moslem

Brotherhood exploited the legislation to the limit from its strongly entrenched position in the workers' syndicates of big firms. The military régime could not change this legislation without running counter to its professed aim of defending the standards of the workers and to its 'Egyptianism', but it attempted to instil into the Labour Department the need for fair and reasonable treatment of foreign employers and workers.

In January 1953 the Government formed a Permanent Council for the Development of National Production, with the task of examining all schemes, and ensuring that they were executed in the correct sequence and used available capital efficiently. Ministries were ordered to submit all projects to the Council, which then gave the Cabinet an expert report on them. The first Three-Year Plan was modestly limited to several small projects of land reclamation and conversion, and improvements to roads and other communications, and it was planned to use State and private capital jointly for industrial development under government direction. Because people with money invested conservatively in land and real estate, some form of State-investment policy was necessary, but the Government went out of its way to reassure private investors.

In these matters the Free Officers were more realistic than revolutionary, but the domestic background to everything was the agrarian reform into which they plunged almost as soon as they seized power. The unequal distribution of the cultivated land of Egypt was an obvious evil; nearly 65 per cent of the land under cultivation was owned by about 6 per cent of the landowners, and 10 per cent was owned by 270 people in vast estates. There was a surplus agricultural population of about 5,000,000, with the result that wages were low, work irregular and under-employment general. Agrarian reform had been discussed for many years but had been frowned on by the King, who was the greatest landowner of all; and it had never had a chance of passage through a parliament which represented the landowning class. The military Government, which faced neither of these obstacles, issued a decree in September 1952, less than two months after taking office, which limited land-holdings to 200 acres, reduced rents by about 40 per cent, increased wages and undertook to distribute the land taken from the big estates in lots of not less than two acres and not more than five.

The Agrarian Law provided only about 650,000 acres from a total of about 6·5 million acres for distribution, and some members of the executive of the Free Officers had argued for a much more drastic limitation to one hundred or even fifty acres. A farm of

200 acres in Egypt, where productivity is very high, still constituted a very profitable holding, but the executive was convinced by expert advice that a more drastic limitation could not be financed or managed and might reduce the countryside to chaos; a limitation to fifty acres, for example, would have meant that about half the cultivated land would need to be redistributed. Even so, the law was revolutionary, for it altered the social pattern of the countryside and broke the power of big landowners who had dominated Egyptian society for decades. The vast estates of the royal family, totalling about 170,000 acres, were later confiscated without compensation. The compensation for other estates was low, but there was certain rough justice in basing it on the land tax, which the owners had fixed to their own advantage. Finally the reduction of agricultural rents enlarged the income of about 4,000,000 peasants and further impoverished all landowners.

The reform brought the régime into conflict with the landed aristocracy which had been the effective power in the land under all previous governments and it was opposed by the Prime Minister, Aly Maher, and by both Bahaeddine Barakat and Colonel Rashad Mehanna in the Regency Council, but the army leaders would not be balked of their plans to 'eradicate feudalism' and to develop industries, to which they intended to channel the funds paid as compensation. They forced the resignation of Aly Maher on 7 September and General Neguib became Prime Minister in a reformed Government consisting mainly of administrators and technicians, and in mid-October he dissolved the Regency Council and appointed the tractable Prince Abdul Moneim as sole Regent.

The upper class was thoroughly alarmed. Politicians, landowners, members of the royal family and disgruntled senior officers began to consult together on means to get rid of the junta. They looked to Colonel Rashad Mehanna who had considerable support in the artillery and might be able to raise a counter military force, but he was promptly seized and held under house arrest. The Revolutionary Command Council then bared its revolutionary teeth, confiscating the property of all members of the Royal House down to the remotest connections.*

On 15 September Major Saleh Salem, Minister of National Guidance, announced that members of the old régime were plotting with a foreign power for the overthrow of the Government, which

* The Government is said to have netted about £75,000,000 by this operation. Half of it was spent on improving Cairo, which in due course was embellished with a magnificent corniche stretching along the Nile from Shubra, a northern suburb, to Helwan, a distance of about twenty miles.

had therefore formed a revolutionary court 'to protect the people'. It consisted of three R.C.C. members, Wing Commander Hassan Ibrahim, Wing Commander Abdel Latif Baghdadi and Colonel Anwar Sadat, who had power to indict anyone for almost any form of opposition or for corruption under the old régime; and its verdicts could not be questioned in any court once ratified by the R.C.C. Although the court boasted of its leniency in giving the accused a trial at all, there was nothing judicial about it. The President, Wing Commander Baghdadi, told one defence lawyer who protested against an untrustworthy witness, 'you forget that this is a Revolutionary Court', and to another lawyer who questioned the correctness of a charge of espionage against his client, he remarked: 'a revolutionary court is not bound by ordinary legislation'. The court's purpose was to break any opposition which might exploit the growing unpopularity of the régime by punitive verdicts and the proceedings were given the greatest propaganda effect.

Those arraigned before the main court – there were other tribunals established for lesser offenders – were people from the old régime who might offer some threat to security. The tough Saadist leader, Ibrahim Abdel Hadi, was charged with plotting against the Government and with complicity in the assassination of the Moslem Brotherhood leader, Hassan el-Banna. Fuad Serag el-Din, two other Wafdist Ministers and the wife of Nahas, Karim Thabet, Dr. Ahmed Mahmud el-Naguib and Mohammed Hilmi Hussein, all members of Farouk's entourage, and Prince Abbas Halim (who was accused of profiting by the purchase of defective arms during the Palestine War) were also charged. Other courts arraigned communists in batches on charges of subversion.

Ibrahim Abdel Hadi was sentenced to death, but his sentence was commuted to life imprisonment. Serag el-Din was given a life sentence, and Karim Thabet, who was also sent to prison for life, was put in irons in Turah Prison. After these harsh warnings had had their effect the sufferings of the prisoners were eased. Ibrahim Abdel Hadi and Fuad Serag el-Din were said to be in ill-health and were given comfortable but strict confinement, and Karim Thabet, who suffered most of all, was in due course released from his irons when the Government decreed the end of all shackles in Egyptian prisons. Some time later they were all transferred to house arrest. The purpose of the trials was served. There was no more trouble from the politicians of the former régime.

# PART TWO

## Chapter 8

# The Origins of the National Revolt

AD THE VICTORY of the Free Officers been no more than a well-organised revolt of discontented soldiers it would not have survived the disrupting influences from within and without their ranks, but the movement was in the direct current of the national movement and the culmination of seventy years of struggle. Colonel Gamal Abdel Nasser had re-made the Arabi rebellion in more favourable conditions and succeeded where Arabi failed, establishing at last the ascendancy of the Egyptians in their own land. When he seized power in 1952 he was the first true Egyptian to rule his country since the last Saite pharaoh submitted to the Persians in the middle of the sixth century B.C.

There were striking resemblances between the Arabi and Nasser revolts. In both cases the officers first petitioned for a redress of grievances and attempted to strengthen the position of the 'Egyptian' officers in the army; for in this context Farouk's favourites were for Nasser what the Turkish officers were for Arabi, and the election of the Free Officers to the committee of the Army Club in December 1951 was a deliberate challenge to the King's men. Just as the Khedive Tewfik sought to turn away popular opposition by calling the Constitutionalists to power, so King Farouk called back the Wafd, and in both cases the radical movement was accidentally strengthened. Khedive Tewfik precipitated trouble by appointing his brother-in-law, Adly Pasha Yeghen, to be Minister, and King Farouk touched off the *coup d'état* by imposing his brother-in-law, Ismail Sherine, on the Hillali Government; and both rulers tried too late to save the situation, in Tewfik's case by making Arabi Minister of War, and in Farouk's case by offering Neguib the post of Commander-in-Chief. Colonel Nasser succeeded where Arabi failed because the balance of forces had, by the passage of time, been tipped in his favour, for whereas Arabi had only the political support of Constitutionalists, whose aims were in essence reactionary, Nasser was supported at first by the radical 'fighting front' which included the Moslem Brotherhood; and whereas the British Government felt compelled in its own interest to intervene to save Tewfik, it felt no similar need to save Farouk.

Unity of popular aims had been achieved by more than half a century of discussion, for the dialogue started by Jemal el-Din al-Afghani had not ceased with his expulsion from the country, and in one of his disciples, Mohammed Abdou, there emerged a man whose spiritual and intellectual calibre left its imprint on national thought. When Jemal el-Din and he were in exile in Paris in 1884 they produced eighteen issues of a periodical which profoundly affected the ideas of the next generation and in which they not only refashioned the concepts of the Pan-Islamic movement but, for the first time, expounded their concept of the role that Egypt should take in the Moslem world.

Mohammed Abdou was not a politician at heart nor a revolutionary by temperament. In course of time he drifted apart from al-Afghani and when he returned to Egypt in 1888 he was appointed judge and slowly established his authority in Moslem law. In 1900 he became Mufti, the highest religious authority in the State, and led the reform of Islam by a series of unorthodox rulings which stirred interest and intellectual discussion throughout the Moslem world. The reform of the ancient religious university, Al-Azhar, the pillar of Moslem orthodoxy, occupied a great deal of his life and he came into conflict with political nationalists in tolerance of British authority, which tended to support his attitude to reform.

It was a significant contribution to national thought that he believed that no compromise was possible with the Khedive, for this had a profound effect on the attitude of the Egyptians to their rulers, whether khedive, sultan or king, but this was incidental to his aim to liberalise Islam and make it a social and spiritual force capable of using the intellectual and material advances of the world. To this end he preached that the gradual transformation of the mind and spirit of Egyptians must take precedence over political revolution. The collaboration of Saad Zaghloul with Cromer can partly be explained by the influence of Abdou.

In the first years of the twentieth century the followers of Abdou constituted a third force in the country, standing between those who supported the British and those who supported the Khedive. While the national struggle kept to its narrow course in resistance to the British, from this third force there grew an intense intellectual debate between those who put the emphasis on Abdou's defence of Islam and those who saw in his belief that there was no essential conflict between the aims of science and of religion the most vital teaching. In course of time this broad division of thought produced the two main streams of Arab nationalism as represented by the radical secularists and the traditionalists represented by the Moslem Brotherhood.

The dialogue in Egypt was strengthened at the end of the nineteenth century by the influx of Christians from Lebanon who, escaping from the stifling atmosphere of the Ottoman Empire, revelled in the freedom of expression they were permitted by Cromer. This led them to support the British and to oppose both the Ottoman Empire and the national movement, providing through their newspaper the one substantial support that Cromer and the British had in public opinion. This political orientation did harm to their standing with the Egyptian movement and obscured the important role they played in modernising the intellectual life of the country. Fares Nimr and Yaccoub Sarruf, who founded the newspaper *Al-Mukattam* and the critical weekly *Al-Muktadaf*, believed in the liberal thought of nineteenth-century Europe and closely followed the progress of science. Jurji Zeidan, who founded the publishing house of Dar el-Hillal, rewrote Islamic history in the form of fiction, books and articles, which profoundly influenced the entire Arab world. Although all appeared to be in opposition to the political national movement, their high intellectual achievement and critical analyses played an important part in fostering the ideas of the movement in the twentieth century and created both intellectual and political unrest in the educated classes.

Abdou had taught them that to support a despot merely because he was a Moslem corrupted religion and the people, and that it was worthwhile to persuade a foreign ruler that the progress of the people could not do him harm. Thus, he deduced that in the State of Egypt, where so much had yet to be achieved both in ideas and material conditions, it was worthwhile working with the British to secure the advancement of the country. This was the policy of Saad Zaghloul during the earlier part of his political career, during which he believed the national movement to be immature and Turkey – another possible ally – helpless in the face of Europe. To those who, like Mustapha Kamal, turned to the French for support, he pointed out how unwilling they had been to give positive support when it was wanted. His disillusionment with the British was gradual and reached its climax with the collapse of the policy of Kitchener, but until that moment he had worked, as he believed, to prepare his country for independence.

One of the most influential writers of the time was Saad's brother, Ahmed Fathi Zaghloul, who translated numerous Western books of liberal thought into Arabic and sought to interest the Egyptians in the position of the individual in society and the rights of one to the other. He also sought to teach them the European concept of nationhood which he believed to be the necessary prerequisite of independence. One of the curious results of Ahmed Fathi's teachings was to create a widespread desire for British education at a time when the struggle against the British was gathering momentum. Another of Abdou's group, Qassim Amin, roused intense controversy by his writings on the emancipation of women, an idea which the political nationalist leader of the time, Mustapha Kamal, strongly resisted, but he created even greater consternation among conservatives by calling for a social and intellectual revolution.

In 1907 the Abdou group, which by this time included people who had taken part in the Arabi revolt together with a new generation of young, educated people, issued a newspaper, *Al-Jaridah*, which proclaimed itself to be 'a purely Egyptian paper' aiming at the defence of Egyptian rights and interests. From this paper there emerged the Umma Party, which deliberately set out to be a third force that aimed to achieve independence by collaborating with and using the British. The party included almost everyone who was later to have some leading part in the political and economic evolution of the country. It was essentially opposed to the power of the Khedive and when Sir Eldon Gorst based his policy on support for the Khedive, the relations between the British and the Umma steadily worsened and they did not revive until the Umma found in Kitchener a Consul-General whose ideas they could broadly accept.

Among this group there was Ahmed Lutfi el-Sayyid, a man whose life bridged the whole period from Jemal el-Din al-Afghani, whom he had known as a youth, to Gamal Abdel Nasser. He was born in 1872, and when the newspaper *Al-Jaridah* was formed he became its editor and continued to direct its policies until it closed down in 1915. He was the third in the line of the great teachers from Afghani and became known as 'the teacher of a generation'.

Lutfi el-Sayyid was a member of the Umma Party and took part in the delegation of Saad Zaghloul from which the Wafd Party was eventually born, but, dismayed by the conflicts within the delegation itself, he took no active part in politics after it. When *Al-Jaridah* closed down he began his long and distinguished teaching career at the University of Cairo. As a teacher and writer his long-range intention was political in seeking the ultimate independence of Egypt, but he differed from the political leaders during most of his long life in that he taught that the people of Egypt must acquire the moral and intellectual capacities to rule themselves. He was concerned to train people to bear the responsibilities of government, and one of his main criticisms of the British occupation was that it had done little to this end. He too was a great admirer of the liberal thinkers of Europe and considered that Egypt could only establish the foundations of its own progress upon those of Europe. He was opposed to autocracy and thought the withdrawal of the British forces of occupation was neither more nor less important than the limitation of the authority of the Khedive.

He did not seek to relate his ideas of progress to those of the Islamic religion, by implication seeking a secular, Egyptian State, and he openly opposed the Pan-Islamic and Ottoman ideals which were current in Egyptian thinking at that time. For him the Arab or Islamic community could only come together as a free association of national units; freedom was all: the freedom of the nation and the freedom of the individual within the nation.

Yet Lutfi el-Sayyid was a true descendant of Mohammed Abdou despite this divorce from religious tenets, for he sought to inculcate moral standards and to achieve a correct relationship between tradition and material progress. From his teachings there emerged the great debate in the Egyptian Press between those who sought to sustain tradition and those who were determined to achieve reform even in conflict with Islam.

Taha Hussein was a leading exponent of the latter school. Just as Mohammed Abdou had devoted a large part of his time to seeking reform of the Moslem University of Al-Azhar, so Taha Hussein sought also to modernise the university, and even risked imprisonment by writing critically of the Koran. A magazine was produced called *Weekly Politics* in which many distinguished politicians, such as Adly Pasha Yeghen, Sarwat Pasha, Mohammed Pasha Mahmoud, and other less powerful intellectuals, conducted wordy warfare against Al-Azhar. Sheikh Ali Abdel Razziq used its columns to advocate separation of religion from the State.

The intellectual ferment was in some degree a reflection of the changing social condition in cities such as Cairo, where the westernisation of customs and manners which had slowly taken place during the British occupation was hastened by the First World War. Egyptian participation in the pleasures of Western life increased greatly, mixed society became more common, and the bar and the cinema began to be common forms of entertainment. The narrow family traditions of the Moslem gradually relaxed in contact with Western society.

The conflict of ideas between traditionalist and modernist was hastened by the Turkish revolution. When Turkey relinquished its claim to the Caliphate after the First World War, abandoned the

Arabic alphabet, and embarked on a programme of secular reforms, the repercussions in Egypt were considerable. Turkey had cut the Gordian knot of Islamic tradition and law at a time when Egypt, her character still greatly influenced by the possession of Al-Azhar, the citadel of Islamic conformity, was philosophically unprepared for the change. The liberal writers did not want Egypt to follow Turkey's course all the way, but argued against the fossilisation of social and political ideas by the conservatives, who believed that the departure of Turkey from the fold of Islam was a grave sin, that all the needs of modern society were revealed in the Koran and the *Haditha* (the traditions of the Prophet), and that the Caliphate was the necessary and correct source of leadership for Islam. It was their view that the abdication of Turkey transferred to Egypt the mission of leading Islam and by implication, therefore, that the Caliphate belonged to Egypt, but the liberals, while opposing the Caliphate, also thought that Egypt had inherited the duty of leadership.

The Wafd Party, which directed the struggle against the British, was able to embrace many different shades of opinion. It was not opposed to modernism – Saad Zaghloul was by no means a narrow-minded Moslem – but it united a mass of Egyptian opinion which was in general, and certainly at its lower levels, essentially conservative. It was, therefore, quite compatible with the structure of the Wafd that it could come to terms with Taha Hussein and with fanatical traditionalists in town and village; but most modernists, or 'westernists', were antagonised by the intransigent and bellicose policy of the Wafd and its narrow struggle for political power, for they believed that it prevented the new Egypt from finding quickly its place in the stream of Western civilisation. The intellectual divergence from Wafdist ideas contributed to the many resignations of leading Wafdists in the 'thirties and 'forties.

By the end of the Second World War yet another generation had reached maturity which also had its intellectual origins in the stream of thought from Mohammed Abdou through Lutfi el-Sayyid, but it had reached the conclusion that the self-respect of the nation, for which men like Lutfi el-Sayyid had argued, could not be achieved gradually when the nation was not free. For them Lutfi el-Sayyid's idea that limitation of the authority of the Khedive (now King) was as important as the withdrawal of British troops was modified to the view that the King and the British were two forms of the same enemy. Their policy was directed primarily towards removing both their enemies and both extreme religious traditionalists and secular revolutionaries could find common cause in this short-term objective.

## II

The Moslem Brotherhood was born during the period of intellectual ferment, partly in resistance to the secular liberal trend in
the country and partly to demonstrate that social progress was
possible within the bounds of orthodox Islam. Its founder, Hassan
el-Banna, began his teaching and preaching mission in the provinces.
He was not an Azharist, trained to split hairs in that formidable
school, but had been raised by his father in strict adherence to
religious practice and was given a traditional education in religious
jurisprudence, theology, syntax and the Koran. He was initiated in
his boyhood into the 'way' of the Hasafiyeh Sufi order and developed
quite early an interest in organising societies.*

Hassan el-Banna was only thirteen years old during the 1919
revolt, but he joined the students' demonstrations and witnessed the
British occupation of Mahmudiyah. At the age of twenty-one he
was sent as a teacher to Ismailia where he was profoundly influenced
by the contrast between the privileged position of foreigners in the
Suez Canal Company and the British military installations and the
poverty of the Egyptian workers. In common with many young
people in Egypt he was deeply disturbed by the dissensions between
the parties after the 1922 Declaration, for he saw that political
power and the fruits of office had become ends in themselves to a
great many politicians, both Wafd and non-Wafd.

When he formed the Brotherhood in Ismailia in 1928, his
primary aim was to revive and purify Islam and the movement
acquired its character from his own orthodoxy and his opposition
to the secular trends of the Turkish revolution. It was less narrow
and sectarian than Al-Azhar: he stated in his memoirs: 'I tried to
make this a broad general movement based on science, education
and a spirit of militancy, which are the pillars of the Islamic mission.
He who wishes a specialised education (here referring to the Sufi
orders), he, and what he chooses, is his own affair'.†

He strongly opposed the modern trends in Egyptian thought and
society, which he believed to be a sinful departure from the teachings
of the Koran. From the 1919 rebellion and his period in Ismailia
he concluded that it was his duty to fight against foreign 'oppressors'
and the egotism of political leaders, and he considered that political

* One of these he modestly named 'The Society for the Prevention of Sin'.
There was a rampageous passion about his religion while still a student. He not
only preached, taught, wrote pamphlets and called the people to prayer from the
minaret; he would wake the muezzin and then shake the people in their beds to
make sure they heard his call.

† Quoted by Dr. Ishak Musa Husseini in his book, *The Moslem Brethren*.

parties should be replaced by a unified Islamic movement – and it was evident that by this he meant the Moslem Brotherhood. Finally he believed that the leadership of the Caliph of Islam should in due time be restored and be Egyptian, a view which was not orthodox but reflected national opinion. It is significant that the oath of obedience to himself as the Supreme Guide was the oath used in swearing obedience to the Caliph. He did not demand the appointment of a Caliph at once, presumably to prevent the movement offering it to a monarch, perhaps Farouk, and to give him time to conquer Egypt and acquire the title himself. By 1945 he was planning to rule Egypt and wanted to use the revolutionary movement in the army to help him to seize power.

He travelled the countryside from his headquarters in Ismailia and by the time he was transferred as a teacher to Cairo in 1934 he had already fifty branches of the Brotherhood. His opportunities were widened by residence in the capital, whence he began to organise Congresses of the Brotherhood and to send missions to other Moslem countries in North Africa and the Middle East; branches were formed in the Sudan, Syria, Palestine, Lebanon and North Africa. The movement took little part in political life beyond sending letters first to King Fuad and then to King Farouk and to all Prime Ministers, exhorting them to lead a pure life, among other things by eschewing alcohol and secluding their wives and daughters, demanding the dissolution of all political parties and the adoption of an Islamic constitution. Sheikh Hassan related in his memoirs that at that time the King and the politicians did not take him or his movement seriously and were ignorant of the extent of his activities.

The Brotherhood became consciously political in 1938, when he described it as a 'Salafite movement, an orthodox way, an athletic group, a scientific and a cultural society, an economic company, and a social idea'. He claimed that the Koran could illuminate the modern age as well as all past ages, and sought to unify the Egyptian people and then all Moslem peoples behind Koranic principles; to increase the wealth of the nation and realise social and economic justice between individuals and classes, to struggle against disease, ignorance and vice, to liberate the Nile Valley, then all the Arab countries, from all foreigners, and to promote international peace. It defined Arabs as Arab-speaking peoples and declared that the work of reviving the Caliphate was at the head of the programme but had to be done in stages. Any country which was guilty of aggression in the past or the present against any Moslem State was tyrannical and must be prevented from further aggression. The movement's weapons, he declared, were the power of faith, the power of unity and then the power of the sword, to be used when nothing else availed. He abjured his followers to avoid domination by notables who could use it for their selfish ends, and to avoid contamination by political parties which by their very existence were contrary to unity.

The power and personality of Sheikh Hassan el-Banna, to which enemies and friends alike testify, the evocative quality of his speeches and the strength of the organisation which he created, were something new and clearly marked out his path to power. He would gather the faithful around him, teach them to fight sin and tyrants, and, when the work of propaganda was complete and the mass of people assembled in their phalanxes behind him, he would, if necessary, loose them in armed action against his adversary. The plan was not far-fetched. He was worshipped by tens of thousands of people and his educated followers wrote of him in terms of adulation. He could have sent hordes of spiritual slaves, most of them souls as simple as the Dervishes who followed in the wake of the Mahdi, hurtling into civil war. In 1939 he began to collect arms and hide them up and down the country, and about that time he formed the secret terrorist wing of the movement.*

In his meetings and in the mosques during the war he told the Egyptians not to help the British and expressed support for Italy and Germany, and in a letter to Aly Maher Pasha, then Prime Minister, he advocated neutrality. He was in contact with army groups opposed to the British war effort and as soon as these activities became known to the police the leaders were dispersed and their activities banned, but their influence was already so great that parliament petitioned for the return of the Supreme Guide and some other leaders from provincial exile.

The situation in the country was similar to that existing during the First World War, when the national movement, unable to act, planned the policy which culminated in the 1919 rebellion, but there were two notable differences. The successors of Zaghloul were now divided in political parties struggling for power, while the resistance being organised underground was as much opposed to the Wafd as to any other party; secondly, a parallel movement of sedition was being formed inside the army, which was hardly affected in 1919. It is nevertheless true that the 1919 rebellion had

---

* The date of the formation of the terrorist wing is not precisely known, but it was in 1939 that Hassan el-Banna began talking of the *jihad* or holy war, and at the Brotherhood trials in 1954 one of the main accused said the wing existed in 1942 and possibly before.

its genesis in the First World War and that the plotting during the Second World War led eventually to the *coup d'état* of 1952.

## III

The radical movement in the army had much in common with the Brotherhood, and in Gamal Abdel Nasser it had a leader as dedicated as Hassan el-Banna; but whereas el-Banna chose the line of Islamic orthodoxy, Nasser sought to unite the two main tributaries of nationalism: Pan-Islamic sentiment and secular nationalism. The idea that the Moslem world should have its 'caliph' survived in both movements. In the beginning the Arab national movement did not seek to break away from the Ottoman Empire, seeking instead a kind of commonwealth status within an empire made more fit for its mission, for the Arabs accepted Imperial Turkey as an extension of Moslem history and considered the Ottoman Caliph and the power of Turkey necessary to the defence of Islamic countries, but even those few thinkers, such as Abdul Rahman Kawekebi, who were prepared to break with Turkey assumed the continuing existence of the Caliphate. (Kawekebi suggested that it should be restored to the Quraysh tribe of Arabia from which the Prophet came.)

The Arabs were already separated from Turkey when the Turks relinquished the Caliphate after the First World War and the orthodox Moslem believed that it must be assumed by someone else. King Hussein of Mecca claimed it for himself, but this was rejected by all the Arabs because he was unable to fulfil the essential condition: ability to defend Islam. The one Islamic State which might be able one day to fulfil that condition was Egypt, but whereas Hassan el-Banna planned to rule Egypt eventually as Caliph, the secularists and reformists in the Egyptian national movement regarded the whole Caliph-concept critically, some, such as Taha Hussein, condemning it outright. Nevertheless, in their belief that Egypt should assume Turkey's mantle as leader of the Moslem world, they were, consciously or unconsciously, accepting the idea of a Supreme Defender of the Faith. The army movement believed in this leadership; Gamal Abdel Nasser, a good Moslem in the reformist tradition, found common ground with secular nationalists in his desire for Western standards of material progress, but he was also at one with traditionalists like the Brotherhood in believing that the Moslem world should be restored to greatness by Egypt.

The seed of the army movement was sown in the late 'thirties by a group of officers who represented almost all shades of national opinion and who began to discuss among themselves what must be done to liberate and revive their country. In 1938, when the young King Farouk was at the height of his popularity, they had already accepted Lutfi el-Sayyid's opinion that the limitation of the power of the monarchy was as important as the evacuation of the British, but when the war broke out and they were all summoned to serve the British in one way or another, they were so against the Allies that for a time the King found favour in their sight by his resistance to Lord Killearn.

He could not, however, drive from their minds entirely their hatred for the Mohammed Aly dynasty, and his eventual submission to the British destroyed any credit he had at first gained. When Lord Killearn sent the tanks to Abdin Palace to impose a Wafd Government in February 1942 he began the destruction of the reputations both of the King and the Wafd, and gave new impetus to the army movement. Nasser subsequently stated that the incident had an electrifying effect on the spirit and sensibilities of the officers. The feeling of humiliation led some officers, including Mohammed Neguib and others in the Nasser group, to offer their resignations, but Nasser and his closest confidant, Abdel Hakim Amer, were not so much concerned with the insult to Farouk as with the offence to Egypt and determined that it must never happen again.

The officers' group met in the Zamalek suburb of Cairo and, wrote Colonel Anwar Sadat, the real revolutionary conspiracy dates from that time.* An attempt was made to co-ordinate the activities of the Moslem Brotherhood and the officers, because the Brotherhood had already its secret wing and was accumulating arms and grenades, but the Supreme Guide sought to merge the officers' movement into the terrorist wing and make its members join the Brotherhood and give the oath of obedience to himself. This Nasser refused, although at that time he had great sympathy for the Brotherhood's militancy.

The officer group was neither homogeneous nor disciplined, and its planning was haphazard. The unstable and adventurous General Aziz al-Misri, its spiritual guide, contacted the Germans and he and Anwar Sadat, with some of the Air Force officers, made arrangements with Rommel to be picked up and flown to the German lines. The plan failed, Aziz al-Misri was interned, and Sadat and another member of the group were caught when two German spies, with whom they had been in contact, were arrested. The Nahas Government helped British Intelligence in probing the

* The references in this chapter to statements by Gamal Abdel Nasser and Anwar al-Sadat are from their books: *The Philosophy of the Revolution* (Nasser) and *Revolt on the Nile* (Sadat).

fringe of the officers' movement and although it failed to destroy it the subversive activities were temporarily halted. Sadat remained in prison until the end of 1944, when, the Nahas Government having fallen, the authorities connived at his escape.

The movement, now the Free Officers, was reformed early in 1945 with Gamal Abdel Nasser in command of all the cells in the armed forces and Anwar Sadat of those adherents outside the ranks. The central committee, the handful drawn together by Nasser in preceding years, controlled all activities, although the civilian wing was never informed of the existence of the army wing. Throughout this period Nasser kept strict rein on the impetuous members of the group. Sadat confesses that when Lord Killearn rebuffed Nokrashy Pasha's request to reopen talks for the revision of the Treaty, he wanted his army group to blow up the British Embassy, and that it was Nasser, reminding him of the reprisals which followed the murder of Sir Lee Stack, who declared that the mistake should not be repeated. Nasser, whose aim was revolution rather than revolt, was 'not a man to be led away by dreams', remarked Sadat.

When the war was over and martial law rescinded in mid-1945, Colonel Nasser reformed his own organisation in five administrative sections: finance, security, propaganda, terrorism, and *combat personnel*. The committee responsible for *combat personnel* and security were the hub of the whole society and only members who had long and trusted membership were appointed to the security section, which determined whether or not proposed recruits would be admitted or existing members expelled, and on which depended the ability of the Free Officers to escape detection by the State and armed security forces and the King's private intelligence network in the army. The committee for *combat personnel* organised cells in the different branches of the armed forces and in some para-military organisations outside the services. At the pinnacle of the structure were Gamal Abdel Nasser and Abdel Hakim Amer, the only two who, it was said, knew the name of every member.

Although the Palestine War disrupted the organisation, it did not collapse. It encountered real danger for the first time after the murders of Nokrashy Pasha and Sheikh Hassan el-Banna, when Ibrahim Abdel Hadi extended his purge of dangerous elements in the country far beyond the bounds of the Moslem Brotherhood. Nasser was taken into custody by the Chief-of-Staff, Farik Osman el-Maadi, but so well had the society maintained its security that no evidence was found against him, and after a warning from Ibrahim Abdel Hadi he was allowed to go free. The King's terrorist fifth column, led by Mustapha Kamel Sidki, approached Nasser with a proposal that they should link their two movements, but Nasser denied that he had any contact with a secret society, and that moment of danger also passed. In response to the Government's new and unlimited powers of arrest without trial the officers tightened their organisation and dropped their civilian wing.

In 1949 the Executive Committee was composed of Gamal Abdel Nasser, Kamel el-Din Hussein, Abdel Hakim Amer, Hassan Ibrahim, Abdul Moneim Abdul Raouf, Saleh Salem, Gamal Salem, Abdel Latif el-Baghdadi, Khaled Mohieddin and Anwar Sadat. There were others very close to the Executive, such as Zacharia Mohieddin and Hussein Shafei who eventually became members of the Revolutionary Command Council, and Aly Sabry, one of the confidants of Nasser, who became his political adviser and eventually Prime Minister. The propaganda section, which had come too far into the open in the early 1940's, went underground, concentrating almost exclusively on a whispering campaign intended to convert soldiers to the Council's ideas and to spread those ideas in the cafés of Cairo and Alexandria. In 1950 Nasser was formally elected President of the Executive Committee.*

The officers rallied to the Wafd Government when it abrogated the Treaty, impressed by militant resistance to the British and apparently unaware that the Wafd was primarily concerned to cover its own mis-government, and they were slow to realise that the liberation phalanxes were disorganised and often completely out of the Government's control. They themselves trained the guerrillas and took a mine from the arsenal with which they intended to sink a British ship in the Suez Canal. By this time their conspiracy was slowly coming into the open. Their struggle with the King, for long confined to their respective intelligence groups within the armed forces, was brought into the open in December 1951, when, in opposition to the King, they elected General Neguib to the Presidency of the Committee of the Officers' Club and secured control of the Club Committee. The burning of Cairo on 26 January 1952 made it apparent to the officers that the moment of revolution was at hand, and their Executive Committee decided on 10 February to overthrow the régime in March. According to Colonel Sadat, the attempt was postponed because Colonel Rashad Mehanna, on whose troops the plan partly depended, deliberately arranged his own transfer to el-Arish to avoid participation.†

* Mohammed Hassanein Heykal who knew him well and had contacts with other members of the Free Officers' Executive did not know until the eve of the *coup d'état* that Nasser had any part in the movement.
† Colonel Mehanna was later made a Regent, and later again put under house arrest for attempting to plot against the military régime.

By July the movement had one thousand members and was clandestine only in the sense that its leaders were unknown. Generals in the army and the Ministers of the Crown knew of its existence. Mortada Pasha el-Maraghy, chief of the country's security, understood its strength and during his six months as Minister in 1952 he warned the King against actions likely to precipitate revolt. Colonel Ahmed Anwar informed Fuad Serag el-Din, the powerful Wafd Minister, that the army would support the Government if it deposed the King, and instead of throwing this self-confessed conspirator into gaol, Serag el-Din discussed with him the possible effectiveness of the Free Officers' movement and consulted him regarding the general to be Commander-in-Chief. Colonel Anwar Sadat, another leading member of the Free Officers, later reported that Serag el-Din 'did not disapprove in principle', but was concerned about the King's right to dismiss the Government and wanted to know whether, in such a case, the army would intervene on the Wafd's behalf.

The Free Officers still did not realise that political authority in Egypt was collapsing and the will to govern largely gone. When the Chief-of-Staff, General Hussein Farid, called his council of war at army headquarters a few hours before the *coup*, Colonel Nasser is reported to have remarked that it would save the Free Officers trouble because they could now take the army commanders all together instead of one by one, but he did not expect the High Command to be docile. Not a hand was lifted to save the King, not a soul stirred by pity or loyalty to risk his life, not a tear was shed outside the Palace. Those who had lived on his bounty sat with folded arms or fled towards the frontier, and the King himself could think of no one to save him – except the American Ambassador, and he was powerless to intervene.

## IV

For Nasser the revolution was the successful culmination of nearly twenty years of searching for what he subsequently described as the correct form of 'positive action' – a search which began when, as a schoolboy, he joined mobs in the street to throw stones at the British. In his reminiscences he wrote that 'within the Arab circles there is a role in search of a hero'; he was himself a revolutionary in search of a technique.

He was born in Alexandria of a lower middle-class family hailing from Beni Mor, a small town in the Assuit province of Upper Egypt, on 15 January 1918. His father was a district post-master earning about £30 a month, which at that time was sufficient for a family but not wealth. Gamal's mother died when he was eight, the age at which he was sent to school in Cairo. He started to study law, but in 1936, when the Anglo-Egyptian Treaty created the need for a larger Egyptian army and more officers, he tried for Military College and was admitted in 1937.

Like most of his generation he was animated from boyhood by the desire to liberate Egypt from the British, but in one respect he must have been unique. Whereas others were content to protest with stones and slogans, he soon realised that noise and violence were not enough and took time off for thought, becoming in due course that rare phenomenon in Egypt, the unknown nationalist, remaining for many years essentially a 'back-room boy'. The role suited his temperament, for whereas he was not a demagogue, he was always imposing in private. (His first speeches as leader of Egypt were harsh and didactic, making no concessions to his word-loving listeners and he acquired the technique of mass oratory only with difficulty.) His temperamental reserve was a help to him at the Military College when he began to move, instinctively rather than consciously, towards the concept of the Free Officers and needed to draw more and more like-minded men to him by personal persuasion.

By the time the Second World War began he was already speaking of 'we' and not 'I', the plural representing some kindred spirits he had brought together. The young officers from the College, on manoeuvres at Mankabad in Upper Egypt, would talk in 1938 about nothing else but their country, its wrongs, its sufferings and its corruption. 'If we started light-hearted conversation,' relates Colonel Anwar Sadat, 'it was invariably Gamal Abdel Nasser who interrupted us to bring us back to graver topics.' Sadat quotes Nasser as saying in 1938, 'We must fight imperialism, monarchy and feudalism, because we are opposed to injustice, oppression and slavery. Every patriot wants to establish a strong and free democracy. This aim will be achieved by force of arms, if need be. The task is urgent because the country has fallen into chaos. Freedom is our natural right. The way lies before us – revolution'. Nevertheless, he advocated patience, preaching a long-term policy to people of gusty and unsteady nature, and this break with the temperament of his people was his characteristic contribution.

He had tried rioting against the British and leading delegations to statesmen demanding unity of national purpose. He has himself described the process:

'For a brief period, positive action in my estimation meant my own enthusiasm and zeal. But this idea changed and I began to see that it was not enough for me merely to be enthusiastic. I had also to inspire others with enthusiasm.

'In those early days I led demonstrations in the Nahda Secondary School and I shouted from my heart for complete independence, and many others behind me shouted too. But our shouts only raised dust that was blown by the wind and produced weak echoes which shook no mountains and shattered no rocks.

'Then I began to think that positive action would be to demand that the leaders of Egypt unite to agree upon a single policy; so we went round in groups, shouting and excited, to visit their houses demanding in the name of Egyptian youth that they agree on a single policy. But their agreement, when it came, dealt a severe blow to my expectations. The policy on which they decided was the Treaty of 1936.'

He described how the Second World War moved his whole generation towards violence. 'I confess that to my excited imagination at that time political assassination appeared to be the positive action we had to adopt if we were to rescue the future of our country. I considered the assassination of many individuals, having decided that they were the main obstacles which lay between our beloved country and its destined greatness. I began to study their crimes and to take it upon myself to judge the harmfulness of their actions. I even considered the assassination of the ex-king and some of his entourage who had such utter disregard for things we held sacred and I was not alone in thinking thus.' There follows in his *Philosophy of the Revolution* his description of his part in an attempt at assassination, his restless night tortured by the memory of the screams of women and children, and his realisation at dawn that the 'method' must be changed. But, even before the attempt, deep in his heart he 'had not been at all satisfied that violence could serve as positive action'.

From that time on, stated Nasser, thinking was directed towards more important and more far-reaching action and he forged a weapon during the next decade without knowing how it could be used. The object was freedom, but he admits that the method of achieving it was not determined until the *coup d'état*. He turned his movement to the services of the Arabs in Palestine, planned to block the Suez Canal in 1951, and toyed for years with the idea of co-operating with the Moslem Brotherhood, but these plans were all little different from a thousand others for positive action that Egyptian nationalists framed through the years and forgot. In the end, Nasser wrote: 'It was not the army which defined its role in the events that took place; the opposite is closer to the truth. The events and their ramifications defined the role of the army in the great struggle to free the nation'.

His main contribution was to hold firm to his purpose through difficult times and know the true moment when it came, cultivating the calm of the sea-green, incorruptible fanatic, and keeping his mind perpetually poised to its purpose. He could talk from his fox-hole in the Faluja pocket to the Israelis who had brought shame on his country and his army, and discuss neither the Palestine War nor the armistice negotiations but how the Jewish underground had fought the British during the Mandate. The Palestine failure was meaningless to him beside the problem of Egypt which had been in subjection through many centuries; it did not matter that a little more bitterness was added to the cup, only to break the cup.

He was deficient in political theory but he had mastered the history of Egypt and the teachings of the great nationalists, whether they were military activists such as Arabi, philosophers such as Mohammed Abdou, or political teachers such as Mustapha Kamal, and he had measured, to his own satisfaction at least, the achievements and failures of all those who had sought to regenerate Egypt, from Sayed Omar Makram who called on Mohammed Aly to right the wrongs of the people, through the Khedive Ismail, to Saad Zaghloul and Mustapha Nahas. The importance of history through all the centuries right back to the pharaohs lay for him in the tragedy of the people; Pharaohs, Ptolemies, Romans and Turks, Mamelukes, Kings and the British, even the Moslem conquerors themselves, all strutted upon a stage formed of the dumb, suffering masses. 'The underlying constant remained the same, never changing. Only the name of the oppressor was different.' The booty of the Mamelukes 'was our souls, our bodies, our wealth and our land'. Evolution in Europe from the renaissance to the nineteenth century took place naturally, but Egypt was 'still living mentally in the captivity of the thirteenth century, in spite of a few manifestations of the nineteenth and, after, of the twentieth century'. 'We live in a society that has not yet taken form.' And after all the suffering and oppression, the fruitless struggle for freedom; 'it would', he says, 'be monstrous to impose a rule of blood'. His conversation was devoid of the concepts and the vocabulary of Western political thought, whether communist or fascist, but alive with the ideas and historical inferences of Egyptian nationalism.

The radical wing of the national movement to which he belonged had gradually drawn away from the political parties and was a loose federation of extreme opinion which had been distilled from the intellectual debate of the preceding decades – in its activism, in direct line from Arabi, through Mustapha Kamal, to Saad Zaghloul. It was this inheritance that Mustapha Nahas and the Wafd had squandered after Zaghloul's death. Nasser took his experience from the failures of his forerunners, concluding from Arabi that the army must be truly national, from Mustapha Kamal that words were not enough, and from the experience of the 1919 rebellion that there was nothing so treacherous to his cause as the Egyptian ruling class.

The similarity between Arabi and Nasser was striking. Both were of modest social standing and village origin. Arabi was educated at Al-Azhar, whereas Nasser went to secular schools, but both were devout Moslems. Both were against foreign domination, but based their movement on opposition to anti-national forces in the army; in Arabi's case against the privileged position of the Turks and in Nasser's against royal favouritism which had corrupted the officer class. Both movements were drawn in the main from the Moslem population but were not anti-Christian, and both got their strength from the village 'middle class' from which many of the great popular leaders of modern Egypt have been drawn.

*Chapter 9*

# The Internal Struggle for Power

A s SOON AS the first and essential acts of government had been performed and the Free Officers' Executive sought to formulate a policy, opinions clashed and a struggle for power began. As the secular and religious extremists pulled in opposite directions in pursuit of power, they revealed how incomplete was the movement's control of the army, which had been almost unanimous in desiring to overthrow the King but was not committed to Nasser's revolution. The Free Officers' intelligence service weeded out enemies but could not inculcate a uniform opinion even in friends, much less the larger body of acquiescent serving men. The small naval force had not been penetrated at all, and the cavalry, aristocracy of the army and officered from the very wealthy landowning class, was not effectively subverted.

General Mohammed Neguib was a conservative turned revolutionary and became, almost by accident, the instrument of resistance to the Nasser bloc. His contact with the Free Officers dating back to 1949 had not taken him into their inner counsels, and when he was offered the leadership in 1952 he hesitated until a few days before the *coup d'état*. It was the understandable hesitation of a spirit more akin to his own generation than to the radical fighting front, to which he was drawn solely by disillusionment with the King and politicians. The front was attracted to him by his gallantry in the Palestine War, his honesty, and his hatred of the corruption and nepotism of the Palace; but in the end it was the King's hatred for him that drove him into the secret army movement.

The Executive were so charmed by his frank and amiable manner that they made him president of their committee on 14 August. It was a romantic touch. The junta would be the nameless ones, the anonymous saviours of the people, while Mohammed Neguib represented them before the world. The people loved him. He coined the slogan, 'Unity, discipline and work', and the easy-going Egyptians thought it wonderful. He wandered about talking to them, listening to their complaints and, what is more, investigating them, until he came to believe from this popular adulation that he was the true leader of the revolution, that it depended on him. In the meetings of the Executive, however, he still had only one vote and was frequently outvoted by the young officers, none of whom was yet forty, and it irked him more and more that he was responsible to the people for policies and attitudes that he disliked. The Free Officers in turn began to consider this cult of personality dangerous when General Neguib, inspired by his popularity, began to make public statements with which they disagreed. As the conflict grew behind the scenes in the autumn of 1952, Nasser and his colleagues began to drop their anonymity, and at the turn of the year they were in the open and the role of Nasser, as chief architect of the revolution, was well known.

The people did not warm to the austere young man. Neguib's pre-eminence was not disturbed and he still held every post of importance, combining Head of State with the presidency of the military committee. In the belief that his popularity made it difficult for the officers to oppose him, he began to exert authority within the junta itself and at this point Colonel Nasser and his colleagues tried to deprive General Neguib of some of his positions. Neguib later wrote: 'Either I should be given the power I needed to govern Egypt in what I considered an efficient manner, or I could resign in favour of Gamal Abdel Nasser. . . . As the President, Prime Minister and the "Leader of the Revolution" I was responsible for every action taken by the government. I had no objection to assuming responsibility for actions of which I approved. But I was no longer willing to resume responsibility for actions regarding which I was either not consulted or of which I did not or could not approve'.* In short, he demanded a right of veto.

When the republic was declared in June 1953 he refused to give up the post of Prime Minister to Nasser, and after long hours of debate the R.C.C. agreed that Neguib should remain President and Prime Minister and that Nasser should become Deputy Prime Minister. In the late summer he objected to the punitive revolutionary tribunals and as the year drew to its close foreign diplomats and others knew that Neguib thought that the 'boys' often behaved very foolishly. He was consciously challenging Nasser, apparently forgetting that the régime was founded on the army which the Free Officers manipulated. He stated that he was asking for no more power than was normally accorded to a president and prime minister, but Egypt was not the United States. He proposed that there should be an elected assembly and a civilian cabinet, in effect for the abdication of the R.C.C. in his favour, and early in 1954 he

* General Neguib, *Egypt's Destiny*.

demanded a chain of command downwards from himself in place of unwieldy government by committee. 'I suggested,' he wrote, 'that he (Nasser) allow me to run things for a few years until he had acquired the experience necessary to succeed me, at which time, I assured him, I would gladly resign in his favour. Otherwise, I said, I would be forced to resign immediately, even at the cost of causing a crisis. . . .'*

The answer of the R.C.C. was to drive Neguib further from authority by deliberate neglect and on 23 February 1954 he sent his resignation to the Council. The R.C.C. accepted it next day, the palace guard around Neguib's humble home at Zeitoun was replaced by infantry and military police, and his three phones were cut.

All those opposed to the régime, the rich, the left wing, the Moslem Brotherhood right, the Wafdist centre, supported Neguib, not because they believed he was the potential saviour of the country but because they calculated that through him they might break the autocratic rule of the R.C.C.; he became the rallying point for counter-revolutionary forces. This was evident in the council discussions on Neguib's resignation, when Major Khaled Mohieddin, a secular leftist, argued in favour of a proposal of Neguib, of the traditional right, for a constituent assembly and a return to democracy. The left wing of the régime as represented by two influential journalists, Ahmed Aboul Fath, who edited the pro-Wafd newspaper *Al-Misri*, and Ehsan Abdel Kuddous, editor of the popular weekly *Rose el-Youssef*, who were very critical of the dictatorial temper of the R.C.C., also wanted an early restoration of parliamentary life, and were opposed to the suppression and imprisonment of communists by the revolutionary tribunal.

Khaled Mohieddin had been responsible for the cavalry during the *coup* and when the R.C.C. accepted Neguib's resignation he put them on stand-by in their barracks, representing to this most conservative element in the army that Neguib's proposals were an effort to restore sane government. He was, in fact, trying to use the cavalry to execute a *coup* which, if not communist, was certainly pro-communist. The cavalry demanded the reinstatement of Neguib and the appointment of Khaled as Prime Minister, and Nasser, playing for time, agreed, securing also the agreement of the members of the Council at Army headquarters. But it soon became apparent that the cavalry officers represented a very small faction and when next Khaled and the other cavalry leaders were summoned to G.H.Q. it was to be warned by the Commander-in-Chief, General Amer,

* General Neguib, op. cit.

11—ME

that their transgressions would only be overlooked if they gave no more trouble. Nevertheless there had been demonstrations in the street in favour of Neguib, notably by the Brotherhood, and the Council invited him to resume the presidency. He did so, but it was not until the communiqué of the R.C.C. was issued on the morning of 28 February that he learnt that Gamal Abdel Nasser was the new Prime Minister, not Khaled.

The President again became the rallying point for enemies of the régime, but whereas, with the defeat of Khaled, the communists were in eclipse, the Brotherhood now thought that they had imposed their will on the R.C.C. and were on the threshold of power. President Neguib, for his part, believed that the will of the people had triumphed over the Council and confidently promised a cheering crowd that he had returned to office to restore parliamentary government. He did not realise that he was only the tool of the opposition, but Nasser recognised the situation for what it was, an attempt to oust the Free Officers by exploiting the popular appeal of Neguib for parliamentary government. Nasser had, however, acquired one advantage over his enemies; they had unveiled themselves, and he decided there and then to destroy them.

On 1 March Neguib flew to Khartoum, taking with him, as a sign of harmony in the R.C.C., Major Saleh Salem, who had done his utmost to discredit him only four days earlier. In their absence Nasser arrested the cavalry ringleaders and some communists and Moslem Brothers, and began a systematic check on the loyalty of the Free Officers, and Zacharia Mohieddin, now Minister of Interior, investigated the loyalty of the police. The Liberation Rally, which had been formed in January 1953 as the embryo of one-party government, made direct contact with the trade unions and was put in readiness to counter any move by the Brotherhood in the streets.

On the President's return to Cairo, General Amer gave a banquet in his honour at which he was allowed to expound, as one in authority, his concept of a parliamentary republic. Press censorship was abolished and it was announced that a constituent assembly would be elected in time to meet on 23 July, the second anniversary of the *coup d'état*. The liberated Press quickly manifested its discontent with the régime; in particular, Ahmed Aboul Fath took the influential *Al-Misri* into open opposition and sought to unite the Moslem Brotherhood and the Wafd in a demand for complete freedom. Politicians of the old régime began to reappear and consult together, ready at last, after the lesson of two years of military rule, to bury their differences in a national front. President Neguib assured them that democracy would be restored.

On 9 March Nasser relinquished the post of Prime Minister and president of the R.C.C. to Neguib who, thus encouraged, pressed for demilitarisation of the Government, the election of the constituent assembly and a referendum to test popular opinion on his own position as Head of State. Nasser replied that there could be no half-measures; if it was to be democracy then it should be real democracy; the revolution was over. On 25 March the R.C.C. accepted Nasser's resolution proclaiming the abdication of the Council on 24 July, the restoration of the political parties and the Moslem Brotherhood, free and direct elections for a constituent assembly and the election of the President by the assembly. The R.C.C. added that it would not form a political party to contest the elections.

President Neguib was thus presented to the country as the man who broke the revolution, and three days later the Liberation Rally and the trade unions organised a general strike in support of the R.C.C. The army and the police held meetings at which they warned him that the régime would not be allowed to collapse. On 17 April he resigned the post of Prime Minister, and Nasser re-formed the Government with two more members of the R.C.C. in his Cabinet. Censorship was reimposed, the decisions of 25 March were cancelled, the re-emerging parties were again suppressed, the cavalry officers who had supported Khaled Mohieddin were put on trial and Khaled was sent to exile in Europe. General Neguib remained as President, but he was discredited with the army as the man who nearly wrecked the revolution and with the public because he was nominally responsible for the reimposition of dictatorship. He lingered in office for some months more, but his effective reign ended on 17 April.

These events in the spring of 1954 defeated the conservative forces fighting for the old order and curbed the secular pro-communist wing of the radical movement, but the Moslem Brotherhood with its mass following and leaders with ambition to rule, and a belief in their right to do so, was still powerful. The Supreme Guidance Council made no secret of its opinion that the military movement was an instrument intended to put the Brotherhood in power. In August 1952 its magazine, *Al-Muslimun*, had stated that the army had successfully accomplished the first task – that of 'lifting the burden from the nation's back' – and the long-term task of establishing a state based on Moslem law and education must be undertaken by 'those who understood the essence of it'; in short, by the Guidance Council. They had suggested to Nasser that the régime should retain power for ten years, in co-operation with, and under supervision of, the Brotherhood. In 1953 the Supreme Guide had proposed to Nasser that the Brotherhood should form a committee to inspect all draft laws prepared by the Government, and when Nasser bluntly refused, Hudeiby had ordered his followers to oppose the régime.

Free Officers who were members of the movement believed there was a common purpose, and from time to time had considered an alliance; liaison was sustained by the fanatical Abdul Moneim Abdul Raouf. Nevertheless the co-ordination never took place and the Free Officers became convinced that Hassan el-Hudeiby was seeking to use the army movement only to further his ambitions. The Brotherhood had to be handled with care, if only because it had both members and sympathisers in the army, but when it began to organise cells in the armed forces and the police, and to seek control of the labour unions, the R.C.C. warned the Supreme Guide to desist and, when the warning went unheeded, smashed the cells by sending some of the members to distant posts and imprisoning the ringleaders.

In January 1954 the Supreme Guide threw aside his pledge to refrain from political activity and at a mass rally at Cairo University, Brotherhood students assaulted others of the Liberation Rally. The Government immediately dissolved the Brotherhood as a political party and arrested several leaders, including Hassan el-Hudeiby, but its clandestine propaganda then called for armed struggle against the R.C.C. At this point the Neguib crisis occurred and the Brotherhood sprang to the assistance of the President, organising violent demonstrations in which nine people were killed and thirty-five injured. During the brief period of Neguib's ascendancy Hudeiby and other leaders were released from detention, and such was the potential power and influence of the movement that Nasser, when he again took control, exempted it once again from the ban on political parties.

This leniency ushered in the final struggle between the military Government and the Brotherhood. The leaders were far from appeased and now turned to their terrorist wing and gave Abdul Moneim Abdul Raouf, who had been dismissed from the Free Officers' Executive, a free hand to organise for armed struggle. They had arms supplied for fighting the British in the Canal Zone, where Nasser was still using guerrillas, among whom were many from the Brotherhood phalanxes.

Nasser's determination to secure an agreement with the British brought the crisis to a head. The activities of the Young Brethren, as the Brotherhood called the resistance groups in the Canal Zone, had become a menace rather than a help to this end, for when

Nasser secured a resumption of negotiations in the spring of 1954 any major outrage in the zone could have halted them. The Brotherhood was quite ready to torpedo the talks and its clandestine propaganda condemned the R.C.C., and Nasser in particular, for treacherous negotiations, although it was well known that the Supreme Guidance Council, if they secured power, would willingly have settled with Britain on terms less onerous than Nasser's. In opposition they contended that the revolution had taken place to drive out the British by force, an attitude which Nasser now found highly inconvenient; overnight he tumbled the militant groups in the zone from the pinnacle of patriotism to the depths of wicked criminality and within a few days they were dispersed or thrown into gaol. Nasser told the British that he had restored security in the zone and hoped to ensure that neither the Brotherhood nor the communists would again disturb the even tenor of negotiations. The Brotherhood, aided by the communists, made every effort to arouse opinion against the régime. Hudeiby toured the Arab countries inflaming the Brethren against Nasser, 'the traitor to the national cause', and Syria became the focal point of opposition outside Egypt.

Nasser struck first at the communists, and by 31 May had 252 in gaol. He told a conference of Liberation Rally leaders that 'Communists can live only in chaos and in this they have the support of the Zionists', and that they were working in the interests of a foreign power. Then he accused the Brotherhood leaders of seeking to seize power and leading the movement into alliance with communists in a campaign of destruction and subversion. When the leader of the Brotherhood Youth Movement defied the Government by calling a mass meeting to fight the régime there were numerous casualties in the ensuing clash with the police. Nasser deprived the Egyptian Brotherhood leaders in Syria of their nationality and attacked those in Egypt more fiercely than ever, warning them in private that if they resorted to assassination the Free Officers had instructions to take vengeance immediately on the Supreme Guidance Council.

Nevertheless, Abdul Moneim Abdul Raouf continued to organise the terrorist groups for the murder of his former friends of the R.C.C. and an attempt on Nasser's life was made on 26 October while Nasser was addressing a Liberation Rally meeting in Alexandria. Mahmoud Abdul Latif, a simple-minded tinsmith from Cairo, sitting six rows from the front, emptied his revolver at the platform, hitting nothing except a light bulb above the Prime Minister's head. While Abdul Latif was seized and taken away, Nasser continued his speech, declaring: 'let them kill Nasser. What is Nasser but one man among many? Whether he lives or dies, the revolution will go on'. The police and the army took to the streets. It was the moment Nasser had been waiting for and before dawn many of the leaders were in gaol; within five days five hundred had been arrested, and before the purge was finished, four thousand.

Realising that the mass of the Brotherhood were decent, simple Egyptians, Nasser set out to destroy the leadership and the terrorist wing which constituted the real evil of the movement. They were shown little mercy by the special tribunal established by the R.C.C. to try them, which consisted of Wing Commander Gamal Salem, Colonel Anwar Sadat and Colonel Hussein el-Shafei, all of whom were on the Brotherhood's list for assassination. The tinsmith, Latif, and three terrorists directly concerned in the plot against Nasser were hanged, but what shocked Egypt and the other Arab countries was that two members of the Supreme Guidance Council, Sheikh Mohammed Farghaly and Abdul el-Kader Oda, the Secretary of the Council, went with them to the scaffold. Hudeiby was sentenced to life imprisonment. The tribunals continued to send the brethren to varying terms of imprisonment until hardly a single prominent member was left at large. Abdul Moneim Abdul Raouf escaped abroad and was never caught.

This was also the end of Neguib's career. During the main trial evidence was given that he had been in contact with the Brotherhood and was prepared to see the Government, of which he was still the titular head, overthrown. On 14 November he was put under house arrest and as there were now no dissidents in the R.C.C. to support him, nor officers in the cavalry to fight for him, no Moslem Brotherhood, Wafdist or communist to call the mob out for him, his imprisonment did not cause a ripple of disturbance anywhere in Egypt. His detention and the destruction of the Brotherhood organisation completed the *coup d'état* which began more than two years earlier. Nasser, its architect, was President, Prime Minister and leader of the revolution and, above all, he was completely master of the Free Officers who secured his position.

## Chapter 10

# The Victory of Nationalism

I

THE FREE OFFICERS regarded the evacuation of British troops from Egypt as their first task. They were so convinced that the British controlled Egypt that they expected the British to use troops from the Canal Zone to save the King and the politicians, and some of Nasser's forces were deployed across the roads to Port Said and Suez to prevent them doing so. The British Government, however, if it had no reason to assume that a dictatorship by young and unknown officers was necessarily good for Egypt or for Britain, had equally no urge to shed anyone's blood in defence of an irresponsible king or of politicians who had usually been just as irresponsible. The British Chargé d'Affaires advised the officers that the retention of the monarchy would help to create confidence and stability, but his main concern was to get an assurance regarding British and other foreign nationals in Egypt, and when it became apparent that the army was taking adequate steps to that end, the British Embassy sat back to assess the new régime and its chances of survival.

This strengthened the influence of those among the army leaders who thought that Britain should be given another chance to negotiate and weakened those who believed that 'the British only understood force'. General Neguib said publicly as early as 14 August that 'Egypt would always treasure the friendship of the British people', and the British Government, warily lowering its guard, released £10 million from Egypt's blocked sterling to help the new Government through its financial difficulties. It gave away nothing else. General Neguib and the junta, who were impatient to be loved for their moderation by the world – and particularly by Britain, were irritated.

They were compelled to moderate courses by the grave economic plight of the country, and fresh conflicts with Britain would have led to new hardships and perhaps total bankruptcy. Both Neguib and Nasser believed that a peaceful settlement with Britain would help them through their immediate economic difficulties and long-term effort to raise the living standards of the people. This moderation was apparent when the military Government approached the Sudan, which General Neguib, who was part-Sudanese, and Nasser and other members of the junta knew well. As they were not bound by a king's ambition to rule the Nile they were able to abandon the constitution put on the statute book by the Wafd in 1951, which assumed the unity of the two countries under the Egyptian crown, and negotiate freely.

Steps towards self-government had been taken in the Sudan during and after the war, and a conference called in 1946 to consider further constitutional developments in the Sudan had recommended the Governor-General to create a legislative assembly to which the majority of members would be elected by direct means in the main towns, indirectly in the more backward areas of the northern Sudan, and from the Provincial Councils of the three southern provinces. This was done in 1948 and half the executive council seats were allotted to Sudanese, and a number of Sudanese under-secretaries were appointed. Although extensive powers were retained by the Governor-General, the elements of democratic government were there. This ordinance had not, however, been approved by the Egyptians, who opposed all constitutional development on the grounds that Britain was encouraging a separatist tendency in the Sudan.

Negotiations between the Egyptian Foreign Minister, Khashaba Pasha, and the British Ambassador, Sir Ronald Campbell, had concluded with a draft agreement in 1948, which would have secured Egyptian co-operation in the Sudan Government, but the draft was rejected by the Foreign Affairs Committee of the Egyptian Senate, principally because Britain was unwilling to give Egypt an equal share in the proposed Government. The pro-Egyptian parties, led by the Graduates of Congress, refused to take part in the elections, so the legislative assembly was dominated by the Independence Front, but when the pro-Egyptian groups succeeded in winning a majority of one seat in the Omdurman municipal elections and gained ground also in Khartoum, the belief was strengthened in Egypt that the Sudanese wanted union. The Egyptians decided to offer self-determination to the Sudan in 1952, and in doing so assumed that they were preparing the ground for voluntary adhesion of the Sudan to Egypt.

In October, General Neguib reopened negotiations, begun by Hillali, with Sayyid Abdul Rahman el-Mahdi, leader of the Ansar sect of Islam and patron of the Umma Party, which wanted independence of the Sudan and opposed the union. Whereas Hillali had been compelled to seek some recognition of unity, Neguib was able to offer the right of self-government with or without unity.*

After discussions with Sayyid Abdul Rahman, Neguib signed an informal agreement with the Umma Party by which Egypt recognised the right of the Sudan to independence and withdrew its objections to the self-governing statute enacted by the Sudanese Legislative Assembly, and the Umma agreed to international commissions to advise the British Governor-General and supervise the election of provisional and permanent Sudanese parliaments. Neguib then obtained the approval of the Unionist parties and persuaded them to form a coalition, known as the National Unionist Party, to present a united front against the Umma, with Ismail el-Azhary, leading exponent of unity, as President.

The British Government could not refuse to negotiate because its own policy was founded on the right of the Sudanese to self-determination, and its principal support came from the Umma Party. The negotiations with the Egyptian Government proved difficult, for it was immediately apparent that the Egyptians aimed to eliminate British influence as quickly and as thoroughly as possible, in the first place by limiting the power of the Governor-General during the transitional phase and then by instituting direct elections throughout the country including the non-Moslem south, which was unfit for that kind of democracy. The British administrators were anxious about the stability and security of the south, where the people, some of whom could remember the Moslem slave traders and most of whom knew of them by oral tradition, were deeply suspicious of the northern politicians. These anxieties were justified later by a mutiny in the south, but the British were in a weak position because the Umma Party, unwilling to have independence frustrated or unduly delayed by British doubts, stood firmly by the

* General Neguib has explained in *Egypt's Destiny* that the British demand for self-determination for the Sudan was considered a trick intended to deprive Egypt of her rights, and that he called 'Britain's bluff' by making the same offer, but the Free Officers, victims of their own propaganda, were unaware that behind the policy even of the pro-Unionist parties was the belief that 'if we got rid of the British we can get rid of the Egyptians when we like'. This view was explained to the author by the leader of the Unionists, Ismail el-Azhary, as early as 1946. General Neguib's autobiography, which concludes shortly after the first Sudanese elections returned a Unionist coalition, states that the election vindicated 'the new Egyptian theory of unity in independence', but it was this Unionist Government and parliament that declared the Sudan independent. The British Government and British administrators in the Sudan made a similar error. The Umma Party, which had co-operated with the British for decades, was regarded as staunch in support of the British connections, whereas, as became clear during the negotiations, it too wanted independence from Britain as well as from Egypt.

agreement with Egypt. The agreement became the basis of the Anglo-Egyptian settlement signed on 12 February 1953.

It provided a three-year transitional period during which a constituent assembly would be elected, the constitution granted, and elections held for the first Sudanese parliament, and an international commission was formed to assist the Governor-General, and another to organise and supervise the elections. These arrangements proved unworkable and the first elected assembly, although controlled by the Unionist parties with Ismail el-Azhary as Prime Minister, cut short the process by declaring the Sudan independent on 1 January 1956. Both Britain and Egypt hastened to recognise and commend the decision.

The Sudan agreement encouraged General Neguib and Major Saleh Salem, who had done most from the Egyptian side to secure it, to prophesy a new era of friendship with Britain, but as soon as it was signed disputes broke out over its implementation. The Egyptians still believed that it was essential to secure unity, and Major Salem and Wing Commander Hussein Zulficar Sabry began to suborn the Sudan on a large scale. They financed propaganda, charging that the British did not intend to fulfil the agreement and that the Umma Party was their tool in a perfidious plot. A statement in the House of Commons that the Sudan had the right to ask for membership of the British Commonwealth once it became independent was taken as proof that Britain was plotting to retain the Sudan, and Neguib said it was a breach of the agreement because the Sudan could only choose independence or unity with Egypt. The British Government had simply stated the principle that an independent country could do what it iiked; but, in any case, there was not a shred of reason to think that the Sudanese had any intention of joining the Commonwealth.

Neguib also accused British administrators in the Sudan of 'bad faith'. It was true that the administrators, almost to a man, were opposed to Egyptian control of the Sudan, and all their worst fears were being justified by the behaviour of the Egyptians, who spared no effort to pervert by bribing the democratic process which the agreement provided for. The administrators underestimated the strength of the desire of the politically conscious urban population to be rid of British rule, but they quickly realised that no useful purpose was served by holding to posts of diminishing power and influence, and they co-operated fully with the Sudanisation programme. The people of the Sudan, seeing the British withdrawing while Egyptian leaders behaved as though they were already their masters, began to oppose the Egyptians; and the National Unionist

Party recognised the temper of the country and declared its support for independence. The British evacuated the Sudan earlier than they intended, but Egypt lost for ever the claim to possess it.

The Sudan renewed distrust between Britain and Egypt just when confidence was required for settling the question of the British base in the Suez Canal Zone. Post-war negotiations between the two countries had usually broken down over the Egyptian claim to the Sudan, so, with that question settled, there was every reason to expect agreement on evacuation. The Egyptian Government assumed that the British Government would plunge into fresh negotiations, but Britain was greatly discouraged by Egypt's behaviour in the Sudan, and in no hurry to concede anything by too much haste. Nasser broke nearly three months of glowering inactivity by an interview given to the correspondent of the *Observer* in which he said that Egypt was ready to maintain the base, and, as the Egyptian army was incapable of doing so, would accept British technicians for a period if Britain did not intend by them a veiled 'occupation'.*

Britain accepted this as a negotiable position and talks began almost at once. They were short-lived. The British wanted to construct a technical agreement through a series of committees which would work from the ground up, but Nasser, viewing this with suspicion, demanded agreement in principle on certain specific points and particularly Britain's intentions to evacuate the base. The British were not ready to commit themselves to total withdrawal, whereupon Nasser brusquely broke off negotiations on 6 May and spoke of 'pulling down the pillars of the temple' around his own head if the troops were not taken away. Because the situation was tense and recollections of the 1952 disorders fresh in mind, British women and children were evacuated from Egypt in May and June.

Nasser kept the country calm. While busy consolidating his power inside the country, he kept informal contact with the British Embassy, directly or through others, and negotiations moved from the conference hall to the dining-table. Mr. Churchill, Prime Minister at that time, still preserved illusions about what he might concede, and when Sir Ralph Stevenson left Cairo on leave, Churchill personally briefed Mr. Robert Hankey, whom he sent as Chargé d'Affaires, with instructions to retain military control of the base. For months the British negotiators argued that technicians in the zone must wear army uniform: it was a small point compared with the number of technicians, the duration of the agreement and

* At this time, the author.

the conditions governing reactivation of the base, but it showed how little the British Government understood the mind of Egypt.

Nevertheless, when Sir Ralph Stevenson returned in the autumn, he and Nasser patiently continued to talk and at the turn of the year Nasser agreed that the base could be reactivated in the event of attack on Turkey. The British had not yet conceded total evacuation of the base, which was essential to Nasser, and early in 1954 he reminded the British Government that they could have no peace in the zone as long as troops remained by unleashing bands of saboteurs and assassins. To discourage co-operation with British troops he put on trial for treason an Egyptian who had served them for many years and had been in jail in Cairo for nearly twelve months, and had him hanged within twenty-four hours of the verdict. This judicial murder reflected the passion still aroused in the R.C.C. by the presence of British troops.

This further incensed feelings in Britain and particularly in the Conservative Party, already annoyed by Egyptian broadcasts which were disturbing British territories in East Africa, but its immediate purpose was served. The British service chiefs and the Government were faced with the need to maintain over 70,000 troops at great cost in a base which had lost much of its value by this planned hostility of the people surrounding it: its local labour force, the food supplies it wanted from the country, and freedom of road communications were denied it, and the installations were deteriorating because there could be no long-term financial planning. The only alternative was a military operation against the Egyptian Government itself, which no one contemplated. In 1954 the British decided to come to terms.

When Nasser emerged from the Neguib crisis in May he turned again to the question of the base. At the end of the month he called a halt to guerrilla operations in the zone; in June the British released a further £10 million of blocked sterling; and the Egyptian Government removed some of the restrictions on sterling trade. On 12 July, when the situation was relatively tranquil, the British Government submitted new proposals in which it undertook to remove all British troops from Egypt and to maintain the base with civilians on contract to British firms. This was decisive for Nasser for it meant military evacuation, and on 27 July the Heads of Agreement were initialled in Cairo. He had won: he had the promise to evacuate for lack of which he had broken negotiations in the spring of 1953.

It was agreed that the British forces would quit the base within twenty months of the completion of the agreement and that the base would be maintained by British civilian contractors for seven years, during which it could be put on a war footing in the event of armed attack on Egypt, on any country party to the Arab Treaty of Joint Defence, or on Turkey. The final agreement was signed on 19 October. Sir Charles Keightley, Commander-in-Chief of British land forces in the Middle East, described the agreement as 'an act of faith' by both countries.* 'The ugly page of Anglo-Egyptian relations has been turned and another page is being written,' said Nasser. 'British prestige and position in the Middle East has been strengthened. There is now no reason why Britain and Egypt should not work constructively together.' Egyptian relations with Turkey, which had been ruptured early in 1954 by the dismissal of the Turkish Ambassador from Cairo, now improved, and Nasser made friendly references to the Turkish Government and people. On 4 November, Egypt and the United States signed an agreement whereby Egypt would receive $40 million in aid.

## II

Thus at the end of 1954 President Nasser was able to look with satisfaction on the little world he had conquered. At home the army was firmly behind him, his enemies were dispersed, in prison, or dead, and the hated dynasty of Mohammed Aly was scattered. The national economy, if not prosperous, was no longer threatened with collapse, and he had secured West German aid in the preparation of plans for a mammoth high dam at Aswan which he believed could be the economic turning point of his new Egypt. The British were busy evacuating the Nile all the way from the Mediterranean to the foothills of the African mountains. Abroad, relations with the Western powers were more promising than they had ever been; and at the same time General Aziz al-Misri, 'spiritual father' of the revolution, was reporting from the embassy in Moscow that the Kremlin was inclined to be friendly.

The goodwill between Britain and Egypt, however, was soon brought to an end by the creation of the Baghdad Pact. Adnan Menderes, Prime Minister of Turkey, arrived in Baghdad on 6 January 1955 and six days later the Turco-Iraqi Agreement was announced in a joint communiqué which said the pact was open to other Arab States if they desired to join. Egyptian newspapers and radio stations attacked Iraq and Nuri Pasha with extreme violence and nationalists in other Arab countries supported the campaign.

* General Sir Charles Keightley commanded the British forces which invaded Egypt in 1956. His and President Nasser's statements were made to the British-owned Arab News Agency.

Despite this, Britain shortly afterwards adhered to the pact and Ministers repeatedly emphasised that it was the cornerstone of British Middle Eastern policy. Yet the final collapse of British policy in the Middle East dates from the Baghdad Pact, after which it suffered defeats culminating in the futile invasion of Egypt at the end of 1956.

It could hardly be otherwise, for the Arab States were at this time dominated by national sentiment which was opposed to the pact. Nuri Pasha's control of opinion in Iraq possibly gave a false impression to Britain; and other Arab leaders, who would have been willing to link their policy to that of Iraq, were afraid of Nasser and Arab opinion.

The Anglo-Egyptian Agreement and the Baghdad Pact were opposing concepts, for the agreement was valueless unless based on growing confidence and co-operation with Egypt; as Egypt was resolutely opposed to the pact, support for it was bound to prevent any reconstruction of Anglo-Egyptian relations. If the British Government intended to base its policy on the Turco-Iraqi Agreement it might just as well have undertaken to evacuate the Canal Zone unconditionally. The nature of the Nasser movement made it impossible for him to accept it, for in aspiring to create a strong and independent Egypt that would lead the renaissance of the Arab world, it firmly believed the emancipation of the whole region from Western dominance was its first task and that the Baghdad Pact offered indirect tutelage.

The British Foreign Office felt that if the Arabs knew the benefits to be derived from the pact, that if only Egyptian propaganda would cease and the matter be explained to the Arabs, they would be happy to join; but the politically minded Iraqis, Jordanians, Syrians or Egyptians – excluding a small minority of political leaders – were not interested in benefits. They saw the pact as a plot to make the entire region once again subservient to Western policy at the very moment when the agreement to evacuate British troops from Egypt brought the Arab Middle East in sight of total emancipation. The Arab nationalists also feared that the underlying intention of Western policy was to force them into peace with Israel, for they believed that the Baghdad Pact, by allying the Arabs with Turkey, which had relations with Israel, and to the Western powers through Turkey's N.A.T.O. connection, would 'soften' Arab policy towards Israel; and they did not believe that Turkey would, as the Baghdad communiqué hinted, join Iraq in opposition to Israel. The principal attack made on Nuri Pasha was, therefore, that he was leading the Arabs towards peace with the Jews. If the criticism was sometimes consciously dishonest on the part of opposing leaders, it outweighed the effect of arguments produced in support of the pact.

Nasser was convinced that the British intended to use the pact to recover the position they were losing in Egypt, and that the pact communiqué was an invitation to all Arab states to break with Egypt and join an Anglo-Iraqi grouping. If that were so, he argued, the protestations of friendship and the signing of the Anglo-Egyptian Treaty were hypocrisy. How otherwise to explain that the British had, as he believed, promoted this defence pact which they knew he opposed immediately after signing an agreement requiring Egypt's collaboration?

While the discord over the Baghdad Pact was at its height, Israel launched a major raid on the Egyptian-held Gaza Strip, which reminded Nasser of his lack of modern arms. He was not prepared to remain militarily inferior to Israel, and did not believe that the 1950 declaration of Britain, France and the United States guaranteeing the frontiers of the Middle East would be implemented effectively against Israel. Therefore he demanded arms with greater impatience from Britain and the United States, and he let it be known that he would get them, if necessary, from the Eastern bloc. In June he received from Britain a limited quantity of excellent arms, including a few Centurion tanks, which had first been ordered by the Wafd Government in 1950, but Nasser thought them insufficient. When another warning that he could get more from Russia went unheeded he announced the Czech arms deal in September, by which Russia undertook to arm him.

The British trade position was also degenerating. A trade mission was sent to Egypt and to other countries early in 1955, but almost immediately after the departure of the mission British cotton buying in Egypt declined sharply from an already low level. In the summer of 1956 an Egyptian mission went to London to seek means of reviving trade and made most encouraging statements. It was already too late for trade. Anglo-Egyptian relations were at breaking point. The Egyptian leaders were convinced that the decline in Britain's cotton buying was economic pressure and that the British Government could stimulate trade if it wanted to, pointing to purchases of Sudanese cotton as evidence that Britain needed cotton and was deliberately trying to weaken Egypt by reducing purchases. This seemed to them to be parallel to the attempt to strengthen Iraq through the Baghdad Pact.

The British Government, on the other hand, thought that it had been rebuffed in every attempt to restore relations with Egypt. It had delivered arms in 1955; was fulfilling its undertaking to withdraw

British troops; and had signed another agreement whereby Egypt would receive £20 million a year from its blocked balances until 1960 and then £10 million a year until the balances were exhausted. The United States had also played its part by giving aid. What had Britain and the Western powers received in return? Egypt had opened the Middle East to Russia, was doing its utmost to wreck the Baghdad Pact, and its radio propaganda had exacerbated troubles in Jordan and was inciting peoples in territories under British protection or control to revolt against 'British imperialism'. But, in truth, the Baghdad Pact, the failure to provide enough arms for defence against Israel and the decline of British trade were all matters fundamental to Egypt beside which sterling releases and American aid did not seem vital.

Plans for the mammoth High Dam north of Aswan constituted another essential point in Egyptian policy, and there were reports that Russia was prepared to provide the foreign currency for the project.* As this would have given Soviet money and technicians an established place in Egypt for at least a decade, the British and United States governments tentatively offered financial assistance late in 1955 and to support Egypt's request for a loan from the International Bank. It was a political move, for in both Britain and the United States the climate of opinion was against helping the Egyptians and the financial position was adverse. The cost of the Czech arms, the large development projects planned or in progress, and the condition of the Egyptian cotton trade, which was supported mainly by its barter deals with the Soviet bloc, made it unlikely that the Egyptian Government could bear the burden of the scheme. The offer was only justified by the need to support the Western position in Egypt, for, by the spring of 1956, Soviet influence had largely replaced Britain's. There was still a substantial British community engaged in trade but little else of the British position remained.

## III

By the spring of 1956 the British and Egyptian governments thoroughly disliked each other. When King Hussein of Jordan dis-

---

* The nature of the Soviet offer was not clear. Colonel Nasser's version late in 1955 was that the Russians had offered to build the Dam, but that he preferred an international arrangement rather than dependence on any one country. For that reason, he said, he negotiated with the World Bank, Britain and the United States, even though the arrangement would be more costly. It is probable that the Soviet offer was only verbal. In the summer of 1956, when the probability of British and American aid was waning, the Russians said they were prepared to give Egypt development aid but were not prepared to help with the High Dam.

missed General John Bagot Glubb from command of the Arab Legion in March and then linked Jordan to the Egyptian-Syrian defence pact, it was the last straw.*

During the last stages of the evacuation of British troops in May, Nasser sent for Sir Humphrey Trevelyan, the British Ambassador, and together they went over old ground in a fruitless search of an understanding. Nasser, supported by Soviet Russia, saw no reason to change his successful Arab policy, and the British Government was in no mood to please him. The celebration of a new constitution and Nasser's election as President coincided with the evacuation of the last British troops and produced a brief truce. Nasser personally invited General Sir Brian Robertson, who had taken part in negotiations for the Anglo-Egyptian Agreement, and Nasser's speeches at the final evacuation of British troops were moderate in tone, paying tribute to Britain's honourable fulfilment of her undertaking. But it was Mr. Shepilov, the Soviet Foreign Minister, who was lionised; Sir Brian was treated only with politeness and respect.

President Nasser may not have been in full control of Egyptian policy at this time, for by coming to the aid of Egypt with trade and arms, Russia had justified anti-British left-wing influences which were now predominant. This was evident in negotiations with Western oil companies; whereas the military leaders had been willing to reach agreement with the companies up to the end of 1954, it was apparent in 1956 that they were conducting oil policy in terms of politics not economics. In the late spring of 1956 Nasser stated that he would grant Mobil thirty-two exploration licences, but would not, in view of the unfriendly British policy, grant any to the Shell subsidiary, Anglo-Egyptian Oil Fields, which were associated with Mobil in the application for sixty-one licences. Mobil, in fact, never got the licences either, because relations with the United States also deteriorated.

There was more fighting between Israeli and Egyptian troops on the frontier in April and increasing talk in Israel of a preventive war. Ill-informed diplomatic comment supplemented by inaccurate intelligence reports after the spring N.A.T.O. conference convinced Nasser that the Western powers were seeking to bring Russia into a U.N. arms embargo which would halt the flow of Czech arms to Egypt, so in May he recognised People's China, calculating that if

---

* Nasser had no part in the dismissal of Glubb Pasha and was surprised to learn of it. Unfortunately, the dismissal occurred when Mr. Selwyn Lloyd, the British Foreign Secretary, was in Cairo trying to improve relations with Nasser, and he left believing that Nasser had known about Glubb's dismissal during their discussions. Mr. Lloyd ran into riots at Bahrein, which again were attributed to Egyptian propaganda.

an embargo were imposed he could obtain arms through Chou En-Lai. The decision was no surprise, for Egypt had growing trade dealings with China, whose mission already occupied a villa of embassy dimensions on long lease.

This did serious damage to the reputation of Nasser among members of the U.S. Congress at a time when negotiations for a High Dam loan had reached a critical stage. They had continued into February – largely by the International Bank, whose president, Mr. Eugene Black, announced 'substantial agreement' with Egypt on 9 February – but were halted when Egypt submitted unacceptable amendments to the aides-mémoires which constituted the draft agreement. The next move was with Nasser, and when Ahmed Hussein, the Egyptian Ambassador to the United States, returned to Egypt for the June celebrations, he drew the President's attention to the serious decline of Egypt's standing in Washington and warned that if he did not take the High Dam loan now he might never get it. It was only after many hours of discussion and argument that he received permission to withdraw the proposed amendments to the aides-mémoires which had paralysed negotiations. Ahmed Hussein announced in London on his way to the United States that Egypt would accept the aid, but by this time the U.S. Congress was already against the loan. The policy pursued by President Nasser over the previous eighteen months, particularly the recognition of People's China, had incensed American opinion. The offer of aid had done nothing to arrest the growth of Soviet influence which was its purpose. Ahmed Hussein informed Mr. Dulles of his Government's decision, but the response was a public announcement that the United States would not give the aid, on the grounds that the Egyptian economy was too unstable to face so large a scheme and that there was no agreement between Egypt and the Sudan over the Dam. Britain and the United States had offered between them $70 million for the first building stage and the International Bank proposed to lend $200 million, but the three contributions were inter-dependent, and were together subject to an agreement with the Sudan regarding the submergence of a large stretch of the Nile banks inside the Sudan and the division of the additional Nile waters which would become available. When the United States withdrew its offer, the two associated offers were automatically cancelled.

President Nasser's anger was revealed in an icy speech made at the inauguration of the Suez-Cairo pipeline on 24 July in which he criticised the United States bitterly and stated that he would announce plans to finance the High Dam without Western assistance. Speaking at Alexandria two days later – the fourth anniversary of the abdication of King Farouk – he announced the nationalisation of the Suez Canal Company and said the High Dam would be built with its profits. Immediately police surrounded the offices of the Suez Canal Company in Cairo and Ismailia and sealed the doors, and in the Ministry of Commerce the new Egyptian Board of Directors held its first meeting.

The Suez Canal Company was regarded by Egyptians as a fraud imposed on them by avaricious powers to serve their own ends. By the building of the Canal, Egypt lost the considerable profits from travellers on the overland route from Alexandria to Suez and then lost the Egyptian share in the future profits of the Canal. In course of time the profits of the Company brought a little financial benefit to Egypt, but as late as 1927 George Young described the transactions as 'disastrous for Egypt, financially, economically and politically'. Even the 1949 agreement between Egypt and the Company gave Egypt only 7 per cent of the profits. George Young commented: '. . . Europe should have constructed this enterprise, that served its own economic interests only, by acquiring the concession to do so from Egypt at a price that would have paid off the Egyptian debt and by compensating Egypt for its loss of traffic with a share in its profits. As it was, Egypt was made to pay heavily both for the concession of the site and for the construction of the greater part of the Canal, and was left with no share in the concern. The sufferings of the Egyptian fellaheen, both in the years of forced labour and the subsequent fiscal exactions to meet interest on the Canal debt, put Europe heavily in their debt, a debt of honour of Europe to Egypt as to which we have not heard so much as we have of the less worthy liabilities of Egypt to Europe. . . . Egypt deserved well of Europe in this matter and was in return most ruthlessly defrauded'.*

President Nasser's statement that the Canal was built on the skulls of Egyptians had some truth. The original concessions provided the right of forced labour for four-fifths of the work, and until it was stopped by Ismail forced labour was used, as Young states, 'on so large a scale and with so little scruple', that it resulted in 'scandalous inhumanity that had shocked not only British but even French public opinion'. No Egyptian government would have renewed the concession on any terms when it expired in 1968, and the Nasser Government had in existence a committee preparing to take over the Company.

As the Company was Egyptian, President Nasser was entitled to

* George Young, *Egypt*.

regard its nationalisation as legal, just as the nationalisation of many concerns in Britain was legal. Its international form gave it a political character but not international status, because Article 16 of the 1866 concession laid down that the Company 'being Egyptian, is governed by the laws and customs of that country', and a subsequent statement in Article 16 that the status of the Company and the relations between its shareholders were to be governed by French law was only intended to meet the legal needs of the Company at a time when the Ottoman Empire lacked a company law and could hardly be intended to contradict the specific statement made earlier in the same clause. Had the Powers and Company accepted the nationalisation and handed over the assets, and thereby secured the compensation promised by the nationalisation law, the Egyptian decree of nationalisation would have been legal; in so far as compensation was offered it was legal; and it could only later have acquired the character of confiscation if its shareholders had been defrauded after the assets had been handed over.

The much more important question of freedom of navigation through the Canal, guaranteed by the 1888 Constantinople Convention, was not affected, for Nasser had not seized the Canal. Egypt had been given 'unfettered control' – the phrase much used during the crisis – when British troops completed their evacuation of the country six weeks before the nationalisation. By Article 8 of the 1936 Treaty, British troops had been stationed in Egypt 'with a view to ensuring in co-operation with Egyptian forces the defence of the canal' because the Canal, while being an integral part of Egypt, was a universal means of communication and an essential means of communication between the different parts of the British Empire. Although the Anglo-Egyptian Agreement of 1954 expressed the determination of both parties to uphold the 1888 Convention, there were in fact only Egyptian troops in Egypt to do so in July 1956, and the conditions for re-entry of British troops did not include obstruction to transit of the Canal.

President Nasser promised on 21 July to respect the 1888 Convention and his ability to do so and the sincerity of his intentions were matters for the future. It could be argued that the international company facilitated freedom of navigation by the excellence and impartiality of its administration, but it could only be presumed, not proven, that the facilities would be extinguished by the inexperience, partiality or maladministration of the Egyptian Company. The one justifiable and existing ground for complaint, the refusal of passage to Israeli ships, predated both nationalisation and the military régime, and began when British troops were stationed in the zone to ensure 'the liberty and entire security of the Canal'. The British had protested against this restriction during and after the monarchy, but the case against the nationalisation was prejudiced by the fact that nothing practical had been done to end it. The embargo on Israeli ships could be cited as an example of what Egypt might do, but the maritime powers, and specifically Britain, had condoned it and established by precedent the right of Egypt to control the Canal in so far as Israel was concerned.

Nasser's speech emphasised once again that the Egyptians were fighting a battle against Western imperialism, which, he contended, was seeking to halt the advance of Arab nationalism everywhere from the Atlantic Ocean to the Persian Gulf. It shattered whatever remained in the West of friendly relations with Egypt, and from that moment Western policy and Nasser were in open conflict. Sir Anthony Eden expressed this conflict in a television address that distinguished between Nasser and the people of Egypt as the enemy, and it was evident in British and French determination to accept nothing less than his humiliation and overthrow. Almost every word or action of the two governments was like an ultimatum; in the build up of troops in the Mediterranean, in the take-it-or-leave-it message of the Menzies mission, in the refusal to negotiate on the Security Council's 'Six Points' for a settlement unless Egypt produced a new offer. The two sides were enemies seeking victory, not a settlement.

The British and French governments protested against the nationalisation in strongly worded notes, which the Egyptian Ambassador refused to accept. On 31 July Sir Anthony Eden announced 'precautionary measures', including troop movements to the Eastern Mediterranean and permission for France to station troops in Cyprus. The United States Government agreed on the need to re-secure international operation of the Canal and in condemning the manner in which Nasser had nationalised the Company, but Mr. Dulles did not think it justified force, and on 3 August he denied any intention of meeting violence with violence. His proposal for a Suez Canal Users' Association, which Sir Anthony Eden presented to the House of Commons as a further challenge to President Nasser, was designed to side-step military intervention, and he undermined a tough Anglo-French policy at the second S.C.U.A. conference by announcing in advance that no American ships would 'shoot their way through the Canal'. He supported Anglo-French demands for international control of the Canal, but Nasser, knowing that Soviet Russia and almost the entire Asian continent were on his side and that the United States was against war, had reason to think Britain and France would capitulate before he did.

Whatever anxieties Arab governments felt, they dared not express them in face of the enthusiastic support which their peoples gave to Nasser, for whom nationalisation was a triumph exceeding that of the Czech arms deal. Jordan and Libya refused to allow their British bases to be used for strengthening of British forces in the Mediterranean, compelling Britain to rely on Malta and Cyprus. President Nasser was alarmed by the strength of Anglo-French reaction, but, counting on international support either to prevent a war or to arrest it when it began, he conducted himself after the nationalisation with a calculated correctness which was intended to reassure the Arab and other Asian states, to deprive Britain and France of any excuse to intervene, and to ensure the maximum support for his case at the United Nations.

The British and French governments froze Egyptian funds by imposing exchange control; Egypt was removed from the transferable sterling account area and 60 per cent of its trade was thereby brought under control of the Bank of England. The British and French governments paid their dues to the Suez Canal Company, but some others paid to Egypt or into blocked accounts while awaiting a settlement. Egypt received only about 40 per cent of the dues, but if she had tried to compel world shipping to pay dues to the Egyptian administration she would have been compelled to deny passage to those ships which refused to do so and the issue of the freedom of transit would have arisen in its most challenging form. The Canal therefore stayed open to all shipping except Israel's; the anger aroused in many countries by nationalisation was minimised and the unhappiness of Arab and Asian governments waned as their anger against France and Britain increased. This was particularly true of India, to whose economy the Canal was vital; the Indian Government believed that Nasser had the right to nationalise the Canal, but was critical of his provocative way of doing so and advised him to be more conciliatory, but, long before the armed intervention of Britain and France, Nehru came to view Anglo-French policy as more dangerous than Nasser's.

Mr. Dulles, Sir Anthony Eden and M. Pineau invited those nations party to the Constantinople Convention and other nations using the Canal to a conference in London on 16 August. They issued a joint statement that they considered 'the action taken by the government of Egypt, having regard to all the attendant circumstances, threatens the freedom and security of the Canal as guaranteed by the convention'. They therefore considered 'that steps should be taken to establish operating arrangements under an international system designed to assure the continuity of operations of the Canal'. The note did not claim a restoration of the rights of the Suez Canal Company, but neither did it acknowledge that the Company was Egyptian or specifically state that it was anything else. It referred to 'its international character' and acknowledged only Egypt's rights 'under appropriate conditions, to nationalise assets, not impressed with an international interest. . .'. The note stated, 'but the present action involved far more than a simple act of nationalisation. It involved the arbitrary and unilateral seizure by one nation of an international agency which has the responsibility to maintain and to operate the Suez Canal so that all the signatories to and beneficiaries of the treaty of 1888 can effectively enjoy the use of an international waterway upon which the economy, commerce, and security of much of the world depends'. In the choice of words, the 'international character', 'interest' and 'agency', the legal issue was evaded and the condemnation of the 'arbitrary and unilateral seizure' was political. The Egyptian action was frequently described as illegal, but the case against it was never seriously pressed on those grounds.

Egypt and Greece did not attend the conference. President Nasser announced his refusal to the Press on 12 August, when he reaffirmed his pledge to maintain freedom of navigation and said he was willing to sponsor a conference wider than that called to London, in order to bring the 1888 Convention up-to-date. Of the nations that assembled in London, sixteen supported a proposal of Mr. Dulles for a Suez Canal Board which would provide international operation of the Canal and co-operation between user-nations and Egypt. Russia, India, Ceylon and Indonesia voted for India's proposal that would have limited the users' organisation to co-operation with Egypt and would have left Egyptian national administration intact. The conference decided to send a mission consisting of representatives of Australia, the United States, Ethiopia, Iran and Sweden, under the chairmanship of Mr. Menzies, the Australian Prime Minister, to present the majority plan to Nasser.

This mission drew more sharply the line dividing the Egyptian position from that of France and Britain. Although the eighteen-power proposals contended that the sovereign rights of Egypt were respected, they proposed to establish a board to run the Canal, and Nasser insisted that this infringed sovereignty. Egypt was to be a member of the board and granted all the required rights and facilities, but the paragraphs which advocated 'the insulation of the Canal from the influence of the politics of any one nation' and 'effective sanctions for any violation of the conventions' were aimed at Egypt. Subsequently, at the second London Conference on 19 September, Mr. Dulles explained that although the Egyptian Government had promised to observe the 1888 Convention, Egyptian administrative control offered 'infinite possibilities of covert violation and practice, in obscurity, of preferences and discriminations'. This argument was never countered by Egypt but a reasonable degree of protection could have been obtained by an international consultative body as proposed by India.

On the other hand, if the need to finance the High Dam had been the main consideration in President Nasser's mind, the Menzies proposals should have carried weight, because as Mr. Menzies pointed out in his concluding letter to Nasser, Egypt's ownership of the Canal would be recognised, she would draw the profits, and the burden of development would be borne by the international body; but Nasser's reply made no concession on the essential point of control. Egypt's right to nationalise the Company, he said, could not be seriously contested, and the proposal was a hostile infringement of Egyptian rights. 'We are convinced,' he wrote, '. . . that the purpose is to take the Suez Canal out of the hands of Egypt and put it into some other hands.' It was evident, nevertheless, that short of relinquishing control, he was anxious to reach a settlement. He reiterated his willingness to participate in a wider conference, contending that in addition to the eighteen nations which submitted the note, there were many other countries which needed the Canal for the bulk of their trade even if they had no ships passing through it, and he re-emphasised his intention to observe the 1888 Convention and to compensate shareholders. 'We believe,' he added, 'that the real insulation of the canal from politics would best be guaranteed by a reaffirmation or solemn and internationally binding commitment in the form of a renewal of the 1888 Convention, either of which, as we have already declared, is acceptable to us.' His Government had no intention of discriminating against the United Kingdom, was ready to enter into a binding arrangement concerning the establishment of just and equitable tolls, the Canal Authority would be independent of the State budget or other limitations, and Egypt would always be ready to 'benefit by the knowledge and experience of highly qualified experts from all over the world'. He reaffirmed Egyptian policy as: freedom of passage, the development of the Canal, and the establishment of just and equitable tolls and technical efficiency; but the Menzies mission was not empowered to negotiate on any of these matters. It had come to claim international control of the Canal.

It was confidently assumed by the maritime nations that the decisive weapon was still in the hands of the Company, to which the large body of British and French pilots were on contract and whose loyalty to the Company had been strengthened by assurances about their gratuities and compensation. The Company had been anxious to withdraw the pilots almost from the outset of the crisis and, had it done so, traffic in the Canal would have been halted. The British Government opposed their withdrawal and Egypt profitably utilised the six weeks delay in securing new ships' officers to train as pilots and in training about thirty Egyptians to supplement an existing corps of twenty-four Egyptians and seven Greeks. On 11 September, after the failure of the Menzies mission, Britain agreed to the withdrawal of the pilots, and Egypt was left with about seventy pilots of whom only thirty-one were fully trained. Although this was believed to be about a third of the total required to run the Canal, the convoys continued to go through without serious hitch.

Britain and France sought to persuade the maritime nations that sterner measures were needed, but they were by no means happy about Anglo-French military preparations. At the second London Conference the majority of the eighteen states clearly regarded the Suez Canal Users' Association as an attempt to find a *de facto* working arrangement with Egypt and not as a new method of coercion, and the association they formed lacked teeth for Britain and France to bite with. It did not even compel the members to pay tolls to the association, thus paving the way for a drift into co-operation with the Egyptian administration. The British and French governments were annoyed at the trivial outcome, and particularly annoyed with Mr. Dulles, at whose behest they had delayed an appeal to the Security Council while the S.C.U.A. gambit was played. They took counsel together on their true purpose, the defeat of President Nasser, and, with S.C.U.A.'s back-sliding and the British parliamentary opposition in mind, cleared the decks for action by referring the Suez Canal Company's nationalisation to the Security Council. The deterioration in the relations between Britain and France on one side, and the United States on the other, meanwhile gave President Nasser much comfort.

The British and French Prime Ministers discreetly snubbed Mr. Dulles by meeting privately in Paris and he responded on 2 October by telling a Press conference that the United States' role was 'somewhat independent' on the problem of 'colonialisation' and there were differences with Britain and France about some 'fundamental things'. Nevertheless, he supported the Anglo-French policy when they tabled a draft proposal before the Security Council on

5 October to the effect that the eighteen-power plan and S.C.U.A. should be the basis of negotiation. Russia supported the Egyptian proposal for a six-power commission to negotiate a system of co-operation between the users and Egypt, which would recognise Egypt's sovereign rights, establish a basis for tolls and charges on the Canal, and provide for a retention of a reasonable proportion of the income for Canal development. The meeting was adjourned until 8 October, while discussions continued in private between Dr. Mahmoud Fawzi, the Egyptian Foreign Minister, M. Pineau and Mr. Selwyn Lloyd in the presence of the Secretary-General.

The moment was opportune for negotiations because Nasser was under pressure from the Arab States and some Asiatic governments to reach a settlement. The failure of a second London Conference to give Britain and France full support, and the evident opposition of many of the maritime nations to their warlike preparations, weakened the position of President Nasser by making the Bandung bloc believe that the danger of an armed attack had so diminished that their task of saving Egypt was accomplished and Nasser could now act to end the crisis. The Arab States were also anxious about Israel. The frontier situation had been uneasy throughout the year and twice Mr. Hammarskjoeld had visited the Middle East on fruitless missions of pacification.

In September about one hundred people lost their lives in Israeli attacks on Jordanian frontier posts, made in retaliation for minor frontier offences, and on 10 October, while the Security Council was still in session, the Israeli army wiped out the Jordan frontier station at Qalqilya. The Arab States again consulted together over the situation, but Egypt, the country most able to help, could do little while threatened by an Anglo-French invasion; Nasser had even withdrawn some forces from Sinai. At Jordan's request, Iraqi forces moved to the Jordanian border, where they halted in response to an Israeli warning that their entry into Jordan would be considered a breach of the Jordan-Israeli armistice. The pressure on Nasser was not, however, enough to make him capitulate, for he had the support of popular opinion in the Arab world, and this was proved in the Jordanian elections in October, when the parties pledged to unite with Egypt and Syria won an overwhelming majority. He had only to satisfy the Arab governments and other friendly nations that he was doing his utmost to be conciliatory.

In private discussions at the United Nations the British Government was no longer as adamant about international control as about machinery to determine when a breach of the 1888 Convention took place and to provide for automatic sanctions if a breach occurred; it was, in short, down to the crux of the matter, 'the infinite possibilities of covert violations'. The French Government, however, was already in close liaison with Israel, and M. Pineau announced on 11 October that there was no basis for negotiation.

This was only twenty-four hours before agreement was reached on Six Principles for a settlement: free and open transit, respect for Egypt's sovereignty, 'insulation of the Canal from the politics of any one country', tolls and charges to be fixed by agreement between Egypt and the users, the allotment of a fair proportion of dues for development, and the settlement of disputes by arbitration. When Britain and France embodied these principles in a resolution to the Security Council on 13 October they added a final clause to the effect that, pending agreement on a régime for the Suez Canal, the Egyptian Government should co-operate with the Suez Canal Users' Association. The Egyptian Foreign Minister immediately rejected this clause and although the Six Principles received unanimous support in the Council, Yugoslavia voted against the S.C.U.A. clause and Russia vetoed it.

Morally, Britain and France had won, and they held that it was now for Egypt to advance proposals for implementing the Security Council's resolution. Dr. Fawzi remained in New York in contact with Mr. Hammarskjoeld, and on 19 October the Secretary-General proposed to Britain and France that discussions should be resumed in Geneva on 29 October. Mr. Selwyn Lloyd replied next day that Egypt should now produce practical proposals and Mr. Hammarskjoeld sent a note to the Egyptian Government on 24 October in which he outlined his understanding of the position and asked for the Egyptian reaction to his interpretation. The Egyptian reply accepted Mr. Hammarskjoeld's views with only one reservation concerning the right of others to take 'police action', but it was sent on 2 November when the British and French planes were already bombing Egyptian airfields.

The British and French governments had in any case decided on 16 October to use force (four days before Mr. Selwyn Lloyd replied to Mr. Hammarskjoeld) during a meeting in Paris attended by Sir Anthony Eden, Mr. Selwyn Lloyd, M. Mollet and M. Pineau. An Indian compromise which went some way towards meeting the Anglo-French case – it provided among other things for co-operation between the Egyptian Canal Authority and S.C.U.A. – was confirmed by the Indian Government on 24 October and probably had Egyptian approval, but it did not halt Anglo-French, or Israeli, plans. On the day after the Paris meeting, the Israeli Prime Minister, Mr. Ben Gurion, told the Knesset that Egypt was 'the main enemy', although the recent weight of Israeli action had been directed against Jordan. On 25 October an Israeli spokesman announced that *fedayeen* activity had been resumed by Egypt, although there was little evidence to support the statement. Next day the Israeli forces began to mobilise and on the 28th the Israeli Government confirmed partial mobilisation. The British Ambassador warned the Israeli Government that an attack on Jordan would automatically invoke the Anglo-Jordanian Treaty, but made no reference to an attack on Egypt, although that also would have involved the Tripartite Declaration of 1950 guaranteeing Middle Eastern frontiers. A Tripartite Committee was actually meeting in Washington at President Eisenhower's summons.

The Israeli forces invaded Sinai on 29 October. The Tripartite Committee met again in Washington, but the British and French governments refused to implement the 1950 Declaration. Mr. Dulles announced that he would refer the Israeli invasion to the Security Council next day, but when the draft resolution was submitted to Mr. Selwyn Lloyd early on the 30th, he objected to stigmatising Israel as the 'aggressor'. That day M. Mollet and M. Pineau arrived in London. Less than four hours later the Egyptian and Israeli ambassadors were summoned to the Foreign Office to receive a joint Anglo-French ultimatum, which instructed the belligerents to order an immediate cease-fire and withdraw to ten miles from the Canal, in default of which British and French forces 'would intervene with whatever strength may be necessary to secure compliance'. They also asked Egypt to allow British and French troops to move temporarily into key positions at Port Said, Ismailia and Suez, in order to guarantee freedom of transit through the Canal. Israel, whose troops were now in strength ten miles from the Canal, accepted the ultimatum. Nasser rejected it.

The Security Council began to debate the United States resolution almost at the moment when the British and French governments were delivering their ultimatum to the Egyptian and Israeli ambassadors in London. When it learned of the ultimatum, the United States persisted in submitting its resolutions, which not only called on Israel to withdraw her forces from Egypt but also called on all members to refrain from using force or the threat of force. Seven members voted for the resolution; Belgium and Australia abstained; Britain and France vetoed it. Next day, at the expiry of the twelve-hour time limit prescribed in the ultimatum, British and French planes began to bombard Egyptian airfields and other targets.

It was evident to President Nasser that militarily he could not win. It had been his view even during the Security Council discussions early in October that the British and French intended to attack Egypt and, as he did not intend to capitulate, the bombing foreshadowed invasion. He therefore ordered his troops in Sinai to withdraw as best they could and he kept his main forces west of the Canal for the defence of the delta, for he could afford to give up Sinai and the zone as long as the central Government remained intact to mobilise international opinion against the invasion. He armed the civilians of Port Said, Ismailia and Suez, stiffened them with some army units, blocked the Suez Canal, kept strict security in Cairo and the delta area and, as though besieged, awaited the relieving force of international pressure. By 2 November the Israeli forces were already victorious in Sinai and the Canal was blocked in several places. The British and French troops landed in the Port Said region three days later.

## IV

Egypt suffered heavily. The Israeli forces captured the entire armament of Egypt's best division and other dumps of ammunition and equipment, sabotaged the oilfields in Sinai, and took away much of the equipment. Egyptian casualties in Sinai were never revealed, but the Israeli Government subsequently released five thousand prisoners; and casualties in the Anglo-French invasion of Port Said were estimated as 650 dead and 2,100 wounded. A native area of the town was razed and some damage was done to the international and business quarter. Anglo-French bombing destroyed a large part of the Egyptian air force and severely damaged fields and landing strips.*

The British and French landings were made in defiance of the U.N. General Assembly, which adopted on 2 November a United States resolution calling on Israel to withdraw behind the armistice line, on other member states not to put 'military goods' into the area, and urged that on the cease-fire becoming effective, steps should be taken to reopen the Suez Canal. Only Australia and New Zealand voted with Britain, France and Israel against this resolution; Canada, the Netherlands, Belgium, Portugal, South Africa and Laos abstained, and sixty-four nations voted for it. This was one of the most solid condemnations ever issued by the assembly on a substantial question.

* John Erickson, Senior Lecturer at Manchester University and specialist in Soviet military affairs, states that the Russians 'to all intents and purposes crippled the strike capacity of Egypt' by withdrawing their 45 Ilyushin 28 strike bombers to Upper Egypt and Syria before the Anglo-French attack. BBC Third Programme Broadcast, *Suez— Ten Years After*, II—'Egyptian Outlook', 7 July 1966.

Britain and France defended their action in a note to the Secretary-General next day, arguing that the need to prevent the Israeli attack on Egypt from developing into a general war made their 'police action' necessary. The Afro-Asian bloc nevertheless secured on the 4th overwhelming support for a resolution demanding compliance with the resolution within twelve hours and, by 57 votes to none, Canada, Colombia and Norway secured acceptance of a proposal to establish an emergency international force to police the Egyptian-Israeli frontier. Before the vote the British and French governments informed the Secretary-General that they welcomed the formation of the force, and the Israel Government sent a note to Mr. Hammarskjoeld accepting the cease-fire, having no reason to do otherwise, since all fighting had already ended on its sector by the surrender or withdrawal of the Egyptian forces. The British Prime Minister, under great pressure from the liberal Press and the opposition, stated on 6 November that the British forces would suspend hostilities at midnight that night but remain in position pending confirmation from Mr. Hammarskjoeld that Israel and Egypt had accepted the cease-fire unconditionally and that the international force would be adequate for its task.

Nasser had lost part of his army and air force, his revenues from the Suez Canal and his Sinai oil, but his Government was intact and almost the entire world, including Russia and the United States, was on his side. His losses could be made good and the United Nations relied on to continue the work of ridding his country of foreign troops. As first step in operation recovery, he accepted the entry of the international force, with only such reservations regarding his sovereign rights as would safeguard his bargaining position without obstructing the action of the United Nations. Within a matter of days the force began to arrive by air and they progressively took over the Anglo-French positions in the Port Said area and moved along the coastal strip into Sinai. The British and French troops completed their withdrawal on 22 December, having failed to get rid of Nasser or secure international control of the Canal.

The French Government was reluctant to yield but could not go on without the British, whose position had become untenable. Their action had split the Commonwealth: the New Zealand and Australian governments supported Britain only by majority decision of their Cabinets; Canada and Pakistan were opposed, although retaining some sympathy for British motives; India and Ceylon were strongly opposed. Arab governments like Iraq, which had no reason to like Nasser and had reason for friendship with Britain, were compelled by popular opinion to condemn the action as flagrant collusion with their enemy – Israel. The Syrian army, which controlled the Government, sabotaged the Iraq Petroleum Company's pipe lines to the Mediterranean by blowing up pumping stations on Syrian territory (incidentally depriving Iraq of four-fifths of its oil revenue) and this action and the blocking of the Suez Canal, through which oil from the Persian Gulf was shipped, forced most Western European countries to ration petroleum. Iraq refused to sit at the Baghdad Pact council table with Britain, but did not break diplomatic relations, as she did with France. Syria and Saudi Arabia broke relations with both countries. In Jordan, British forces were withdrawn from the vicinity of the capital and some of their stores were seized by the Arab Legion.

Britain had never been in so weak and friendless a position in the Middle East and in a large part of Asia. This difficulty might nevertheless have been faced for some time longer had it not been for four factors. Britain was split in a manner perhaps not equalled since the height of the Irish question decades earlier; Russia, which had been in difficulties in the United Nations by the even worse case of its invasion of Hungary, was threatening intervention either by volunteers, rockets on London or military action; the United States was in opposition to the Anglo-French policy; and finally, the economic position of Britain was deteriorating, largely as a result of the decline of oil supplies and the unwillingness of the United States to help. The run on sterling reached such dangerous proportions that the devaluation of the pound was imminent. These troubles caused dissension in the British Cabinet itself. Of the reasons given by the British Government for its action, two – the Russian menace and the desire to safeguard the lives and properties of British citizens in Egypt – were false. The amount of Russian arms in Egypt was known approximately before the nationalisation of the Suez Canal Company, and there was little reason to suppose that Russia intended military action when her political penetration was making steady progress. The Anglo-French military action only strengthened Soviet influence in the Middle East. Nor was there any danger to British lives and property until the invasion, far from safeguarding them, put them in jeopardy. From 3 November onwards the Egyptian Government began to sequestrate or seize all British and French property and to intern at home or in improvised camps all holders of British or French passports, including numerous Maltese who were British citizens. Jews who had British or French passports or were stateless were forced to leave, and selective expulsions of the British, Maltese and French took place. Egypt stated subsequently that only 3,000 were expelled, but many thousands more were compelled to leave by administrative pressure or because they were deprived of their means of livelihood, until very few were left. No British or French civilians lost their lives and very few suffered physical ill-treatment or serious hardship in prison or internment. Britain and France lost pre-eminent positions in the economic, social and cultural life of Egypt. The British base in the Canal Zone was seized as war booty and the Anglo-Egyptian Agreement was terminated. Early in 1957 all British and French banks and insurance companies were Egyptianised, and during the course of the next few months were taken over, together with some other important firms. The holdings of Britain and France in many firms were compulsorily bought out, their schools were seized and all their professional people, such as doctors and accountants, were expelled and their practices taken by Egyptians. As for the Suez Canal, it stayed nationalised on Nasser's terms and, to use the words of Sir Anthony Eden, 'in the unfettered control of one nation'. The balance sheet for Britain and France was total loss.

President Nasser said in a speech at Port Said in December 1957: 'The battle of Port Said resulted, of course, in the confirmation of our ownership of the canal, our economic independence, and the Egyptianisation of the property of the aggressor'. The Suez affair completed the work of the Egyptian movement that started far back in the days of Mohammed Aly, by ending, presumably for ever, the dominant position of foreigners in Egypt and greatly reducing them in numbers. The large Maltese community shrank to negligible proportions and many Greeks, Italians and Armenians departed of their own free will. There are now many Russians, Czechs and Germans, and some Japanese and Chinese, but they are unlikely to acquire the residential status of the people who left. In short, the Port Said invasion did the work of Egyptianisation in a year. This President Nasser would have taken a decade or more to accomplish.

The United Nations completed the victory for Egypt during 1957 by clearing and reopening the Suez Canal at a cost to the maritime nations of £10 million and by forcing the Israeli troops to withdraw behind their frontier. The United Nations Emergency Force took over the policing of the Gaza Strip and the Sharm el-Sheikh headlands on the Gulf of Aqaba, thereby giving Nasser the peaceful Israeli border he wanted. The Russians replaced the arms he lost in the fighting. All he was compelled to concede was the passage of ships through the Gulf of Aqaba to Israel. Egypt suffered economic difficulties caused by the decline of Western trade, but these compelled the country to a degree of austerity which, in the long run, need not have done her harm.

## Chapter 11

# Egypt in Arab Affairs (1): Union with Syria

---

## I

BY TAKING THE Suez Canal Company and finally getting rid of the British, President Nasser had achieved Egypt's national aspirations and was free at last to devote himself to wider interests, none of which was more important to him than the Arab world, the inner circle of policy to which he had referred in his *Philosophy of the Revolution*. His attitude to it was inbred from the intellectual and philosophical discussions of the 'twenties, from which national opinion had come firmly to believe that Egypt had the natural right to lead, and it was coloured by the secular struggle for power he had won in Egypt. The rights of nations to be free was a principle imposed on him by God, like a supreme Commandment, and to no area was his commitment more immediate than the Arab countries to which he was linked by language, religion and, to some extent, race. Their condition was in varying degrees akin to that of Egypt before his victory, for only the small Aden colony was in formal subjection to a foreign power, Britain, the others having chosen by policy, alliance or treaties to accept a subservience ranging all the way from Lebanon's cautious collaboration with the West to the outright dependence of petty sheikhdoms in the Persian Gulf and South Arabia, which, in Nasser's view, were essentially colonies. He wanted this whole area released from every commitment, so that it could move freely into the third world of uncommitted nations, play its part with some of its former greatness, and achieve the benefits to which this would entitle it. The interests of powers, the United States because it desired the Arabs to bolster resistance to Russia, and of Britain, which still had established positions on the perimeter and substantial dependence on Arabian oil, stood in his way, but this he expected and purposed to resist; what seemed to him of more importance was the self-interest of ruling groups who sought to preserve their power in alliance with the Powers, just as the class-interest of Egyptian leaders had done before. The strength of these

rulers depended on territories or oil revenues and he did not expect
them to sacrifice either to further a policy of Arab liberation or
achieve Arab unity. It followed that if the ultimate enemy was the
foreigner, the immediate target of attack must be the Arab leaders
who supported the foreigner to preserve their own power.

Israel was a special and related case because it existed by the
conquest of Arab territories and had been helped to victory and
sustained by Western powers, he believed, as a bridgehead against
the Arab nation. Palestine had a particularly evocative appeal, too,
because it was the region where the Arabs had defeated the earlier
religious imperialism of the Crusades. Even more, the loss of the
lands of the Palestine people touched the heart of every Arab, and
the diaspora of intelligent and articulate Palestinians kept alive the
passion that might otherwise have cooled. To the broad philosophy
of liberation there was therefore added the more pressing claim to
recover Palestine from the Jews, a claim which held everyone to the
cause when some might have found Nasser's nationalism too remote
for concern. Palestine gave so sharp an edge to the national movement that the Arab ruler who could perhaps be accused of collaboration with imperial powers was because of it exposed to the greater
charge of outright treachery.

In the middle 'fifties none but the most pragmatic and intelligent
Arab leaders recognised the impossibility of early reconquest, and
popular opinion never gave it a thought; but for people like Nasser,
whether he recognised it or not, time was the essence of the question,
for they could not go to war with Israel while conducting a revolution to overthrow collaborating rulers. From the outset they needed
to pursue the revolution in the confidence that an Arabia freed of
reactionary rulers could then combine to defeat Israel, or to
diminish the revolutionary urge so that all rulers could combine
temporarily to pursue a successful Palestine policy. Both courses had
their disadvantages for President Nasser; the first in that it postponed
indefinitely the victory against Israel, for which Arabs insistently
called, and the second because, in his opinion, the 'enemy' rulers
would never combine effectively against 'their imperialist masters'.
He preferred to pursue revolution, but he dared not tell the
Arabs that he had shelved the hope of victory for a long time to
come.

While he was consolidating the military régime and his own
position, Arab nationalists believed that he was luke-warm towards
'Arabism' and solely concerned to revive Egypt, even if it meant
coming to terms with Israel. They were also against his dictatorship,
because democracy was an essential part of their creed, inspiring

their resistance to autocracy among Arab rulers. The Pan-Islamic movement also was bitter about his repression of the Moslem Brotherhood and was further embittered when he executed the two Brotherhood leaders, Oda and Farghaly, in 1955. The Arab rulers were in doubt about him for different reasons; they were not averse to an Egyptian dictator extricating them from promises to exterminate Israel that they could not fulfil, but they did not like a government which dethroned kings, confiscated the property of the rich, and used trade unions to unseat a president. To follow Egypt in the path of moderation was one thing; to follow along the path of revolution was another.

Nasser was not unduly disturbed by this. He was now free to take the lead in Arab affairs to which his success against the British entitled him, and he was confident that nationalists would swing to him because he achieved Egyptian aspirations. As for the politicians, he had contempt for them and their criticism, likening their bombast to the empty protestations with which Egyptian leaders had thrust their forces ill-armed and unprepared into the Palestine War. The Arab world, as he saw it at the time, consisted of a small and unimportant Lebanon, an irresponsible and ill-governed Syria, Jordan a satellite of Britain, Saudi Arabia ruled by a tribal royal family which squandered the nation's great oil-wealth, and Iraq, yet another reactionary monarchy but more dangerous than all the rest, because in Nuri el-Said it had the most able Prime Minister. He intended to struggle against them all and he did not expect any politician to welcome his efforts until forced to do so by popular opinion.

The Egyptian revolution had changed the balance of power in the Arab Middle East by breaking the unnatural alliance between the puritanical King of Saudi Arabia and the licentious Farouk, who had combined to limit the ambitions of the Hashemite kings of Iraq and Jordan and moulded the Charter of the Arab League to this purpose. The Free Officers were inclined to think less of the Saudi than the Iraqi king and were too busy putting their own house in order to spend much effort fostering royal rivalries. At first they were more concerned by Abdel Rahman Azzam Pasha, the fervent pan-Arab Secretary-General of the Arab League, who sometimes committed Egypt by word and deed to policies they did not like; and when they replaced Azzam by Abdel Khalek al-Hassouna, an obedient administrator, they had for once an ally in Nuri Pasha el-Said of Iraq, who had long complained of Azzam's initiatives.

Nuri was the veteran leader of Iraq, a man powerful and active

in government and not given to idle speech, who was making some
sense of the Iraqi economy by the relatively wise use of the country's
oil revenues, but to the people of Nasser's generation he was the
arch-collaborator who preserved at all costs the British connection
for the sake of the Hashemite dynasty and his own power. Their
uncompromising minds could not understand the wisdom of his
compromises; they measured his careful and rational statements
against the wordy patriotism of other leaders and found him
wanting; and he, in misplaced contempt for popular opinion, rarely
explained himself. Nasser, viewing him with the eyes of his generation, thought him a pillar of the old order that had to be changed,
but he could not escape the fact that Nuri was a pillar, not a broken
reed like the rest. For the time being the Arabs would be stronger for
the combination of Nasser and Nuri, of Egypt and Iraq. Therefore,
despite all his reservations, Nasser told a journalist in August 1954:
'Nuri has returned to power in Iraq and is likely to stay for some
time. Now we must try to reach an understanding with him.'*

Real co-operation between Iraq and Egypt would have changed
the mould in which Arab politics had been set ever since the formation of the Arab League in 1945. Egypt had then taken the lead and,
in agreement with Saudi Arabia and Syria, had secured a charter
which weighted the League against the Hashemites on behalf of
King Farouk, who did not want the kings of either Iraq or Jordan
to rival him in royal status, and of King Abdel Aziz ibn Saud, who
was even more opposed to the Hashemite family because he feared
they might one day try to recover the Arabian kingdom he had
taken from them. Damascus was traditionally opposed to Baghdad
and therefore to Iraqi ideas of a 'fertile crescent' combining Syria
and Iraq, and as Lebanon leaned towards Egypt and Saudi Arabia,
these four states controlled league policies and, in practice, gave
Egypt effective leadership.

This combination no longer existed in 1954. The obstructive
ambition of King Farouk had disappeared with his abdication;
King Abdel Aziz of Saudi Arabia and King Abdullah of Jordan
were both dead, and there were boy kings on the Hashemite thrones.
Egypt's ties with Saudi Arabia and Syria were much weaker and
the military régime had not forged new ones that would necessarily
prevent better relations with Iraq. The obstacle in 1954 was different
in nature, arising from the revolutionary purpose of Nasser himself
and reflected in foreign policy.

Nuri, who prided himself on being a practical man, saw no sense
in vague concepts of neutrality in world affairs and sought solutions

* To the author.

to immediate problems in alliance with the Western powers.* Because of its proximity to Russia and the consequent vulnerability of its northern oilfields, Iraq consistently held the view that the Arabs should preserve Western friendship, and to that end he had tried to mediate between Britain and Egypt. During the monarchy the quarrel with Britain had not seriously damaged Egypt's relations with the Western powers, but the first major pointer to a change occurred in 1950 when the Wafd Government professed neutrality between the two world blocs. They regarded neutrality simply as a bargaining position against Britain, but the policy had already taken root in Arab national opinion and, in 1954, had become the corner-stone of Nasser's foreign policy.†

Nasser was aware of the rift between his and Nuri's ideas, but the summer of 1954, when he was certain of final agreement with Britain, seemed propitious for 'realism', however temporary. He sent Major Saleh Salem on a tour of the Arab countries to project a reasonable image of the army régime, in the course of which Major Salem met the Iraqi leaders, the young King Feisal II, Crown Prince Abdulillah and Nuri el-Said at Sarsank on 15 August. Salem announced after a brief conference that there had been 'total accord' and Nuri said privately that he had found nothing to oppose in the opening Egyptian statement, but it soon became evi-dent that Salem had gone far beyond the intentions of the R.C.C. Syrian newspapers reported him as saying that he had withdrawn Egyptian objections to the union of Syria and Iraq, which was what Nuri had understood him to say and meant that Iraq had permission to fulfil the greatest Hashemite ambition; but there was a crucial Egyptian qualification: union had to come by agreement of the two peoples and this was impossible to determine.

When Nuri el-Said arrived in Cairo a month later he found Nasser's willingness to tolerate plans for a 'fertile crescent' or any-thing like it depended on Iraq's willingness to bring its policy in line with Egypt's 'neutralism', for Nasser was not prepared to have Syria brought into the orbit of British policy via Iraq and was

---

* In the early days of the Arab League, Nuri el-Said proposed that Iraq and Egypt should agree to postpone their claims against Britain in order to secure Western support for the Arab cause in Palestine. The Egyptian Government not only refused but took its case against Britain to the Security Council at the very moment when the General Assembly was debating the Palestine question and the sympathy of Britain particularly important.

† The Moslem Brotherhood had done a great deal to strengthen popular support for the neutral policy by telling the Arabs that Britain and France were aggressors against the Islamic peoples, citing the Koranic verse: 'He who attacks you, attack him in like fashion and know ye that Allah is with the pious'. At the same time it emphasised that Russia had not been guilty of aggression against the Arabs.

opposed particularly to Iraqi plans to join the Turco-Pakistan pact. Nuri once again argued for an alignment with the West, which he said would mobilise maximum resistance to Israel, but without avail, and the 'agreed viewpoint' they announced at the end of their meetings was an agreement to differ; all Nasser had conceded was that Iraq could make defensive arrangements against Russia if she wished, as long as no attempt was made to drag the whole Arab world into a new Western alliance.

Nasser wanted the evacuation of British air bases in Iraq, in accordance with his policy of liberation everywhere, and revision of the Anglo-Iraqi Treaty became urgent once Britain agreed to take her troops from Egypt. Nasser made contact with Moussa Shabander, the Iraqi Foreign Minister, when he and his Arab colleagues were in conference in Cairo in December 1954, and Shabander gave a Press conference on the 13th to announce that Iraq was ready to sign an agreement similar in form to the Anglo-Egyptian Agreement, but providing that British air bases could be reactivated in the event of an attack on Iran. This provision was the peak point of Nasser's 'realism', never to be reached again, for it deferred to Nuri's anxieties about Russia and conceded a point raised by the British in their negotiations in Cairo; they had then asked that the Canal Zone base could be reactivated in the case of an attack on Iran as well as Turkey, and the R.C.C. had agreed only to the latter. If Iran were now conceded in an agreement with Iraq, a member of the Arab Collective Security Pact, which was also covered by the reactivation clauses, this presumably meant that Nasser had agreed that the Canal Zone could after all be used to defend Iran.

Nasser had approved the Shabander statement; Nuri Pasha informed the Iraqi Chamber of Deputies that the Anglo-Iraqi Treaty would be replaced by a new bilateral agreement which would provide for the security of Turkey and Iran, and that Iraq would not accept any commitment without the approval of the members of the Arab Collective Security Pact; yet, still, all was not well. Moussa Shabander contracted pneumonia on his return to Baghdad and did not resume his post on recovery. He had promised Nasser that Iraq would not join the Turco-Pakistan pact before there had been another meeting of Arab Foreign Ministers, but Nuri was not prepared to submit his policy for approval. The visit to Baghdad of Adnan Menderes, Prime Minister of Turkey, was imminent, and although his ambassador to Iraq announced on the eve that it would have nothing to do with Middle East Defence, Menderes and Nuri Pasha signed what became known as the

Baghdad Pact on 6 January 1955. The announcement ended all hope of agreement between Iraq and Egypt.

Nasser unleashed a propaganda campaign against Nuri, the violence of which did not stop short of inciting the Iraqi people to murder.* He summoned the member States of the Arab Collective Security Pact to a meeting in Cairo on 22 January and the Egyptian delegate fiercely attacked Iraqi policy. Those countries unwilling to endorse the Egyptian statement in case it drove Iraq from the Arab League, persuaded the conference to send a delegation to Baghdad to patch up the quarrel, but the mission failed. Saudi Arabia, Syria and Yemen, which most strongly supported Nasser, formed a system of bilateral defence agreements and joint commands linking them with Egypt, which effectively restored the original grouping of states within the League. Lebanon and Jordan tried to hold a middle position but their influence was negligible, and eventually Jordan also joined the defence grouping. The first effect of the Baghdad Pact was, therefore, to restore Egyptian control of the League and thrust Iraq into isolation.

## II

The majority of politically minded Arabs, effective public opinion, were wholeheartedly on Nasser's side about the Baghdad Pact but otherwise had mixed feelings about him. The Baath movement in Syria with its radical social doctrine and concepts of unity and liberation was giving nationalism a clear political form, whereas Nasser was barely articulate, vague and personal in his *Philosophy of the Revolution*. Time was to prove the Baathist philosophy imprecise and Nasser's vagueness precise, but, for the time being, people were puzzled; and more immediately the sentence of death on the two Moslem Brotherhood leaders and Egypt's reticence about Israel worried them.

The Arab-Israeli frontier had been quiet. The Israelis had occupied the disputed Al-Auja demilitarised zone, which had strategic importance on the route out of Sinai to Beersheba, without any more harm to themselves than an Egyptian protest to the United Nations. There were some incidents on the Gaza border, where Palestinian frontier guards made sporadic raids on armed Jewish settlements, but none was serious and the Egyptian forces in

---

* The Egyptian propaganda campaign defeated itself at the time. People in Iraq who were doubtful of, or even opposed to, Nuri Pasha's policy, rallied to his support in anger at the arrogance of Cairo Radio. Nuri Pasha stayed in office longer than he had done before. It was nevertheless the beginning of the end for him.

the whole region consisted only of the brigade permitted by the Egyptian-Israeli armistice. Egypt was important to the Arab boycott of Israel because it kept the Gulf of Aqaba closed to ships bound for Eilath and denied the use of the Suez Canal to Israeli cargoes, but this was pre-revolutionary policy offering no new reason for the collapse of the truce.

During the 1954 troubles on the Jordanian frontier Cairo Radio pledged support against Israeli aggression anywhere in the Arab world and for the day when the Arabs would drive Israel into the sea; it could do no less; but Nasser was restrained in public, and in private conversations with non-Arabs he seemed to accept the fact that one day there must be peace, admitting that his army was too weak to attack Israel and expressing doubt whether other Arab States would give him enough support. He did not mean that he was prepared to promote a settlement, as some foreigners imagined, but it did mean that he could foresee circumstances that might make one necessary. His nuances escaped the Arabs and they felt uneasily that he was reluctant to fight the war of reconquest which they considered the ultimate duty of every leader.

At this moment of Arab hesitation, Mr. Ben Gurion, newly returned to office as Israeli Minister of Defence, decided to resolve their doubts by launching a big attack on Gaza on 28 February 1955. Nasser, the Egyptians and the Arabs all concluded that he had re-entered politics in order to start a new phase of aggression. No Egyptian government had much interest in the Gaza strip, which was about five miles wide and twenty-five miles long, pinned against the sea by Israel and totally indefensible, and it sheltered a quarter of a million despairing Palestinians for whom Egypt, with its own large population, could do little. Nevertheless, Egypt was responsible before the world for its administration and before the Arabs for its defence, and when Ben Gurion's half-battalion attacked the Egyptian headquarters in Gaza town and wiped out a truckload of reinforcements approaching along the single road through the strip, Nasser found himself in the front line.*

He was in no shape to face trouble with Israel, for his own army was imperfectly armed and trained, and he was in violent dispute with Iraq and doubtful of his relations with some other Arab States. He was alarmed when his troops on the frontier demanded permission to retaliate in strength and to keep them quiet he instituted

---

* The situation was sufficiently tranquil enough for Mr. Henry A. Byroade, who arrived on 27 February 1955 to take up his post as U.S. Ambassador in Cairo, to set himself the task of seeking Egyptian support for a settlement with Israel. The deterioration of the situation began with the Israeli attack on Gaza the next day.

more intensive training of a guerrilla force – the *fedayeen* – for limited counter-action; he even invented an imaginary victory over the enemy at a place called Sabha in order to satisfy opinion at home. But most of that year he tried to keep the frontier quiet. In September he proposed the withdrawal of both his and Israeli troops from the armistice line to prevent clashes, and he accepted a U.N. plan for the demarcation of lines and a mixed force to patrol both sides, a plan which was still-born because Israel refused to accept a patrol on its side. He was willing to accept a scheme for utilisation of the Jordan river and its tributaries, which had been prepared by Mr. Eric Johnston, President Eisenhower's personal envoy, modified to meet Arab objections, and commended in its modified form by Egyptian engineers, but Jordan, Syria and Lebanon rejected it and their co-operation was essential.

Efforts at pacification were nullified by the trivial *fedayeen* raids and the publicity given them in Egypt, which gave Israel fresh excuses for attacks on Gaza and Egyptian territory. Then, in order to intensify its blockade of the Gulf of Aqaba, the Egyptian Government announced in July that ships proposing to enter it had to give seventy-two hours' notice. In November the Israeli army made its fifth onslaught, and in the following month it attacked in strength the Syrian positions on the eastern shores of Lake Tiberias. This compelled Nasser, who by this time had his defence agreement with Syria, to inform the Secretary-General of the United Nations that if there were any similar attacks he would be compelled to support his ally.

By the end of 1955 the stage was set for the 1956 invasion. The Israeli Government was determined to open the Aqaba Gulf to Eilath, its southern port for the Asian trade; its people were incensed by the *fedayeen* raids; and the Czech arms deal, signed in the summer, was a threat that one day the Egyptians would be strong enough for the long-promised war to drive Israel into the sea. Those in Israel who called for a preventive war seemed justified.

Nasser had little to show to his credit from the confrontation with Israel in 1955, yet the 'role' found its 'hero'* – and he emerged the most popular leader in the Arab Middle East. Misgivings about his firmness were dispelled by Egypt's involvement, which the Arabs desired and he could not escape, and he had startled and delighted them by the Czech arms deal, which had broken the Western monopoly in the supply of arms; and he had done so without any of the harm to themselves that they thought might ensue. It was to

* In *The Philosophy of the Revolution* Nasser said there was a 'role in search of hero'.

them a supreme act of liberation from unwritten tutelage, and the hope of a war of Palestine reconquest was more and more reflected in his independence of Western policies and friendship with Russia. By comparison the petty victories of Israeli raiders were unimportant.

The rapid growth of 'Nasserism' began in 1955 and it imposed popular pressures on Arab governments greater than any they had experienced before and frustrated British and United States policy. Turkey and Britain, with United States encouragement, tried to convince Lebanon and Jordan that they had everything to gain by joining the Baghdad Pact, but the great weight of popular opinion was against it. The Lebanon, attempting to hold a middle position between Iraq and Egypt, cautiously considered a British suggestion that it should only join the Economic Committee, but was afraid to give even this timid lead against Nasser before knowing what Jordan would do. The visit of the Turkish President to Amman in November 1955 was interpreted by public opinion as an attempt to bring Jordan into the pact and to break Arab solidarity against Israel. Nowhere was feeling stronger than on the west bank of the Jordan, the most solid enclave of support for Nasser, and when it became known that the Chief of the British General Staff, ostensibly in Amman to discuss financial aid for the Arab Legion, was far advanced in persuading the Government to join, four Palestinian Ministers resigned because the Cabinet would not promise to submit the Jordanian terms for joining to Egypt. A new government formed to pursue the matter was compelled to resign within a week by an outburst of popular fury in Jerusalem, Amman and other towns, which was encouraged by Cairo Radio but was spontaneous in origin. More serious rioting in January ended all hopes of bringing Jordan into the pact, halted Lebanon's tentative approaches, and confirmed for ever that Baghdad was the beginning and the end of Arab participation.

These events warned King Hussein that the minds of his people, notably of the Palestinians, were so captivated by President Nasser that he could not hope to turn back the tide, and, holding in check his impetuous temperament, he trimmed his policy to the need of survival. Nasser, quick to take advantage of the situation, persuaded Saudi Arabia and Syria in January 1956 to join with him in offering aid to end King Hussein's financial dependence on Britain. The offer was not immediately taken up but, in pursuit of a more popular image and animated by admiration for Nasser's strength, King Hussein abruptly dismissed Glubb Pasha, the commander of his Arab Legion, who was believed by the Arabs to be the real power in Jordan and was blamed unjustly for the Palestine débâcle in 1948. His course was then set for popular government, and in free elections at the climax of the Suez affair a parliament containing strong radical-national elements was elected and a Government formed under Suleiman Nabulsi, who called himself a socialist.

If Nuri Pasha continued to persuade Britain and the United States to restrain and contain the ambitions of Nasser, the behaviour of King Hussein more truly reflected the anxiety of other Arab rulers. Nasser's belief that public opinion would in time compel them to come to heel was apparently justifying itself faster than expected, and he became more than ever confident that his ability to impose on the Arabs policies against the Western powers would force them to accept him on his terms. This confidence led him to take the risks that resulted in the Suez invasion.

Arab affairs in 1956 took second place to his breath-taking brinkmanship. The Israeli invasion of Sinai made certain that every Arab government would stand by him when the crisis came; no government dared to be lukewarm in his cause. (When it became known that Nuri Pasha wanted Britain to use the nationalisation of the Suez Canal Company as an excuse to overthrow Nasser – with the obtuseness of age he thought he would fall at the first push – he signed his own death warrant.) The Syrian army cut the oil pipeline from Iraq to reinforce the blocking of the Suez Canal. Everywhere the entire weight of opinion was against Britain and France.

When he emerged from the Suez crisis, Nasser was ready to press forward with his revolutionary policy and turned to Jordan where the elections appeared to make change inevitable. He desired Hussein's overthrow or, as temporary second-best, that he be brought to heel by the Nabulsi Government; and this seemed possible when Hussein and Nabulsi accepted on 19 January 1957 the offer of Arab aid to replace British subsidies. When Britain and Jordan decided in most amicable fashion in March to end their treaty the Arabs gave Nasser credit for liberating another state.

It was ironical that at this moment of apparent triumph the reaction was already beginning. King Hussein was disenchanted with his radicals and King Saud had taken fright at the growing power of Nasser which, he rightly concluded, bode him no good in the long run. The struggle between King Hussein and Nabulsi came into the open in April, and Saud, forgetting for the moment his anti-Hashemite sentiments and his ties with Egypt, supported Hussein against the pro-Egyptian radicals; and President Shamoun, seeing Jordan and Saudi Arabia drawing closer to Iraqi policy, began to repair his fences with the Western world. Nasser launched so violent a propaganda campaign against both Hussein and Shamoun that, in June, Jordan and Egypt broke diplomatic relations. Egypt found herself alongside Syria in isolation.

Hussein dismissed the pro-Egyptian groups in his Government, imprisoned Nabulsi and many other people for plotting against the throne, and accepted United States aid in place of the money which Syria, Saudi Arabia and Egypt had promised but never paid. King Saud did not break openly with Nasser but he helped King Hussein with money and edged closer to the pro-Western governments of Iraq and Lebanon. Public opinion clearly was not, after all, strong enough yet to overthrow the rulers, but Nasser only concluded from this that the effort should be greater.

### III

Ever since the first military *coup* in 1949, Syria had been ruled unsteadily by military factions, but in 1957 the Government consisted of a broad political 'front' which was intended to prevent more revolts by uniting the competing army groups. The Baath Party, which had given Arab nationalism a political ideology in post-war years, was the dominant and dynamic influence out of all proportion to its membership. As early as 1955 it had set aside its doubts about Nasser's policy and Egypt's role in nationalism, concluding that faults in both must be rectified if unity was to be achieved. Michel Aflaq, co-founder with Salah Bitar, explained that they reached the conviction that unity could not be achieved unless Egypt participated, because Egypt, if excluded, would successfully obstruct the movement; Bitar said that Nasser's mind was awakened to Arabism in 1953 or 1954, but 'the Arab idea never went very deep in Egypt; the ordinary Egyptian does not yet *feel* Arab. We, in the Baath, always hoped that union would foster in Egypt the same sentiments that fired us'.* These hard-headed sentiments were reinforced by the manifest success of Nasser, who had captured overnight more Arab support than the Baath had won by years of work and propaganda, for the Baath was as deficient in leadership as it was rich in words and the Arabs saw Nasser *doing* what the Baath only talked about. The party leaders therefore decided to use Nasser's reputation to carry them to power in Syria, which they could not achieve on their own; they became his most enthusiastic allies and persuaded the National Front Government to make union with Egypt part of their programme.

Syria was the geopolitical fulcrum of the Arab Middle East, for

* Quoted by Patrick Seale, *The Struggle for Syria.*

the control of which unceasing efforts were made by big Powers and neighbours: by Britain and France, by Iraq and Jordan who posed rival Hashemite claims, by Egypt and Saudi Arabia seeking by influence to exclude all Hashemites; and when Russia found that friendship for Nasser increased its influence, Syria was caught in the cold war. The opportunist Baath Party, in its search for support, made alliance with the communists in Syria. This alliance proved of greater advantage to the latter, who were much better organised, and within a short time the pro-communist Chief-of-Staff, General Bizri, appointed party members to key posts in the army. As the army still determined the character of the government the Baath took fright.

Nasser was already concerned about the instability of Syria and he was not willing to see a communist take-over however much he might seek to use Russia against the Western powers and Iraq. He had played no small part in securing the return of Shukry el-Kuwatly as President, not because he had any great admiration for Kuwatly, a right-wing politician of the old school, but because he thought him the best of a poor lot of Syrian leaders and, when Kuwatly was in exile in Alexandria, he had reached an understanding with him about the broad lines of Arab policy. Now Kuwatly also became alarmed by the communists in the Army Command and, fearing that they intended to seize power, he urged Nasser to take counter-action. In this he found himself in the unusual position of making common cause with the Baath Party.

The National Front Government had already approached Nasser to carry the Joint Military Command much further on the road to unity and by the end of 1957 Kuwatly and the Baath pressed urgently for outright union. Nasser, who had no illusions about the difficulty of ruling Syria, told the Syrian Government that union was premature and only agreed to the formation of committees to study it, but, under pressure from his allies in Syria and conscious that union would be a formidable counter-stroke against the Arab governments which were trying to isolate him, he gave his consent early in 1958.

The new constitution was promulgated in a matter of weeks and Nasser was elected President of both Egypt and Syria, which became respectively the Southern and Northern Regions of the United Arab Republic. A new Cabinet was formed with Syrian and Egyptian vice-presidents and some Ministers appointed for the whole republic and others for the separate regions. The process of merging the Foreign Services began immediately and Zacharia Mohieddin sent picked Egyptian security officers to Syria. Field-Marshal Abdel Hakim

Amer dismissed twelve leading communists from the Army Command, and when General Bizri protested his resignation was accepted before he offered it. In line with the Egyptian Constitution, the political parties of Syria were dissolved and Khaled Bikdash, the able secretary and leader of the Levant Communist Party, departed with some of his close associates for Prague and Moscow.

The union was received with unparalleled enthusiasm by Arab opinion everywhere and Nasser became overnight the most popular leader of modern times. When he visited Syria his welcome exceeded anything he had ever known in his own country. Nor did his reputation suffer by his suppression of the Communist Party, because nationalists considered it an alien, materialist philosophy directed from outside the Arab world and in opposition to the pan-Arab movement, which remained faithful to Islam.

Nationalism seemed poised now to achieve its objectives, even perhaps the reconquest of Palestine. The ideology of the inefficient Baath Party was now allied to a dynamic leader who had the most powerful Arab country at his command and the great majority of people from the Tigris to the Nile were willing to follow them even against the will of their own leaders. Radical oppositions took heart. The governments of Iraq and Jordan realised at once the danger threatening them and hastily fabricated a federation to demonstrate their fidelity to unity, but it was regarded everywhere as a political expedient and made no impact on opinion. When it was discovered in Syria in March that King Saud had paid cheques on British banks totalling £1,900,000 sterling to further a plot to break the union, the effect of this revelation on the Saudi royal family was so disastrous that the King was compelled to yield authority to Prince Feisal, who promptly brought Saudi policy back into line with Egypt's.

President Shamoun and his Foreign Minister, Charles Malek, had progressively broken with the Lebanon's cautious and traditional neutrality in Arab affairs by developing a policy which so favoured the Western powers that it was manifestly opposed to Nasser. They thereby revived tensions between the Christian and Moslem communities that were never far from the surface, for Lebanese political attitudes were divided broadly between Moslems who supported a pan-Arab, pro-Nasser line, with whatever collaboration with communist powers that that entailed, and Christians who looked to their co-religionists of the Western world for protection against Moslem domination. There was, however, a small but strong Christian minority which supported the pan-Arab movement, and together with the Moslems they were encouraged by the union to work more openly against Shamoun. It was fertile ground for President Nasser, who sent money, arms and agents into Lebanon. Sporadic disorders reached serious proportions by May and, enlarged and confused by the Christian-Moslem conflict, were approaching civil war by the end of June. The Lebanese Government complained to the United Nations that arms and men from Syria were causing the trouble, but U.N. observers who were sent to study the situation reported no 'massive infiltrations'.

The troubles in Lebanon were at once a warning to Nuri el-Said and an excuse that he could exploit if necessary to break through Syria to the aid of Shamoun. He showed little concern about unrest in his own country and was confident that the army would be loyal enough to handle it and march on Lebanon. In July he called a brigade to move towards the Syrian frontier, and on the night of 13 July 1958 it was camped with its arms outside Baghdad. This brigade entered the city in the early hours of the next day, murdered the royal family and Nuri Pasha, and seized the government.

It seemed at the outset that the new Government of Brigadier Abdul Kerim Kassem would support President Nasser, who would then control the three most powerful countries bridging the region all the way from the Nile to the Tigris. The position of Lebanon and Jordan was desperate, for the Christians of Lebanon had now no support against the Moslem hinterland, and in Jordan there was doubt about the loyalty of the Arab Legion, the only defence of the King and Government against civil revolt. The *élan* of the pro-Nasser national movement was now so great it could hardly be restrained and the danger that the exuberant confidence of President Nasser, the Baath and Kassem might lead one or all of them to invade could not be discounted. King Hussein and President Shamoun immediately called for help, and American troops of the VIth Fleet landed in Lebanon and British troops flew into Jordan. The operations were covered by article 51 of the U.N. Charter and were approved by the General Assembly, to which the Jordan delegate reported U.A.R. threats of aggression.

The danger to both countries was removed. On 21 August an All-Arab resolution calling for Arab good-neighbourliness was passed by the U.N. Assembly, and the Secretary-General flew to the Middle East to see that the resolution was carried out. It was not so easy to end the bitterness caused by the civil strife in Lebanon, however, and even after General Shihab was elected to replace President Shamoun on 31 August, disorders, violence and confusion continued until Shihab took office in late September. Nor had the revolt entirely failed, for Rashid Karame, one of its leaders, was appointed

Prime Minister. He formed a strongly pro-Nasser Government, which provoked a general strike and fresh disorders in which there was serious loss of life until he reconstructed his Cabinet in a more balanced way. The Karame Government restored normal relations with the United Arab Republic and the American troops withdrew in late October. The British forces left Jordan on 2 November.

The gains of Nasser were considerable. He controlled Syria, the Hashemite royal family of Iraq and Nuri el-Said were dead and replaced by a military Government which he assumed would collaborate, and the Lebanon had swung from opposition to cautious support of his policy; and although British troops had prevented the overthrow of King Hussein, they had also demonstrated his dependence on foreign intervention and damaged his reputation with the nationalists. The road seemed open to the rapid conversion of the entire Arab world to his radical policies and to the union of peoples which he advocated. The Arabs responded to his word and their governments to his whip.

The cracks in the radical front were, however, quickly apparent in both Syria and Iraq. Kassem was far from pleased that the first reaction of the Baghdadis was to assume that Nasser had liberated them and would be their leader, and he was in no hurry to confirm the offer, made in Syria by his closest colleague in the revolt, Brigadier-General Abdel Salam Aref, of union with Syria and Egypt. The Baath Party in Syria was dismayed to discover that, far from being imposed as the ruling caucus, Nasser insisted that it be disbanded along with all other parties, and their disgruntlement helped to make unworkable the clumsy cabinet system improvised at the time of union. In October, Nasser announced a new Cabinet for the entire United Arab Republic in which fourteen Ministries out of twenty-one, including all the most important, were allotted to Egyptians, and the Syrians thereupon concluded that a Nasser takeover had begun. Nothing could be more offensive to the Syrians and the Baath, who considered themselves historically and in spirit the generators of the Arab renaissance.

At this stage Nasser was mainly concerned with making the united Government work, but the fact remained that every action demanded further submission by Syria. The Syrian High Court was replaced by a Council of State on the Egyptian model; laws governing a State of Emergency were unified with those in Egypt, which gave Nasser sweeping powers; the competition of superior Cairo newspapers drove all but five Damascus journals out of business; and the free exchange of currencies, from which Syrian trade might have benefited, had soon to be abandoned because the Syrians took advantage of cheap planes to Cairo to create a thriving black market in the already weak Egyptian pound.

From the moment of union the Syrian landowners were alarmed at the prospect of agrarian reform on the Egyptian model and their fears were confirmed in September when the law was promulgated and Egyptian experts arrived to direct its application. There were backward, semi-feudal areas in Syria which could well have done with reform, but it was applied to the Gezira, in the north, where the farming had been cited as a good example of private enterprise.* Before the year was out there were severe shortages and a flourishing black market in commodities, the movement of Syrians to Lebanon was restricted, and many essentials normally home-grown had to be imported. All this was blamed on union government policy, although at that stage agrarian reform could have done little harm except perhaps to confidence; the real cause of the economic difficulties was a succession of bad harvests. Disillusionment and unrest progressed so far that Nasser sent a three-man mission to see what could be done about it. When he returned to Syria himself in 1959 he received a good welcome, but it lacked the spontaneous enthusiasm of the preceding year and was more a tribute to his continuing *mystique* than to the union.

A National Union was formed in July, again on the Egyptian model, to replace the disbanded political parties, and became the popular base for the régime, and 40,000 members were elected to local councils in both regions. This was another attempt by Nasser to create a grass-roots democracy to replace the Western system; the local councils were to elect provincial councils, which would elect a national council, from which Nasser would choose a National Assembly to replace the assemblies of both countries, dissolved at the time of union.

The Baath Party did so badly in the local elections that it blamed the interference of the security forces for its failure, although it had seldom done well in popular elections in the past. Despite the fact that it had Ministers in the Government, it had continued to operate clandestinely after being ordered to disband, and it was now stirred to more active and subversive opposition to Egyptian domination. In an effort to secure more co-operation, Nasser sent his right-hand man, Field-Marshal Amer, as governor of the Northern Region in October, giving him instructions to conciliate Syrian opinion, and when Amer opened an office for complaints several thousand were received within a few days. He told the business community that he was intent to improve trade and proceeded to reduce customs duties

* Doreen Warriner, *Land Reform and Development in the Middle East.*

14—ME

on a large range of capital goods and luxuries, and his efforts were helped by a good harvest; but neither harvest nor concessions could overcome the political resistance of the Baath and other political groups. In December he advised Nasser to accept the resignation of all the leading Baathists from the Government. This counsel of despair had considerable importance, because it meant that Nasser, the activist, had failed to come to terms with the nationalism of the Baath, of which he should have been the natural ally in the radical evolution of the region.

Nasser was now governing Syria and controlling its international and inter-Arab policy without any real attempt to consider Syrian attitudes, and in doing so he had to turn it into a Police State under his own intelligence service and senior army officers. The one Syrian on whom he relied was, significantly, Colonel Abdel Hamid al-Sarraj, a taciturn and withdrawn young man who had been Chief of Military Intelligence as early as 1955 when he was only twenty-eight. He was an efficient administrator, dedicated to Nasser, and his ability and loyalty were devoted to catching the enemies of the union, which he did with such success that the hatred he engendered became embarrassing to his master. Unrest was so widespread that Nasser was nevertheless compelled to make him Minister of Interior early in 1960, and then President of the Executive Council of the National Union in September, thus making him, in effect, his viceroy. Sarraj quickly filled important Ministries with colonels whom he could trust to work with him under the Egyptians.

## IV

While the difficulties in Syria multiplied, the hope that the revolution in Iraq would bring that country into union, federation or at least close political association with the United Arab Republic faded. Although at the outset Nasser approached relations with Iraq with his former caution, the Baath worked hard to bring it into union, but their enthusiasm only made Abdul Kerim Kassem reflect the more on the advantages of independence. The communists at his side worked hard against Nasser, for their party, with Soviet encouragement, had opposed him ever since he broke their influence in Syria. Kassem relied on them increasingly and their first victim was General Abdel Salam Aref, who had been Kassem's partner in the *coup d'état* and was made Commander-in-Chief and Deputy Prime Minister after it; Aref, the principal advocate of fusion with the U.A.R., soon fell from favour, and he was arrested and sentenced to death for conspiracy in February 1959. In the following month a pro-Egyptian revolt by Colonel Shawwaf in Mosul was defeated with much bloodshed and punished with brutality. Nasser's relations with Iraq as a result of these events were as bitter as they had ever been in the days of Nuri el-Said.

Nasser now appeared a less evil figure in the eyes of King Hussein and King Saud, both of whom approved his attack on the communists; and the quarrel with Iraq and his difficulties in Syria made it unlikely that either he or Kassem would have power to harm them. Jordan resumed diplomatic relations with the United Arab Republic in August 1959 and King Saud paid a State visit to Cairo in September, during which the two leaders agreed to renew 'unrestricted and absolute' co-operation. But Nasser's relations with both countries remained cool rather than cordial, for he had by no means changed his opinion that the kings should be overthrown. In August 1960 Huzzah Majali, the Jordanian Prime Minister, was murdered by a bomb placed in his office by agents instigated by Syrian intelligence and prompted by Cairo propaganda, which had arraigned Majali, the Prime Minister who had tried to bring Jordan into the Baghdad Pact, as 'an imperialist agent and traitor'. Troops were massed on both sides of the Syrian-Jordanian frontier and King Hussein condemned Egypt before the United Nations General Assembly, and he described Nasser in a broadcast from Amman as a madman, a jester, a red agent, a dictator, a small Farouk, a ruler thirsty for blood, and a conspirator. Cairo Radio resumed its campaign against King Saud as well as Hussein. The very strength of King Hussein's riposte showed how far Nasser's domination had declined from its peak in 1958, when the union with Syria and the revolutionary upsurge had brought it to the threshold of success everywhere. Even public opinion was dismayed by inter-Arab quarrels, which were as bitter within the revolutionary camp as between it and the monarchies, and by the impending failure of the Syrian-Egyptian union.

The union was, in truth, collapsing. Another bad harvest and economic restraints intensified the unrest caused by the ubiquitous police methods of Sarraj. The cash-conscious Syrians brought some of the difficulties on themselves by smuggling as much money as they could into Lebanon, compelling the Government in February 1961 to impose restrictions on the Syrian pound as rigid as those already applied to the Egyptian, and in July a series of decrees imposed widespread nationalisation and state-control of private firms. Behind the scenes, Egyptian and Syrian experts had made great strides in planning the future development of the Northern

Region, but their work counted for little with the Syrians beside the immediate impact of the new laws.

Under pressure of events and from natural inclination, Nasser had destroyed every centre of political power except his own, thereby excluding the Syrians from any say in the running of their country and driving into opposition every political group, including those like the Baath who had supported him, until he had only the tight-knit security organisation of Sarraj to support him. Clandestine opposition in Syria meant working within the army, and this too was ripe for revolt. The Egyptian officers, insensitive to the intense pride of their Syrian colleagues, had taken it over and riddled it with intelligence spies, whereas the Syrian officers, who had gone to Cairo to undertake the parallel work of fusing the two forces, were left idle at empty desks. Nasser recognised the danger in the summer of 1961 and got rid of Sarraj, the focal point of discontent, by making him Vice-President and Commander-in-Chief and removing him to Cairo, but it was already too late. Field-Marshal Amer called a halt to some of Sarraj's more onerous police methods, but in so doing weakened security by depriving Egyptian military intelligence of an efficient indigenous organisation. His own Syrian Chef-du-Cabinet protected the plot being manufactured around him. Sarraj resigned on 26 September and escaped to Damascus. Two days later army units stationed at Qattana revolted and marched the twenty miles into Damascus where they were quickly joined by others. Nasser sent troops by sea towards Lattakia but recalled them before they got there, and the 150 paratroops who flew to Lattakia were taken prisoner by the garrison they were sent to help. Yet such was the strength of the idea of unity that the Syrian officers who had seized power offered to preserve the republic on new terms. Nasser refused and union was over.

Nasser's reputation with the Arab peoples never completely recovered from this resounding failure even though no one arose to challenge his leadership. Never again would the public accept him without question, whatever his mistakes or virtues. The cohesion of the radical Arab front was broken by the conflict between him and the Baath Party, separating him from the national ideology which had conditioned the Arab mind, and this forced on radicals and revolutionaries alike a choice they were reluctant to make. As for Egyptians, they forgot overnight the pan-Arab enthusiasm of the days of union, turned inwards again to the Nile, and would have given anything for Nasser to drop the name United Arab Republic and call their beloved country Egypt once again.

Nasser's conclusion from these events was entirely contrary. The collapse of the union, he said on 28 September, 'is an act which affects our long struggle for our Arabism and for our Arab Nation. It affects the call for Arab nationalism for which our fathers and our forefathers were martyred. It is an act which affects all the slogans we have issued. It affects our present and our future lives' : and again, on 5 October, 'I am confident . . . that this first experiment in Arab unity will not be the last. . .'. He told the Egyptian people, who waited anxiously for him to say that he would concentrate on their affairs and leave the Arabs and the world alone, that his failure lay in too little, not too much, revolution.

## Chapter 12

# Egypt in Arab Affairs (2):
# The Yemen War

## I

IT WAS NOT in the nature of President Nasser and the people
close to him to believe that the failure in Syria was due in the
last resort to the offence they had given to the Syrian army, and
a few months of careful thought brought them to something less
than a quarter-truth, that the machinations of imperialists, neo-
colonialists and other formalised figures of Satan, using reactionaries
and duped revolutionaries, had brought their disaster about. It was
a curious conclusion, for the leaven in the lump of opposition to
Nasser in Northern Arabia was everywhere the communists,
whereas the Western powers, in their search for stability, were
inclined to consider three years of Nasser's stability in Syria as
something worthwhile; and they had this in common with Arab
opinion, they could see no one able or likely to replace him. But,
having reached the conclusion, Nasser came to two further decisions:
that he had been right to state in his letter to King Hussein in March
1961 that there was a 'real and profound current leading to an
integral Arab union of which the constitutional form is to us of less
importance than the will of the Arab peoples'; and that it was therefore correct to use any possible means to enable the Arab peoples to
impose their will.

There was no other course open to him at the time, for the
opposition of the monarchies had been reinforced by the resistance
of the revolutionary governments of Iraq and Syria. The hopes of
people and the fears of governments had, in their decline, left him
weaker than ever before, even though the strength of Egypt and his
own influence were together greater than any that stood against
him. This was soon evident in 1962 when Jordan and Saudi Arabia
combined to contest Egyptian dominance in the Arab League by
demanding that its headquarters be moved from Cairo; it was not
until 31 March, after great efforts by the Secretary-General, that a
meeting was assembled in Riyadh. His opponents under-estimated,

however, his power to command the Arab mind, which might now be critical but had not turned against him, and when he proclaimed his Charter of Arab Socialism in May, in which he stated that the much-desired unity could only be achieved by the extension of the Egyptian revolution to all Arab states, he recovered much of his popularity. By contrast, there was little popular response to the Islamic Charter produced at King Saud's instigation by a conference of world Moslem leaders held after the Mecca pilgrimage which, by criticising false nationalism based on atheistic doctrine, implied condemnation of Nasser's policy.

He hoped that his failure in Syria would be reversed by another *coup d'état* and used agents, money and his adherents in an effort to bring it about. This was a reversal of traditional Egyptian policy, which had always sought only to prevent Syria from alliances with Jordan and Iraq, and never to secure control for itself, but its only effect was to create unrest when the Syrian Government was trying to restore amity. In June it offered him federal union, but he refused because he was preserving the fiction of the United Arab Republic, still referring to Syria as the Northern Region. He was also disturbed by the close relations between Iraq and Syria, which signed a defence agreement in January and abolished visas in April; in August, Kassem sent a force to the frontier to defend Syria in the unlikely event of an attack by Egypt.

That month the Egyptian military attaché in Lebanon defected to Syria with a list of agents working there, and while the agents evacuated the Levant *en masse* the Syrian Government summoned a meeting of the Arab League in the Lebanon town of Shtaura to complain of Egyptian interference in its affairs. The meeting brought the Arab League to its nadir. The Egyptian delegation consisted of three Syrians, refugees in Cairo after the collapse of the union, who would certainly have been gaoled if they returned home, and Syria, Jordan and Saudi Arabia were in full cry against Egypt. The police were called in twice during the riotous sessions and, when the Egyptian delegates finally walked out, the meeting collapsed with a resolution suspending discussion of the complaint because of the absence of the Egyptian delegation. A full-scale campaign was then launched to prevent the re-election of Abdel Khalek Hassouna as Secretary-General because he was an Egyptian, and it was only to prevent the total collapse of the League, which would have affronted Arab opinion everywhere, that the opposition states granted him another term. The civil war which began in the Yemen in the late summer completed the paralysis of the League; the royalists and the republicans both claimed the seat, and with the revolutionary governments supporting the latter and the monarchies the deposed Imam, Hassouna was driven to inform the members that it was useless even to summon a meeting.

The Israeli problem went by default during this internecine strife. The year started with a meeting in January at which secret decisions were taken to resist Israeli plans to divert some waters of the River Jordan for irrigation and industrial use. Hassouna warned the League States that Israel had already built the pumps and was well advanced in the work on pipes and ditches. Egypt continued to improve its own military potential, obtaining forty new MiG fighters from Russia, starting work on a factory to build frames for jet aircraft, and successfully firing four one-stage rockets with enough range to reach Tel Aviv, but nothing practical was done to impede Israel's work on the river.

There were no less than eight plans for the utilisation of the head-waters of the Jordan, beginning with the Ionides project of 1939 and including the Johnston Plan of 1955, and Arab and Israeli counter-proposals.*

The Israeli plan proposed to take 920 cubic metres of the 1,300 cubic metres available, and although the scheme in progress envisaged drawing only 180 cubic metres, the Arabs feared they would eventually take the full amount, impoverishing arid Jordan in the process and making possible further large-scale Jewish immigration. Arab governments had so far few grounds for inter-national protest because the amount of water Israel proposed to take did not exceed the amount supplied by the Dan tributary inside its own borders, but the Arabs could prevent Israel taking more water by diverting the main tributaries, the Banias and the Hasbani, and reducing the flow into Lake Tiberias. To do so, however, they required to prepare the technical plans, raise about £70 million mainly from Kuwait and Saudi Arabia, and spend three years on the work; and as Israel was unlikely to sit back with arms folded while the scheme was executed, they had to co-ordinate military plans to fight the war likely to ensue.

The collaboration needed for such an effort proved impossible and after the August meeting the League Committee of Experts, formed to devise plans, was compelled to cancel its meeting. Israel was able to operate with complete impunity. In mid-March it put the largest force since its invasion of Sinai into a punitive attack on the Syrian frontier and suffered no more than censure by the Security Council for doing so. Renewed tension at the end of the

---

* See G. H. Jansen, 'The Problem of the Jordan Waters', *The World Today*, February 1964, for a succinct survey of this complicated problem.

year prompted the Syrian Government to proclaim a military alert and the Israeli Prime Minister threatened to invade Syria unless its troops stopped molesting Israeli farmers at work south-east of Galilee. Lacking the means to sustain a larger conflict the Syrians gave way, and the farmers planted their crops unmolested.

These events demonstrated that when inter-Arab relations were so bad that even the League could not function, it was quite impossible to put any restraint on Israel; or, more precisely, that it was impossible to pursue revolution and fight Israel at the same time. President Nasser was mainly responsible for the state of affairs by his decision, after the collapse of the Syrian union, to pursue the revolution by any and every means. He had driven all his opponents to unite against him. King Saud made Egyptian workers so unwelcome that most of them left his country and he added to Egypt's financial difficulties by demanding that Mecca pilgrims should pay their fees in hard currencies, of which Egypt was very short, and publicly insulted Nasser by refusing to accept the pilgrimage carpet which Egypt provided as cover for the *Kaaba*, the holy rock at Mecca. Four Saudi princes defected to Egypt and called from Cairo for the overthrow of their own monarchy. On 7 August the Maghreb Press Agency reported that a Lebanese hairdresser and two armed Palestinians had been arrested and fifteen more Palestinians were sought in connection with a plot to assassinate King Hussein during a State visit to Morocco; the Jordanian Prime Minister accused the U.A.R. of responsibility for this plot and another to murder himself. Kassem drew closer to Russia, which gave him a lot of arms on credit, and renewed his dalliance with the communists.

At this moment of isolation, with no support except that of remote Algeria, which had come newly independent upon the scene, Nasser was challenged by the civil war in Yemen, and with only popular opinion and his own convictions to sustain him, he felt compelled to commit his country to it.

## II

Immediately after the union of Egypt and Syria, Yemen asked to be associated with the United Arab Republic and Nasser agreed to a federal connection under the title of the United Arab State. This absurd connection between the revolutionary core of the Arab world and a repressive feudal monarchy could only be explained by Nasser's conviction that it was perhaps easier to remove kings who worked with him than those who stood against him.

Prince Mohammed el-Badr naïvely assumed that he would have

Egyptian support when he succeeded his father, the Imam, and that meanwhile he might get more aid from the Powers by playing Egypt's neutral game. He began to align his policy before the union. In the course of a world tour he signed a ten-year trade and technical agreement and established diplomatic relations with People's China, and he arranged for a Soviet economic mission, headed by the Cairo ambassador, to visit Yemen.

The federal link with the U.A.R. was always tenuous, expressing Prince Mohammed's will to follow Nasser more than the deed of union, and it was soon evident that Imam Ahmed regarded it as a doubtful experiment. Although in 1958 he ordered the withdrawal of the British Chargé d'Affaires, it was soon apparent that he did not like the sudden invasion of Chinese and European communists that followed the agreements in Moscow and Pekin.* In 1959 he turned to the United States for supplies of wheat to relieve famine. As he thrust Prince Mohammed and his policy further into the background his own relations with President Nasser cooled rapidly, and when Badr asked for 1,000 Egyptian troops to repress the powerful but troublesome Hashid tribes, Nasser replied that he would help to meet aggression but not to repress the Yemen people. The Imam recalled his representative from Cairo in June 1960, which effectively put an end to the federation, although it was not formally terminated until President Nasser remembered to issue a decree to that effect in December 1961.

He was quite happy to quarrel with Imam Ahmed because trouble was so widespread in Yemen late in 1960 that his overthrow seemed imminent. A curfew was declared in central and southern areas in July, but bomb incidents multiplied in spite of it and culminated in Hodeida in 1961, when the Imam was shot four times and gravely wounded. He recovered enough to broadcast an appeal to his people to 'follow his son', Prince Mohammed, but on 9 September he died.

His reign had been a byword with the Arabs for its cruelty and despotism, but his ruthless strength had held his tribal country together for fourteen years. Prince Mohammed who succeeded him represented himself as a modernist, a friend of President Nasser, and on terms with Russia, People's China and the United States, in accordance with 'positive neutrality', but whatever this meant to the Yemenis it did not change their mind about the Imamate or make them fear him. Only eighteen days after his father's death, the

---

* *The Economist* reported on 25 July 1959 that there were already 700 Chinese and 200 European communists in this small country, which was not given to welcoming strangers.

Yemeni army shelled his palace guards into submission and executed those members of his family who were caught.

Colonel Abdullah al-Sallal emerged as leader of the revolution, with the rank of Prime Minister and presidential powers, and Dr. Abdel Rahman el-Baidani as Deputy Prime Minister. They were both adherents of President Nasser and they appealed to him for help. Small contingents of Egyptian troops landed by plane. Foreign correspondents reported on 8 October that all resistance was at an end.

The overthrow of the Imamate was welcomed everywhere in the Arab world except by the rulers of Jordan and Saudi Arabia, and even there popular opinion was against the official policy. For President Nasser it was a matter of principle that he must intervene to sustain the revolution against a reactionary monarchy in accordance with the will of the Arabs. His action restored his image as the supreme revolutionary leader, dimmed by the collapse of the union with Syria, and it had the incidental advantage, it seemed to him, that intervention would be brief and cheap.

In this, he and his advisers revealed considerable ignorance of the mountains of Yemen and the character of its people. They had been conquered before but the conquerors had always come to terms with them, and even the formidable Imam Ahmed had ruled through careful acceptance of the rights and responsibilities of the principal tribes and their fanatical Moslem sects. Nor was it true that Prince Mohammed had died under the rubble of his palace; he had escaped over the wall with five of his bodyguard, made his way to the Saudi frontier, gathering tribal forces on the way, and he met foreign pressmen to announce his determination to overthrow the republican régime. He returned to the mountains of Northern Yemen, where he was joined by his uncle, Prince Hassan, and other members of his family. By the end of the year there were 13,000 Egyptian troops controlling the central triangle contained between Sanaa, Taiz and Hodeida, and there was civil war in the mountains.

With arms and money from Saudi Arabia, the spasmodic advice of a few freebooting British officers anxious to bloody Nasser's nose, and the support of warlike mountain tribes who armed themselves from raids and ambushes at the expense of the Egyptians, the odds were not as much against the royalists as most people first supposed. Those countries such as the United States which recognised the republican Government on the principle that it controlled the country acted in error. The progress of the war in terms of territorial conquest was probably as confusing as reports made it out to be, for with no firm front and fighting confined largely to roads and passes through mountains, where both victory and defeat were transient things, royalists and republicans spent a lot of their time behind the enemy lines. The Egyptian forces were neither trained nor equipped for mountain warfare and they felt the cold severely when the first winter hit them in the heights. The Egyptian air force worked hard to clear their way with bombs and gunfire, but did more harm to villages than to fighting men, who vanished into their fastnesses at the sound of a plane and emerged unscathed. Slowly but surely the number of Egyptian troops increased: 20,000 in 1963, 40,000 in 1964 and 70,000 in 1965; but they still could only win battles without permanent value, moving to the northern or southern frontier, advancing and retreating over routes that were constantly cut by their enemy. The royalists could not conquer the central plateau with tribal forces and the Egyptians could not hold the territory around it. In February 1965 they mounted a major offensive to capture Harib, near the southern frontier with Beihan, in South Arabia, but within a month it was recaptured and President Nasser withdrew his forces to the plateau and sat tight. It was stalemate.

Under pressure from public opinion, Jordan recognised the republican régime during a period of goodwill to Egypt in 1964, but Saudi Arabia stood by the royalists, and as neither Britain nor the South Arabian Federation recognised the Sallal régime the entire frontier was open to assistance for the royalists. Prince Feisal, who was in control of Saudi Arabia owing to the illness of King Saud, proposed in January 1963 that all outside interference in Yemen should cease, confident that if this were done all pro-Egyptian politicians would soon be at the mercy of the tribes. In March, U Thant pursued this offer by sending his assistant, Mr. Ralph Bunche, to Cairo and to the republicans, and Bunche reported that President Nasser agreed to withdraw his forces if Saudi Arabia stopped helping the royalists. When the Secretary-General confirmed that he had received messages from the U.A.R., the Yemen and Saudi Arabia agreeing to end hostilities, the Security Council agreed that a U.N. force of 200 men should be sent to create a buffer zone between the Yemen and Saudi Arabia. The force was totally inadequate over such a distance in rough terrain, but, in any case, the mission failed because there was no will on either side to end the war before victory was achieved. Britain countered complaints that federal planes from Beihan had bombed Yemeni territory by proposing that a peace zone should be created between the Federation and Yemen, but the suggestion was coldly received by Yemeni republicans. The sole purpose of talk of disengagement seemed to be to prevent war spreading to Saudi Arabia, for in January Egypt was accused of bombing Saudi towns, and two days later Prince Feisal announced general mobilisation. In February Mecca radio reported joint manoeuvres with U.S. paratroops, and in June Feisal asked for U.S. air protection.

When Nasser initiated talks in 1964 to end inter-Arab quarrels in order to re-establish a common front against Israel, Prince Feisal took advantage of the better atmosphere at an Arab Summit Conference in Cairo in January to work for peace, and Nasser sent Field-Marshal Amer to Riyadh in March. The joint communiqué at the conclusion of their conference announced agreement of the two states to resume diplomatic relations immediately and that neither country had ambitions in Yemen. This was taken to mean that Prince Feisal, who was primarily concerned to get Egyptian troops out of the Arabian peninsula, was willing to persuade the royalists to compromise in order to bring about the withdrawal. In September, Nasser and Feisal agreed to work for a settlement, and with this encouragement republicans and royalists agreed in conference at Erkwit, in Sudan, to cease fire and hold a peace conference in November. The conference never took place because the republicans would not agree to any representatives from the Imam's family.

The next effort for peace took place in August 1965 at Jeddah, where President Nasser met Feisal (who was now King, having replaced his brother who was deposed by the family in the previous November) and agreed to an immediate cease-fire, the withdrawal of Egyptian troops by 23 September, the formation of an interim government, and a plebiscite to determine the country's future government. In accordance with this agreement the republicans and royalists each sent twenty-five delegates to a peace conference at Haradh, in Northern Yemen, in November, but with the republicans insisting that the future government must not be royalist, and the royalists unwilling to have a plebiscite before Egyptian troops withdrew in accordance with Nasser's undertaking to King Feisal, the conference ground to a halt in late December. The cease-fire, a practical expression of the military stalemate, was all that survived.

The Saudi Arabian Government concluded from the fact that relations between President Nasser and King Feisal deteriorated almost immediately after the Jeddah conference and a visit paid by Nasser to Moscow, that Egypt was no longer interested in a settlement because Moscow had given the required assurance of arms and financial aid to sustain the Egyptian military effort in Yemen, and that Russia had done so to sustain Nasser's pressure on the

South Arabian Federation until the British withdrew from there in 1968. Whether this was true or not, it must have been clear that, if withdrawal took place, the tribes of Yemen would impose their will without regard to revolutionary theories and perhaps even royalist wishes, and that three years' effort by Egypt would be thrown away. This disaster was all the more likely because the passage of troubled time had eroded the unity of the republican camp, in which more and more leading members came to regard any form of government as less important than the conclusion of what appeared to be a civil war without end. Military stalemate encouraged this attitude because the dissident republicans saw that in fostering compromise they might save their skins if the ultimate outcome was not absolute republican victory. Above all the insular and proud Yemenis resented the dominance that the Egyptians were compelled to impose in order to keep their army in the field and the Government functioning, with the result that the republicans were split between those who wanted the Egyptians out and those so committed that they dared not face the prospect.

Both the interest and the image of the Egyptians in Yemen required a strong republican government which demanded their presence. Field-Marshal Amer and Colonel Anwar Sadat worked hard to reconcile differences, and in 1964 President Nasser went to Yemen himself to put his whole weight behind a revised constitution. The result was only a fluctuation between repression of dissenters and compromise with them, and each period of repression drove republicans into exile, the royalist camp or the grave. Sallal, the apostle of the strong hand, first drove Baidani out of office and then had him lured to Cairo where he was put under house arrest.*

In 1964 Egypt kept Sallal out of Yemen, either in Cairo or ranging far and wide from Bonn to Pekin, while an attempt was made to restore cohesion to the republican Government. When this failed, General Hassan al-Amri was made Prime Minister and Sallal returned briefly to proclaim no conciliation and a tribunal to try dissenting Ministers. The Deputy Prime Minister, one of the dissenters, was murdered in February; he was reputedly the leader of a republican 'third force' which wanted a peace settlement with the royalists and the withdrawal of the Egyptians. Seven of his followers escaped to Aden where they appealed to Nasser and King Feisal to impose peace. The repressive policy coincided with the last major offensive against the royalists at Harib, which Nasser had foreshadowed in a speech on 27 February, and both together were intended to force a military and political settlement. This phase

* By 1967, Baidani was back in favour as Yemeni Ambassador to Lebanon.

ended with the recapture of Harib by the royalists, the regrouping of the Egyptian forces out of harm's way on the central plateau, and the formation of a moderate republican Government under Ahmed Mohammed Noman, who was stated to have demanded a conference with the royalists as a condition of taking office. He announced 'a return to peace in all parts of Yemen' and implied the withdrawal of Egyptians by promising the formation of a strong national force to assure the country's safety. Even Sallal stated that the Government was determined to end the war.

The purpose of domestic conciliation at this stage was to create a unified republican front for negotiations with the royalists, but there were both Egyptians and Sallal, and his followers, who thought that those already half in mind to sell the pass were the wrong people to seek terms. Sallal was soon at cross purposes with Noman and created a Supreme Council of the Armed Forces which arrested some of Noman's supporters. Noman flew to Cairo on 1 July and three weeks later a new Government, again under Hassan al-Amri, took office, and it directed the republicans at the abortive Haradh peace conference.

The refusal of President Nasser in 1966 to pursue peace efforts requiring some compromise with the royalists was assumed to mean that he had decided to stay in Yemen until the British fulfilled their undertaking to withdraw from Aden in 1968 and that Russia had promised him the aid to make it worth while doing so. He paid for this in a steady withering-away of republican support; former Yemeni supporters toured the Arab world protesting against the Egyptian occupation, and staunch supporters like Hassan al-Amri became increasingly critical.

The weakness of the Egyptian position in Yemen arose from the fact that there never had been a simple division between the royalists and the republicans, for there were those in the royalist camp who were by no means dedicated to the restoration of the Imam's family, and in the republican camp there were people with tribal affiliations with those on the royalist side. In theory, this should have helped towards compromise, but the forces for compromise had common ground mainly in the desire to get the Egyptians out, and this Egypt could not afford without abdicating the revolutionary purpose proclaimed as the reason for entering. The propagation of the republican idea could not change the essentially tribal and Moslem-sectarian structure of the country which would, and will, determine the final settlement. Nasser could only impose a settlement to his liking, or at least save face, by political and military authority which most Yemeni republicans resented.

When Hassan al-Amri tired of his role in 1966 there was a real danger that the republican Government might itself withdraw its request for the Egyptian presence and thus deprive it of all justification. Sallal was therefore sent back from Cairo to stiffen the Government. He found that Amri as well as Noman and the hard core of republican support was against him. Amri, Noman, and about forty other politicians flew to Cairo where they were promptly detained; Sallal announced complete support for Egypt and demanded the trial of the 'traitorous' party in Cairo, and he tried and hanged several prominent Yemeni political and military men.*

Sallal formed a new Defence Council on which the majority were Egyptians and at his side there was not one republican politician of importance. The Egyptian decision to 'defend the revolution' had become straightforward occupation against the will of the Yemenis and had so far not achieved victory over the royalists. The only result was to prevent the Yemenis from holding a tribal conference which would have been their natural and traditional method of solving their problems.

## III

The wheel of Egypt's fortunes in the Arab world took another turn on 8 February 1963, when Abdul Kerim Kassem was overthrown and killed and the pro-Egyptian General Abdel Salam Aref became President of Iraq. President Nasser said that Iraqi-Egyptian relations would now 'go to the farthest limit'. The situation proved not to be so clear cut, for the *coup d'état* had been engineered by the Baathist underground, which was in close touch with Nasser's Syrian enemies, and in March the Syrian Baathists secured control of their Government also. Close collaboration with Egypt therefore depended on President Aref's ability to influence or impose his will on the Iraqi party which was dominant in his Government.

As both President Nasser and the Baathists believed in the union of revolutionary forces the prospects of progress in that direction should have been improved by the change, and when the Iraqi Government was quick to propose 'military unity' of the five 'liberated' states, Iraq, Algeria, Syria, the U.A.R. and Yemen, he could not refuse to accept delegations from Iraq and Syria to discuss the formula for bringing it about. His unofficial but authoritative

---

* There were reports that Amri was considering an appeal to the United Nations *against* Egypt. He and his party were said at first to have gone to Cairo for consultations, but Noman's son, an envoy of the republican Government in the Arab States, said publicly that they had been hustled on a plane and flown to Cairo against their will.

spokesman, Mohammed Hassanein Heykal, set the tone of Nasser's approach to the discussions by a scathing attack on the Syrian Baathists in his newspaper *Al-Ahram*. Nasser pitched his demands high, no less than his own final and authoritative say in government; he had no faith in the Syrian Baathists' concept of 'party democracy' whose will the president would execute. Nevertheless, when the conference reassembled in April the agreement went beyond military union to federation on Nasser's terms. They agreed that the president – who would certainly be Nasser – would be elected in five months, after which there would be a twenty months' transitional period to complete a federation.

When the Syrian party took stock of the agreement and realised that for twenty months Nasser was going to have undisputed authority, it got cold feet. Not only did the referendum never take place, the Baathists began to repress the Nasserites, who had been encouraged to show their heads by the Cairo decisions. In July, when the referendum should have been held, those Baath moderates who had sought to appease Nasser were removed from government and party office; and Nasserite officers then attempted a *coup d'état* which failed and twenty-seven were executed. This was the bloodiest aftermath of any Syrian revolt.

The Baathists also had the bit between their teeth in Iraq. Despite President Aref's personal commitment to a pro-Egyptian policy, they worked closely with the Syrians, and the 'international leadership' of the party, which was effectively a combination of the Iraqi and Syrian party leaders, openly proclaimed their intention to direct the policy of both countries. The Deputy Prime Minister, Ali Saleh Saadi, formed a National Guard of civilians to counterbalance the army, and its members terrorised the public; opponents, or suspected opponents, were thrown into prison indiscriminately, many were tortured and some, notably communists, were executed.

Inevitably the terror drove the army to action, and Brigadier Abdel Rahman Aref, acting for his brother the President, swept the National Guard from the streets and the Baathists from office. Although, in Syria, Ali Saleh Saadi and his extreme group were unwelcome to the more sophisticated leadership of Michel Aflaq and Salah Bitar, Syrian anger with the Iraqi Government was intense. By contrast, Iraq's relations with Nasser were restored.

These events had an important, if temporary, effect on Egyptian policy. They proved that revolutionary régimes would not necessarily combine to overthrow imperialism and feudal rulers everywhere in the Arab Middle East. Syria was now isolated in the Arab world, but the continuing authority of the Baath international

15—ME

leadership was evidence of the deep rift in the Arab radical national movement, and Nasser found himself fighting his own kind more than the 'feudal' rulers whom he considered his target. He therefore concluded that, for the purpose of resistance to Israel – the diversion of the Jordan waters was still the dominant inter-Arab issue – he must temporarily work with the monarchies to produce unity of action and give time to destroy the Baathist régime in Syria.

To this end he introduced the 1964 truce in inter-Arab relations. The moment was timely, for Arab public opinion was dismayed by the bitterness of the conflict in the revolutionary states and the monarchies were reassured by the knowledge that the conflict of the radicals prevented a united front against them. President Nasser called them to a summit conference in Cairo in January 1964 and they all came, albeit Syria reluctantly.

The summit restored Nasser's influence overnight by enabling him to work once again with King Hussein and Prince Feisal while preserving popular support, for most Arabs were concerned with the threat from Israel more than ideological concepts of revolution. He called for a halt to inter-Arab disputes while a plan to counter Israel's use of the Jordan waters was formulated, and as a mark of good faith he halted propaganda against Jordan, Saudi Arabia and Syria. The Syrian leaders were the odd-man-out, diminishing their attacks on Nasser with obvious unwillingness and maintaining their propaganda against the Iraqi Government with accustomed virulence, but they suffered in Arab opinion in consequence. The summit policy was regarded everywhere as a high and hopeful moment in Arab affairs and the subsequent departure from it created widespread disillusionment.

When it was not arresting, trying and executing communists and Baathists, President Aref's Government modelled Iraqi domestic policy on that of Egypt in every respect, and it would have moved willingly towards closer ties with Egypt except for Nasser's customary caution. In May, however, he agreed to work towards unity through a joint Presidential Council and joint Military Command, and then in December he agreed to the formation of a 'Unified Political Leadership' as the 'highest political authority in both countries' – which preserved the myth rather than the method of their unity. The Ruler of Kuwait and Prince Feisal promised some of their oil money for a United Military Command and engineering works to divert the Arab tributaries of the Jordan river. Prince Feisal was nevertheless reluctant to lower his guard. He brought a British officer to train his bedawin gendarmerie for internal security and got rid of the Egyptians who had been training the Saudi Army.

King Hussein avoided his mistake of 1956–57 by keeping firm hold on his domestic situation also, but he welcomed the Egyptian initiative because the political opposition of the west bank of the Jordan was diminished when he had good relations with Nasser. He withdrew his opposition to the 'Palestine entity', the idea of preserving the identity of Arab Palestine in an organisation of Palestinians As most of Arab-held Palestine was now part of the Jordan State, King Hussein had opposed it because he believed its intention was to create a state within his State and eventually to divide Jordan. He now agreed to the formation of the Palestine Liberation Organisation with a former lawyer and diplomatist, Ahmed el-Shukairy, as its president. In international affairs he moved closer to Egypt's neutrality by establishing diplomatic relations with Russia, and by July there were six communist missions in Jordan. Relations with President Nasser became cordial; he spent four days with him after the January summit conference, recognised Republican Yemen in July, and was Nasser's State guest in August.

The problem of Israel provided the cement of this fund of goodwill, and when the second summit conference assembled in Alexandria in September, the Arab leaders got down to the practical problems involved. Only Syria advocated plans to crush Israel there and then; the others devised plans to divert the Jordan river and create the defences to withstand Israeli counteraction. The Palestine Liberation Organisation was authorised to create an army of Palestinian volunteers, to which the Arab governments were pledged to give support. An overall fund of £25 million was levied to provide additional defences for Lebanon, Syria and Jordan under a United Arab Command.

But the suspicions generated by earlier quarrels were dormant, not dead, and this became apparent when General Aly Amer, commander of the United Command, proposed that units of his force – when assembled – should be stationed in Lebanon and Jordan in advance of any trouble. As this force might in time consist mainly of Egyptians, neither Jordan nor Lebanon was willing to have it on its soil, with all that could mean in terms of interference in internal affairs, except at their own request and in abnormal circumstances. This reduced Amer's task to planning the logistics of united action by the Arab armies. The problem of Yemen was also left to Nasser and Feisal to settle between them.

Even so, 1964 demonstrated how effective Egypt's leadership could be in Arab affairs if consultation and compromise preceded action. If the object had been an Arab policy which took account of different political and social patterns in the region, and moved slowly towards united action in spite of them, collaboration might have overcome the difficulties outstanding at the end of the Alexandria summit. Nasser said later that the 'reactionary' states were useless partners but he had put them on trial in the one enterprise for which there was no likelihood of early or successful results, and in all other matters, Yemen and South Arabia, the Persian Gulf, and international policy in general, he demanded their obedience. The peak of goodwill and co-operation therefore withered away in 1965 and collapsed in 1966.

The first break in the front was caused by President Bourgeiba of Tunisia who, with more conceit than wisdom, decided to break the deadlock on the Israeli question. He toured the Arab Middle East in the spring of 1965 to make a frank appraisal of the problem with Arab leaders, including President Nasser, and, influenced by their confidential assessments of the difficulties facing Arab plans, notably the opposition of the great Powers, he proposed publicly that the Arabs should enter into negotiations with Israel on the basis of the United Nations resolutions. Quite apart from the fact that there was no evidence that Israel would make any concessions, it was most untimely to present the proposal when the Arab States were, for the first time for years, approaching unified action over Israel's utilisation of the Jordan waters. Confident that no Arab leader would publicly support the proposal, President Nasser loosed on Bourgeiba all the vituperation at his command and effectively drove him out of the Arab conference. Bourgeiba boycotted the Arab summit in Cairo in May and again in September at Casablanca, rejecting a written request for his return from some members at Casablanca with a letter which condemned the 'dictatorship' of Nasser in Arab affairs.

The negotiations over Yemen which Nasser and Prince Feisal began at Alexandria were impeded so much by mutual suspicion that it took eleven months to reach the Jeddah agreement, and before any attempt to implement its terms could be made, Cairo criticism of Feisal recommenced. Feisal, shedding his fears of Cairo, had taken his own initiative in international affairs by receiving Mr. George Thomson, the British Minister of State at the Foreign Office, after Nasser had refused to do so in Cairo; and there were rumours, soon to be justified, that Saudi Arabia was buying an entire air defence system and missiles from Britain and the United States. He considered he was entitled by the new-found tolerance in inter-Arab relations to pursue a course that, in his view, did no harm to Arabs and even strengthened them, but President Nasser concluded that he was exploiting tolerance to execute a pro-imperialist, anti-national movement. When Feisal paid his first State visit to Iran in December and jointly announced with the Shah their support for a conference of Islamic Heads of State, Nasser was convinced of the truth of his suspicions, for he regarded the Shah as an enemy of the Arab cause and of himself in particular, and the proposed conference as a plot to undermine his command of Arab nationalism.

The concentration on Israel at the Alexandria Conference had disguised the fact that Saudi Arabia and Egypt were in fundamental conflict over the Arabian peninsula. This conflict was reflected in the Yemen dispute, although here too discussion in terms of royalists versus republicans clouded the real issue of Egyptian penetration. It was a principle of Saudi Arabia's policy that the peninsula was its sphere of influence and should be kept closed to the revolutionary intentions of Egypt, Syria and Iraq, even to the extent of excluding Egyptian military people, school teachers and experts who might subvert the Saudis. From the outset of the Yemeni civil war the object of Feisal's policy had been to get the Egyptians to withdraw because, in his view, the Yemen was only the bridgehead to Arab revolution in his country.

The danger foreseen by Feisal increased in 1965 through Arab League policy in the Trucial States of the Gulf and developments in South Arabia. Egyptian policy was directed towards a 'liberation struggle' in both areas. Cairo was the home of Aden politicians opposed to both the British and the South Arabian Federal Government, and from it and Yemen, the National Liberation Front and later the Front for the Liberation of South Yemen which absorbed it, directed a terrorist campaign against the British and the Arabs who worked with them.

The British Government suspended the Aden constitution in order to counter this campaign, but shortly afterwards announced the intention to withdraw British troops in 1968 and withheld an offer of protection to the independent government which would then take over. This put a premium on Egyptian troops in Yemen, for if they could secure an independent South Arabian government favourable to Egypt, it could ask for military support just as the Yemeni republicans had done, and the troops could overrun the tribal areas of the Federation and Aden.

The situation in the Persian Gulf required more circumspect action. According to President Nasser, most of the rulers there qualified as feudalists entitled to overthrow, not least because they were tied to Britain by various forms of protective treaty, but there did not exist a popular movement strong enough to overthrow them.

Their territories were almost entirely desert, with diminutive populations, and they had no natural resources until oil brought wealth in varying proportions to some of them in the last few years. The League recognised that the only practical policy at this stage was to support the impecunious rulers and weaken British control, firstly by giving them financial aid and, secondly, by accusing Britain of encouraging an influx of Iranians to de-Arabise the region.

The British had sponsored and given £1 million to a Development Fund for the Trucial States, the main purpose of which was to direct some money from the oil-producing states to constructive purposes in others less fortunate. The Arab League sent missions to the Gulf in 1965 and offered aid directly to some of the states. A British proposal that it should be channelled through the Development Fund was refused because the League would not thereby gain the influence with the rulers that it sought. It then called on League members to contribute to its own Arab Gulf Special Development Fund. Sheikh Sakr bin Sultan al-Qasimi, the Ruler of Sharjeh, was inclined to turn to the League, but had to take refuge in Cairo when, with prodding from the British, his family deposed him. In July the first conference of the Rulers of the Gulf States brought together rival family chiefs in amicable discussion of economic problems and they approved fifteen new development projects, at an overall cost of £2,500,000. In the following year Bahrein and Sharjeh agreed to take small British forces from Aden.

Opponents of Nasser held the view that his policy in the Gulf was designed to secure control of oil revenues, others that it was governed in the Gulf and Aden by his personal lust for power. Both views underestimated his intelligence and the complicated pattern of his ideas about the 'liberation struggle'. He knew that political changes on the Trucial Coast were unlikely to give him early access to oil income, and very recent history had shown that revolutions did not necessarily play into his hands. In Aden, it was true, he was poised to impose a government of his choosing by military force, but in the Gulf he could hope only to achieve influence by using the Arab League to break British power. All of this was part of his great design to liberate the entire Arab world, a design he had pursued in Algeria and in Yemen, so far at cost rather than material benefit to himself or his authority. If he had come to identify himself with the liberation struggle, to consider that he alone had the strength of will to lead it to success, to see everyone who saw a different line of progress as his enemy, this was not the same as seeking to impose his own rule on the region; indeed, it is highly probable that Nasser has never changed his first opinion that Egypt's dominance over the Arab world is impossible, and that 'unity of aims', in which like-minded governments act in unison under his influence, is the ultimate aim of his policy.

Whatever the motivation of Nasser, its objective was in total conflict with that of King Feisal, who saw Saudi Arabia as the natural heir to British influence in the Gulf and South Arabia. What irked Nasser was his belief that the British Government, in its undertaking to evacuate South Arabia and its efforts to modify its position in the Gulf, seemed prepared to see Saudi Arabia take over some of its responsibilities and to protect the petty states. The Saudi arms deal with Britain* and Feisal's proposal for an Islamic Conference appeared to him to be a grand design to defeat his own concept of liberation. King Feisal had, in effect, established a counter-policy, and with it a claim to lead the Arab world; this had been evident at the Casablanca summit in 1965, where the initiative had been taken from Nasser for the first time.

Nor was it still possible for President Nasser to appeal with confidence to Arab popular opinion, which now knew that radical Arab nationalism did not necessarily produce the millennium expected of it. Far from producing unity of purpose, the front of revolutionary states had been torn by dissension as bitter as any of its own quarrels with the monarchies; Iraq and Syria had suffered disorder, bloodshed, and economic decline; even Egypt was in acute economic difficulty, which was depriving the people of some of the gains they had earlier made. There was an increasing demand among the educated public for a period of tranquillity, stability and reconstruction, as the enthusiasm which greeted the 1964 inter-Arab *détente* had demonstrated. Support for Nasser was still widespread and exceeded the support any other leader could claim, but it was no longer uncritical: there was neither enthusiasm for nor interest in the proposal for an Islamic Conference, but there was some anger at the bitterness of the quarrel about it.

President Nasser came to the conclusion that King Feisal was the spearhead of the 'imperialist counter-offensive', manifested by the fall of Nkrumah, the defeat of the extreme left in Kenya, and the eclipse of Sukarno in Indonesia and, always referring to the proposed Islamic Conference as an alliance, he equated it with the ill-fated Baghdad Pact and fought it as strongly. The paper-thin accord with Jordan broke under the strain when King Hussein approved the conference idea. He had his own troubles with the Palestine Liberation Organisation, which interpreted its brief to

See Chapter 13, III.

mean that it had authority over the Palestinians who constituted about two-thirds of the Jordanian population, and when its demands were refused by the King, it began to attack him as a traitor. The P.L.O. broadcasts were delivered from an Egyptian station with the approval of the Egyptian Government.

Two events in the spring of 1966 widened the gulf between the two blocs in the Arab world: in Syria, the 'international leadership' of the Baath Party was overthrown by an aggressive, left-wing group which cultivated closer relations with Russia and quickly secured an agreement for the building of the long-desired mammoth dam on the Euphrates river; and Prime Minister Kosygin visited Cairo. Syria immediately revived the proposal for united action by the 'progressive' states, Egypt, Syria, Iraq, Algeria and Yemen, and Algeria, which was now receiving large supplies of arms from Russia, echoed the call. The Syrian Government then initiated moves to end the Baath Party quarrel with President Nasser, which was the major obstacle to the plan.

The decisive issue before the Arab leaders was the proposal to hold another summit conference at Algiers in September, when they would have been compelled to discuss the 'solidarity' agreement they had initiated in Cairo in January 1964, reaffirmed at Casablanca in 1965, and destroyed in 1966. Whether it would take place depended on President Nasser, and he announced in July that he would not confer with those Arab rulers whom he described as 'the reactionary tools of imperialism'. King Feisal withdrew his offers of financial aid to the League's Palestine policies, Syria and Egypt moved closer together and in November they signed a defence agreement, to which Iraq gave its support. The polarisation of the Arab world between the 'conservative' and 'progressive' states was then complete.

President Nasser had returned to his policy of overall revolution, whatever that might cost to the Palestine issue, for it meant that united action to save Palestine was indefinitely postponed. He contended that a united purpose was in any case impossible and that this had been proved by the League's failure to execute its plans against Israel or to secure Saudi and Jordanian support for the 'liberation' of South Arabia and the Gulf States. He challenged the Arabs to support the 'revolutionary upsurge' with all their old enthusiasm right through to the overthrow of the 'reactionary' rulers who, he believed, stood between them and their hope of a free, united, socialist Arab world.

## Chapter 13

# Foreign Relations

I

EGYPT'S FOREIGN POLICY was almost non-existent prior to the Anglo-Egyptian Agreement of 1954. Pre-revolutionary governments had acted in concert with the Arab States against those countries supporting Israel, but never to the damage of their vital interests, and when the last Wafd Government adopted neutrality as a policy, it did so only to bargain for a settlement with Britain and without the ideological conviction of the Arab nationalists who advocated it. During their first two years in power the Free Officers were too busy finding their own philosophy, planning the development of the country and trying to achieve the national 'aspirations', to do more than act in the way that seemed best at any particular moment. They genuinely believed that the Anglo-Egyptian Agreement ushered in a new and constructive era of relations with Britain and the Western powers, and when they contemplated closer collaboration with the Soviet bloc they saw no reason why this should create insurmountable difficulties, any more than they expected their support for liberation movements in Africa and Asia to disturb their Western friends unduly. The Baghdad Pact, coming hard on the heels of the Anglo-Egyptian Agreement, challenged these simple assumptions when the officers were free to construct their own policy at last. 'Reaction to events,' as President Nasser frequently called his policy, dates from that time, and was pursued by Egypt as leader of the Arab liberation movement and participant in the world-wide anti-colonialist struggle, but always in uneasy balance with national self-interest, the main ingredient of all foreign policies.

The Baghdad Pact demonstrated that efforts to free the Arab world of foreign influence meant conflict with Britain primarily, and with other Western powers. It also opened the door to Soviet Russia but Egypt's domestic policies did not encourage the Soviet bloc; the Government was persecuting the communists, its economic policy, agrarian reform apart, was conservative, and its financial directors were orthodox, even bourgeois. There were, however, both civilians and military men with pro-Soviet sympathies in positions of influence, and the régime was nationalist and therefore qualified, according to Lenin, as a forerunner of socialist revolution. In any case the Government had secured the withdrawal of British troops and, if it survived, had a good chance of embroiling the British everywhere.

The gains to Western policy in the autumn of 1954 were correctly assessed by the Russians as illusory, for the loss to the British position by the withdrawal of British troops from Egypt could only be profitable if the co-operation it implied was pursued afterwards. The plans for a Baghdad Pact made this unlikely; Israel was restive, and the Western powers could only reiterate their 1950 pledge to guarantee the frontiers, a pledge which the Arabs distrusted and which the French and Americans were unlikely to honour in the case of an Israeli attack on Egypt. Russia responded by giving support to Arab opposition to the Baghdad Pact (and its sincerity was taken for granted because the pact was a defence against Russia), and then offered to arm the member states of the Arab Collective Security Pact, which was directed against Israel. The formal offer of arms was made to Egypt in January 1955 and Moscow became less friendly towards Israel. Soviet policy had nothing to lose and everything to gain; any loss to the West was its gain, and if the West resisted Arab nationalism the situation became doubly favourable. In this situation the dominant influence of Egypt in Arab policies gave it primary importance to the Soviet Union.

The Soviet policy was pursued effectively in trade. Western, and particularly British, purchases of cotton had declined sharply because of the development of synthetic fibres and the high price of Egyptian cotton. Britain, which bought about a third of the annual crop before the Second World War, purchased so little in the crucial 1954–55 season that it failed to be listed among the buyers. The substantial adverse balance of Egyptian trade with Britain was only made possible by releases of blocked sterling, and this was almost exhausted. Economists and officials of the Ministry of Commerce, even those with no particular sympathy for Russia, advocated trade with the Soviet bloc to fill the gap. The door had been opened in 1954 by Egyptian purchases of Romanian oil, which had to be paid for in cotton, and in the 1955–56 season the Soviet bloc, including People's China, bought one-third of the crop. Nasser explained that this expressed neutrality in trade, because the Western bloc still took one-third and the uncommitted nations the other third, but the controlled buying of the Russian group could more effectively be manipulated than the trade of others, which bought separately as countries or through private traders. Soviet purchases kept the price high enough to obstruct buying by Britain and other Western countries.

The Czech arms deal of 1955 and the collapse of British and French trade in 1956 encouraged the trend; Soviet trade with Egypt, which had been negligible in 1954, increased elevenfold by 1957; in that year Egypt bought £18½ million from Russia and sold £35 million, an aggregate increase of £35 million over the previous year. Russia alone bought one-fifth of the 1956–57 crop and one-quarter of the next crop. Egypt signed trade and payments agreements with most Eastern bloc countries and China, and was granted credits for industrialisation. Russia helped with supplies of oil, wheat and maize, and gave credits for other consumer goods during the shortages after Suez, restored the equipment lost to Israel during the Sinai campaign, and supplied three submarines to the Egyptian fleet. In November 1957 Field-Marshal Amer secured credits of £62 million at 2½ per cent for development projects approved by Russia, to be executed by Soviet experts with Soviet materials. In 1958 Russia undertook to provide the foreign exchange and experts for the first stage of the High Dam at Aswan.

The twentieth Soviet Party Congress in 1956 formally confirmed this policy of trade and aid which, in effect, reverted to the Tsarist system. Prior to 1955, Russia sought to secure influence and power in the Middle East through the communist parties in the Arab countries, but the 1956 Congress put the emphasis on the Arab national movements. This was a sharp change; 'a careful examination of Soviet writing shows that before 1955 neither the Soviet Government nor the Communist Party made any formal or outright statement in support of Arab nationalist aims. Pan-Arabism and Arab unity were, on the contrary, officially described as ideologies of the national bourgeois intelligentsia. . .'.*

Soviet pragmatism did not change the *intention* of Egyptian policy, which was still to resist both foreign domination and the international, godless ideology of communism, but its emphasis was changed by reduced dependence on Western economic associations and increasing dependence on Russia. New factories did not require Western spare parts, the substantial proportion of cotton exports committed to the Eastern bloc for repayment of credits and arms reduced the amount of hard currencies available for purchases elsewhere, and with the passage of time it became difficult, if not impossible, to change the pattern of trade quickly.

Nasser tried to preserve his economic neutrality by developing

* Geoffrey Wheeler, 'Russia and the Arab World', *The World Today*, July 1961.

other markets, in Japan, West Germany and India, and by trading as best he could with Britain and France, his enemies of 1956; and he did not relent in his persecution of communists. But he had so little space for manoeuvre after Suez that he was driven into tacit alliance with Russia by the lack of support elsewhere. United States opposition to Britain and France during the Suez affair was quickly recognised as opposition to their policies rather than friendship for Egypt, for Mr. Dulles was just as displeased by Nasser's relations with Russia as he was at the time of the Czech arms deal and his recognition of People's China. During 1957 the U.S. Government was slow to release the $42 million it held for Egypt, although it was a year of extreme difficulty; only half the amount had been freed by the end of the year. Even more repugnant to Nasser was the evident determination of the United States to fill the gap left by Britain's loss of influence.

Although Mr. Dulles had first expounded at Teheran the idea of northern-tier defence, which took shape in the Turco-Pakistan pact and then the Baghdad Pact, he gave it only half-hearted support when it encountered bitter opposition in the Arab world, but in 1957 he rallied to its support. He also made a frontal attack on the concept of neutrality by the Eisenhower Doctrine, which, in effect, sought to bribe Arab States by offering aid to those which declared themselves against communism. It was directed most immediately at Syria, where the communists seemed on the threshold of seizing power, but it was misconceived because the Soviet Government was now more concerned to promote its influence with Arab governments, bourgeois or not, than to promote the fortunes of the communist parties. The Arab governments were themselves repressing their indigenous communists; even in Syria the uneasy Baath-Communist alliance was approaching breaking-point. The only effect of the Eisenhower Doctrine was to put Russia's realistic policy in an even better light by contrasting its peaceful trade and aid with American efforts to drag the Arab world into the 'cold war'.

In this way, starting from the innocuous concept of neutrality, Egypt's policy took shape under external pressure between 1955 and 1958. Because those pressures always seemed to align the so-called conservative Arab States against him, they reinforced Nasser's belief that he must work for the liberation of the Arab world from its own 'feudalists'. His dedication to the Bandung principles and close relations with Mr. Nehru and President Tito were largely theoretical pursuit of an ideal, and in practice he sought economic co-operation wherever he could find it, but the active expression of his policy was in Arab affairs. It brought him into conflict with the Lebanon for the first time, when his opposition to President Shamoun's pro-Western policy and ambition for a second term of office helped to provoke the civil war and the intervention of the American Sixth Fleet; similarly the dedication of Jordanian radicals to him and not to King Hussein precipitated British intervention there. Equally, his acceptance of union with Syria was in part resistance to the Communist Party.

The extension of Soviet influence, the strong position of the Syrian communists, and the economic dependence of Nasser made the Kremlin over-confident at the end of 1957. Nasser's destruction of communist ambitions in the newly formed United Arab Republic early in 1958 therefore came as a shock. The Soviet leaders renewed their campaign for the Communist Party after the revolution in Iraq later in the year, and the twenty-first Soviet Communist Party Congress in January and February 1959 reflected their increasing opposition to President Nasser's brand of Arab nationalism by affirming strongly that local communist parties were the only consistent champions of national unity. Khrushchev told the Congress that the communists were the most devoted and courageous fighters against colonialism and that the opposition by 'some countries' to the communist and other progressive parties was reactionary. In another speech in March he said, '. . . the interests of the majority of the Arabs are indivisible in the struggle against the colonial yoke. But after a country has freed itself from foreign domination the interests of people cannot be ignored. For the interests of all Arabs cannot coincide. Therefore the attempts under the flag of nationalism to ignore the interests of separate classes of the population and the interests of the working people are futile'.*

Nasser concluded from the behaviour of the communists in Syria and Iraq and from these statements that the Soviet Union had supported him only in order to establish its own influence by replacing his leadership of Arab nationalism by that of the Communist Party; that the only difference between Soviet and Western imperialism was that Russia used the party as its instrument whereas the West used 'feudal' rulers. In an interview with the editor of the Indian magazine *Blitz* he said, '. . . information which we have obtained disclosed a basic communist plan to take over Iraq and establish a Soviet State in that strategic Arab region. This would be followed by the destruction of unity between Syria and Egypt. The final communist aim was to establish a 'Red' fertile crescent composed of Iraq, Syria, Jordan, Lebanon and Kuwait which would enable communist influence to penetrate not only to the Persian

* *Izvestia*, 17 March 1959. Quoted by Geoffrey Wheeler, op. cit.

Gulf and the Gulf of Aqaba but also to the Indian Ocean. . .'.*

As his statement to *Blitz* showed, he had resisted Soviet plans, but as he could not rapidly modify his economic commitments to Russia he set about redressing the balance as best he could. Despite the fact that Britain and the United States had frustrated his plans in Jordan and Lebanon, he concluded a financial agreement with Britain over Suez in January 1959, established diplomatic relations at mission level in December, and secured a technical aid programme from the United States worth £50 million, of which £17 million was received that year. He signed more trade agreements with the Eastern bloc, including a three-year £30 million agreement with Czechoslovakia, and he received three more submarines from Russia, but he banned the barter of cotton against imported goods, the method primarily used by the Soviet bloc, with the result that the Western powers, India and Japan together took 55 per cent of the 1959–60 cotton crop as compared with Soviet bloc purchases of 60 per cent in the preceding season. He refused to attend or address the communist-sponsored Afro-Asian Solidarity Conference in Cairo in December 1958 and waged unremitting war against the communists in the United Arab Republic in both 1958 and 1959.

The reason for this policy was spelled out: the authoritative Cairo newspaper *Al-Ahram* accused Khrushchev in January of interfering in U.A.R. affairs; in March, Cairo Radio said Soviet policy had changed, and the government news agency said Russia was trying to dominate the Arabs; on 30 March President Nasser himself publicly accused Russia of supporting the opposition mounted by the U.A.R. communists. When Khaled Bikdash, the Syrian communist leader, was allowed to attack the U.A.R. at a Pekin rally, President Nasser withdrew his chargé d'affaires from China for a month.

He had by this time made his point and won American aid into the bargain, so with Khrushchev's help he began to patch up the quarrel. Although the wounds took some time to heal, the effect on trade was immediate, for the Soviet bloc took no less than 70 per cent of the 1960–61 cotton crop. Nasser believed that he had restored the balance of his relations with the Powers, and the Soviet Union concluded that it had been premature in making a frontal attack on him; suspicions remained, but tolerance prevailed. The start of the work on the High Dam at Aswan in January 1960 provided a public occasion for a public burial of the hatchet, which

* BBC Summary of World Broadcasts, 20 April 1959, quoting Cairo Radio, 18 April 1959.

Russia did spectacularly by offering to provide the foreign currency requirements to complete the Dam. When Nasser attended the autumn session of the United Nations that year he was studiously cautious to balance his cordiality towards Khrushchev with some friendly Western contacts; in particular he agreed with Mr. Macmillan to raise Anglo-Egyptian diplomatic relations to embassy level; and he supported the United States in its strong opposition to the Soviet 'troika' proposal for the Secretary-Generalship. His position had been greatly strengthened by the United States, which had not only agreed to provide more capital aid but had undertaken to provide wheat worth £21 million, to be paid for in local currency; this was an offer of vital importance because Egypt was chronically short of foreign exchange.

The United States recognition of the importance of the economic factor in Nasser's foreign policy, as reflected in the decision to provide wheat against Egyptian currency, restored some Western influence. There was no other source, because Western Germany could not provide it, and Britain and France, although trading with Egypt, could still play no part; indeed France's enmity towards Egypt over intervention in the Algerian war of liberation was reciprocated by Nasser. American aid gave Nasser some leeway in dealing with Russia, which at that time was opposed to his collaboration with Tito in fostering a bloc of neutral states, a 'third force', which seemed likely to impede the extension of Soviet influence to the small and emerging nations. Nor had the friendly gestures of 1960 led Nasser to release any of the leading communists he had locked up. The Soviet Press castigated the U.A.R. for its anti-communist policy and the *Moscow Journal* allowed a Jordanian communist to use its columns to link Nasser and Kassem (who had turned against the Iraqi communists at this time) as dictators who were 'undermining national independence'. Heykal replied in *Al-Ahram* that Soviet Russia was one thing, communism another, and Russia should keep its nose out of the affairs of friendly states. In June, *Pravda* commented in threatening tone that Egypt should realise that he who paid the piper called the tune. There was also a degree of ill-feeling over work at the High Dam, where Russia was suspected of deliberately delaying supplies for purposes of political pressure, and the Russians accused Egypt of delaying an agreed training programme at Aswan in order to keep out communists. Khrushchev personally intervened to cool tempers.

## II

The Bandung Conference in 1955 and the political philosophy of Mr. Nehru had lifted President Nasser's pragmatic neutrality to the nobler and more difficult search for a middle way in world affairs, and if in practice he was compelled to do some bazaar bargaining with the Powers, this did not alter the fact that non-alignment was the guiding principle of his foreign policy. He admired Tito as neutral within communism and Nehru as neutral within the British Commonwealth, and sought to model his policy on their kind of independent action. There was already within the national movement, with the exception of the Pan-Islamic wing, considerable sympathy for Nehru and the Congress Party because of its long struggle for the independence of India, culminating in the creation of a powerful independent state in Asia; the movement had always avoided an alliance with Pakistan despite the fact that it was a Moslem country. Nasser had also found in Nehru a firm ally against the Baghdad Pact.

The Non-Aligned Conference at Belgrade in September 1961 was the high-water mark of the Bandung movement, when it seemed for a moment that the loose affiliation of states might become a force in world affairs. It was not looked on with favour by either of the two great Powers; and, as though to snub the conference, Russia resumed nuclear testing on the day before it started. The Western bloc were incensed by the final communiqué's failure to condemn the Soviet action, for the non-aligned movement was supposed to be totally against nuclear testing, but of the seven statesmen who did condemn it, President Nasser was one of the most forthright.

Non-alignment is weak because it gives an excuse for avoiding decisions; on the principle that they stand neutral between the world powers, non-aligned nations avoid moral verdicts, to which their philosophy should commit them, for purely selfish reasons. Thus they refused to condemn Moscow, although they had condemned Western powers for the same offence, because most of the emergent nations were unwilling to offend Russia, from which they expected help. The final test of non-alignment came in 1962 when China seized Indian territory by force in circumstances which showed that the operation – the building of a road from Sinkiang – must have been started immediately after the Bandung Conference.* Whatever the legal claims of China, there could be no justification by the principles of Bandung for the method chosen, yet only ten non-aligned states expressed sympathy and support for India, and they

* See G. H. Jansen, *Afro-Asia and Non-Alignment.*

were states whose non-alignment leaned towards the Western powers. Egypt was not one of these, although President Nasser was the first to react to the Chinese invasion. Within a few hours he sent a message to Nehru suggesting that he, Nasser, might keep in touch with both sides in order to mediate, and in so doing he set the example by which the non-aligned bloc, by favouring mediation, avoided the need to condemn China. In almost every case, including those states which supported Nehru, the uncommitted nations committed themselves in accordance with their own interests and in so doing they destroyed the 'third force' they thought they had created at Belgrade. Tito merely expressed hope for a peaceful settlement. No later efforts could put together again the triumvirate, Tito, Nehru, Nasser, which led the neutral states.

In Africa, Nasser's non-alignment was translated to mean support for the liberation struggle, but in effect it usually meant a commitment to the policy of Soviet Russia, which had no position to lose. In his *Philosophy of the Revolution* Nasser stated that Africa was one of the three circles of Egyptian interest, and his propaganda to East Africa had been embarrassing to Britain long before the Suez affair. Cairo became the place of refuge for political refugees from many parts of Africa until over the years they formed an astonishing collection of people, often of opposing opinions but all dedicated to the overthrow of one régime or another. The rebellion in the Congo provided a straightforward case for the application of Nasser's principle of liberation everywhere and he committed Egypt wholeheartedly to support of Lumumba and against Tshombe and, of course, the Belgians. In 1961 he nationalised Belgian property worth £15 million and the Belgian Government broke off diplomatic relations; in June he broke relations with South Africa.* His closest collaborator in Africa was Kwame Nkrumah of Ghana, whose aggressive, pan-African nationalism was far removed from Nehru's grand design for non-alignment, and together they led the extreme wing of the national movement in the continent, notably in the Organisation of African Unity. In 1963 he broke relations with Portugal over its 'imperialist policies' in Africa at the behest of the organisation, and in 1965 he was one of the few rulers to terminate relations with Britain over the Rhodesian issue.

In none of these acts, with the possible exception of the break with Belgium, was there any real advantage to Egypt or the Arabs, except to the extent that they might obstruct the influence Israel

---

* The nationalisation of Belgian property was not, however, a simple act of solidarity with the Congolese. It enabled him, just as had the Suez affair, to speed the process of excluding foreign financial interests from Egypt.

16—ME

was acquiring in a number of African states. In December 1964 the policy did positive harm when President Nasser rounded on the United States for its attempt to stop him supplying arms to the rebels in the Congo. Referring to its aid, he said that it could go and 'drink the Red Sea' – or go and drown itself – if it liked. The American Government, which was already incensed by the shooting down of one of its planes and the burning of its embassy library in Cairo, promptly announced that the wheat aid programme would not be renewed.

This foolhardiness led foreign opinion to the conclusion that Nasser had an insatiable ambition to be leader of the continent, but it is unlikely that Nasser was so ill-informed as to believe that any Moslem from north of the Sahara could dominate Black Africa. It is far more likely that the conviction that he was part of Africa's struggle for liberation hardened after the break with Syria in 1961, when he became convinced that he must strengthen his revolutionary purpose in all fields. If so, his policy suffered a severe setback when Nkrumah was overthrown, President Kenyatta acted firmly against his left-wing opposition, Nigeria established a right-wing military government, and in many African countries resentment grew against Russian, Chinese, Cuban, and even Egyptian, interference.

The unilateral declaration of independence by the Smith Government in Rhodesia revived the ardours of the African states, and Nasser played his part, but the climate had changed as more and more of the newly independent countries were compelled to concentrate on their domestic problems. In 1964 Nasser's interest swung back sharply to the Middle East.

## III

The restoration of full diplomatic relations with Britain did little practical good to the association of the two countries, and the break over Rhodesia did small harm because consular and trade relations were maintained. Britain had neither the means nor the desire to give aid in anything like the amount commensurate with Egypt's needs, and as President Nasser, who wanted trade, did not have the sterling to buy from Britain, and as Lancashire did not want his cotton, there was no compelling reason for him to try to be on good terms. On the contrary, it meant that he had nothing to lose by attacking British positions in the Persian Gulf and South Arabia, which were part of the old world he wanted to sweep away.

During 1964 British policy in South Arabia was under constant attack from Egypt, whose open support for terrorism in Aden incensed the Government. When the Labour Government was elected, President Nasser thought that it might have a more acceptable policy for Arabia and in his speech to the National Assembly in November he responded to a conciliatory message from the new Foreign Secretary by amicable references to Britain. He expected that Britain would respond by sending a Minister to whom he could present his case for radical changes in British policy and when this did not happen the acrimonious campaign was resumed. In May of 1965 *Al-Ahram* published secret documents which Iraq had received from Sergeant Percy Sydney Allen, who had been gaoled in England for selling them, and the part-truths they revealed did harm to Britain's relations with her friends in the Middle East. Nevertheless, Nasser's confidant, Mohammed Hassanein Heykal, visited London 'unofficially' in July to arrange for the visit of a British Minister to Cairo. He departed saying he was successful, but on 6 August, the day after his return to Cairo, he announced in *Al-Ahram* that 'no bilateral agreement could change the fundamental clash of interests'. President Nasser had changed his mind.

The British Foreign Office went ahead with plans for Mr. George Thomson, the Minister of State, to tour the Middle East, primarily for talks with Saudi Arabia which was negotiating for an air-defence system and shared the British desire to limit Egyptian penetration of the Arabian peninsula. It was hoped that Thomson would see Nasser in Cairo on his way out, but the day before he left London the British Government suspended the constitution in Aden. Nasser thereupon refused to receive him. He nevertheless continued on his way to Riyadh to meet King Feisal, and in December Saudi Arabia signed letters of intent for Britain to supply an entire air-defence system costing £100 million and another for missiles from the United States. This convinced Nasser that Britain and the United States were now directing the Middle Eastern phase of a world-wide 'reactionary counter-offensive'; this and Aden killed any immediate hope of re-establishing relations with Britain.

A month later, Field-Marshal Abdel Hakim Amer went to Paris at the invitation of the French Government and was received with great cordiality by President de Gaulle, who paid warm tribute to Nasser. The restoration of good relations with France had begun ten months earlier when M. Edgar Faure, former French Prime Minister, visited Cairo at the request of the U.A.R. Government and, after a round of talks with President Nasser and other Egyptian leaders, announced that relations between the two countries would improve. The one remaining obstacle was France's friendship with

Israel, which had been evident in close collusion over the Suez affair
and in the supply of arms by France; but de Gaulle had not been in
power at the time of Suez and by conceding independence to Algeria
he had removed the major source of conflict. Even more important
to Nasser's concept of world affairs was President de Gaulle's
increasing independence of the United States, which made France a
potential associate of a 'third force'. Further, arguing from the
premise that Israel was an instrument of Western policy in the
Middle East, it seemed possible that an independent de Gaulle
could now be persuaded to end, or at least minimise, French support
for Israel.

By contrast, Egyptian relations with Western Germany deteriorated during 1965 because it had supplied arms worth $80 million
to Israel. When it became known that Herr Walter Ulbricht,
Chairman of the East German Council of State, had been invited to
Egypt, the Federal Government warned the U.A.R. that under its
Hallstein Doctrine it could not maintain relations with any country
which recognised East Germany. When Herr Ulbricht arrived he
was given all the honours if not the formal title of Head of State,
but his country was not given recognition. Nevertheless, West
Germany broke relations with Egypt and recognised Israel, and the
Arab States, energetically prodded by Egypt, withdrew their
embassies from Bonn.

This quarrel was essentially with the United States because Nasser
believed that the arms had been supplied to Israel at the instigation
of Washington; just as President de Gaulle's independence of
American policy was reason for friendship, so Bonn's subservience to
Washington gave added justification for the break. West Germany,
however, was a good source of trade and aid, and in the failure to
recognise East Germany, and in the retention of consular and trade
relations, the outcome was a compromise preserving Egypt's
essential interests.

The U.S. decision to withhold wheat supplies added virulence to
the campaign against Bonn and Egypt's relations with the United
States remained at a low ebb all the year. President Nasser probably
calculated that Washington would be reluctant to abandon its one
important counter-balance to Soviet influence and there was, in fact,
a conflict of opinion in the State Department about the wisdom of
doing so. In the event the difficult economic situation eventually
compelled Nasser to be more conciliatory and in November President Johnson reciprocated by announcing a partial resumption of
wheat supplies.

Russian relations were cordial. The completion of the first stage of the High Dam and the diversion of the Nile in May 1964 gave Khrushchev the opportunity for a display of Russian-Egyptian friendship and he promised to lend Egypt about £100 million. (In a public reference to Arab unity, however, he did not abandon the critical attitude he had expressed in 1959.) When Khrushchev's offer of more aid was given as one of the reasons for his overthrow, it created some anxiety in Cairo, but Russia did not overtly change its policy and in the following year undertook to deliver 300,000 tons of wheat to cover the short-fall in American supplies.

Behind the scenes the Soviet Government reverted to the decision of the twentieth Party Congress to support the bourgeois national governments of the Middle East, and this was confirmed by a meeting of Arab communist representatives, which *Pravda* reported to have been held in December 1964. Local communist parties were no longer regarded as the spearhead of Soviet penetration and were precluded from becoming identified with opposition to bourgeois national governments; but local communists were advised to perform useful Soviet services as expert political advisers inside the ruling nationalist-revolutionary parties.

This deliberate policy of penetration was pursued in Egypt almost immediately. In May 1965 the clandestine Communist Party was reported by the Cairo Press to have voted to dissolve itself and support President Nasser, and many communists were released from detention, ostensibly for the presidential referendum taking place that month.* As this was an unpalatable decision for many communists who had been in detention for years, some refused to accept it and went underground again as adherents of the Chinese Party. In the late summer fourteen of them were arrested for plotting to overthrow the régime and establish an Egyptian People's Republic.† Those who accepted the party decision joined the Arab Socialist Union and some of them were appointed to positions of importance in the Press and the State.

---

* Lotfi al-Kholi, himself a leading member of the A.S.U. and editor of the left-wing Cairo periodical *Al-Talia*, stated in the October 1966 issue of the *World Marxist Review*, published in Prague, that a 'revolutionary vanguard party' with a mission to 'lead the Arab Socialist Union and the entire UAR people to socialism' was being formed within the union. On 13 October the independent Beirut newspaper *Al-Nahar* printed for the first time the text of the statement issued in April 1965 by the Central Committee of the Egyptian Communist Party, announcing the dissolution of the party and instructing the members to join the A.S.U. The statement said the members would not cease being Marxists by joining the union. In Syria, where the Government was much weaker, the Communist Party kept its identity and advocated a popular front.

† A Moscow broadcast in Arabic on 10 September applauded the news that eight of the underground communists (described by Moscow as 'adventurers') had been sent to prison for plotting against the State.

President Nasser, concerned about Egypt's critical economic condition, which had worsened after the cessation of United States aid, visited Moscow in August. Perhaps because the economic relief he had sought in Moscow had not been forthcoming on the scale he needed, when he returned to Cairo he replaced his faithful Prime Minister, Aly Sabry, by Zacharia Mohieddin, who was not only a good administrator but in earlier years had proved himself a highly efficient Minister of the Interior, notably in the destruction of both communist and Moslem Brotherhood cells. Mohieddin was briefed to impose a number of unpopular measures which would cut domestic consumption and make the economy more acceptable to the World Bank and the International Monetary Fund. In this he was partially successful, for the Bank and the Fund resumed their interest in Egypt's affairs, and President Johnson undertook to provide some help with wheat.*

His pragmatism was, however, a potential danger to the Soviet position. Despite Soviet aid for the High Dam, American economic help had, up to then, been greater than that of Russia and considerably more important in feeding the people. By the end of 1964 Egypt was the largest *per capita* consumer of American surplus food; U.S. loans financed more than 60 per cent of all land-reclamation undertaken after the revolution and the construction of more than 3,000 miles of paved road. President Nasser made Aly Sabry Secretary-General of the Arab Socialist Union, the ideological base of the Government, and continued to give him the utmost public support, and his own speeches maintained their anti-imperialist message; but Russia was aware that public speeches were not as important as hard economic facts and became anxious to ensure that economic needs and Mohieddin's method of tackling them did not weaken the Soviet-Egyptian connection. Nasser was still considered by Russia to be supremely important as the *de facto* leader of the Arab national movement and the potential possessor of influence in Africa; and, by the end of 1965, he had acquired the additional advantage of being willing and able to check the penetration of People's China.

Egyptian influence also reduced Iraqi antagonism towards Russia. Then in the spring of 1966 the left-wing Baath faction seized power in Syria. This faction was in close liaison with the Syrian communists and its policy was warmly commended by Khaled Bikdash. As it provided the opportunity for the close collaboration which

---

* In March 1967, however, President Nasser told the editor of the Beirut newspaper *Al-Shaab* that he had withdrawn his request for wheat aid from the U.S. under the Food for Peace Programme because his request had been unanswered for a year.

Soviet policy sought, the Russian Government immediately agreed to build the big Euphrates Dam. The Soviet position was now extremely strong; it had excellent relations with Egypt, it was helping the republican Government in Yemen, its relations with Iraq were improving, Syrian relations were cordial, and it was supplying arms to Algeria. The 'union of progressive forces' which both Syrian and Iraqi leaders advocated was now very much to the Soviet purpose. It only required Nasser to keep in line.

When Prime Minister Kosygin visited Egypt in May 1966 there was only one obstacle to the 'union of progressive forces': the enmity between President Nasser and the Baath Party. After the visit the Syrian Government renewed the demand for it more strongly than ever and was supported by Algeria. In July President Nasser announced that he would not take part in the proposed Arab Summit because he would not sit at the same table with reactionary rulers. Contacts between the Syrian and Egyptian governments then led to a Defence Agreement in the autumn. The gap in the 'progressive front' was, at least for the time being, bridged. It was the fruit of Nasser's policy plucked by Russia.

## IV

Neither President Nasser nor the Kremlin contemplated at that time an early war between the Arabs and Israel. Nasser's opposition to King Hussein was absurd if he thought that in a matter of months he would want the Jordan Army to open a second front in Palestine, and the Russians were doing so well on the political side that they had no wish to jeopardise their position by a war that might get beyond their control. But the Palestine problem is like an unexploded bomb in Middle Eastern affairs waiting to destroy the policies and reputation of all comers, and within a day of Egypt's defeat the Arabs were asking why Russia had not saved her. As the war only lasted four days the request was unreasonable, but in any case Russia had never intended her policy of arming the Arabs and talking against Israel to commit her to the defeat of Israel.* President Podgorny flew to Cairo and Mr Kosygin talked hard and fast at the United Nations to restore the Soviet grip on U.A.R. policy, but neither President Nasser nor other intelligent Arabs could unlearn the lesson that, as far as Russia was concerned, Israel and the Palestine problem were not expected to obstruct the pursuit of Soviet aims.

The war put President Nasser's foreign and Arab policy in doubt

* Communist Party Congresses in Moscow are the only places outside the United Nations where Arabs and Israelis sit round the same table.

at almost every point. His revolutionary Syrian allies got into the fighting on a major scale when Egypt was already defeated but the 'imperialist stooge' of yesterday, King Hussein, threw everything he had into a second front at Nasser's request. France, the one major Western country with political credit in Egypt, gained more credit by her tactful neutrality but President Nasser knew that the last delivery of French planes to Israel took place almost on the eve of war. The body of Afro-Asian non-aligned opinion was as muted and ineffective as it had been when India was attacked by China.

The balance of Egyptian foreign policy was uneasily set between its own inescapable needs on the one side and, on the other, an idealistic pursuit of non-alignment and opposition to colonialism and imperialism. When war came the balance was seen not to exist, for non-alignment and anti-colonialism had deprived Egypt of too many potential friends and of those that remained only Russia and one or two Eastern bloc countries had much importance. Further, public opinion everywhere was much less in the Arab favour in 1967 than it was in 1948, so that even in India the Government was criticised for its so-called anti-Israeli policy.

President Nasser's conduct of international affairs was largely responsible for this state of affairs because it ignored the fact that small powers must have friends and pay in one form or another for the friendship. There are distinct limits to non-alignment. It seemed to work in Egypt as long as both the United States and Russia gave economic support but when the United States was driven to turn against her, Nasser was compelled to depend on the other, a situation totally contrary to his intended policy; and if both found it unnecessary at any time to give support the effect could be disastrous.

As it is, Soviet policy in the Middle East has been greatly helped and Western policies obstructed by Egypt. President Nasser would say that those struggling against 'imperialism' must take what help they can, but it is certainly not non-alignment and the calculated penetration of the national movements by pro-Soviet communists clearly has imperialist connotations. There is no reason to suppose that President Nasser is not aware of the danger of furthering Soviet aims; Russia was a natural ally against Western positions he was attempting to destroy, but he did not hesitate to resist Communist attempts to take over Syria and Iraq in 1959 and could no doubt do so again. He cannot do so alone, without the support of friendly countries—and in this respect the help of small, struggling nations in Africa and Asia is not important now or likely to be for a long time to come.

## Chapter 14

# In Search of Socialism

## I

W HEN PRESIDENT NASSER consolidated his position at home at the end of 1954 he began a conscious search for a theory of government and the ideological framework to contain it. He started by divorcing the political cadres of Free Officers from the army, because the work of conspiracy was done and they could be a danger in the future when a new system of government was created. Those officers appointed to civilian Ministries were given the choice of staying where they were or returning to the army, and most of them chose the Ministries because of the higher pay and status their posts gave them. This caused discontent among officials whose promotion was blocked and sometimes led to inefficiency, but the destruction of the cadres compensated for the disadvantages.

The junta began to disintegrate during the struggle for power and the Revolutionary Command Council was abolished. Those members who talked too much or too actively pursued their own ideas were removed, some of them to take positions which preserved the semblance of high office, and those who were the obedient executants of Nasser's policy remained. In the formulation of policy, however, Nasser consulted this rump of the Free Officers' Executive and some civilian advisers concerned with economic and financial affairs.

In January 1956 he proclaimed a new constitution which provided for a National Assembly, a Cabinet of Ministers and a President. It gave the President complete executive powers, including the power to appoint or dismiss Ministers, but the Assembly was given the right to initiate or amend legislation and of arraigning Ministers, and it was laid down that if the President overruled the Assembly twice, he had to refer the matter by referendum to the country. Nasser was duly elected President by 99·99 per cent of the votes.*

According to the constitution the candidates for the Assembly should have been selected by the National Union, the popular

---

* The result threw doubt on the elections, for any casual observer could see that the country was not so overwhelmingly in favour of the régime.

organisation that was to succeed the Liberation Rally, but they were selected by President Nasser and one or two close associates. The elections, delayed by the Suez affair, did not take place until 1957, and the Union – the one party of this one-party Government – came into existence later.

When the Assembly met its discussions did provide some salutary criticism of the Government's domestic policy and to that extent was a step towards the new democracy that Nasser sought to create; it bore some resemblance to tribal custom, according to which the leader had to consult the elders of the tribe or, if necessary, the tribal assembly. Nasser contended that the Egyptian system was different from that of the 'people's democracies' of the communist countries in that it derived from Islam and from Arab nationalism, and protected the right of private ownership. The late Dr. Hassan Abou el-Seoud, a distinguished lawyer, explained in the course of his study of agrarian reform that Egypt's ideology placed it between the two world camps. He wrote:

'We cannot ignore that ownership is an instinct and we cannot understand why we should deprive men of the fruit of their hard work.

'We believe in equality, but we can never ignore that, in their qualities, men were never and can never be equal; that *de facto* equality is only chimerical.

'Islam is based on democracy and does not recognise monarchy. The leader of the people must be elected by the majority. It does not allow any dictatorship, be it that of an individual or a so-called class.'

The Government was nevertheless authoritarian. Opponents could not join the National Union, which was the only route to the Assembly, and the majority who voted Nasser to the Presidency would not have been allowed to vote him out of it. It was a Police State in which no one was allowed to organise opposition, and critics risked interrogation and possible arrest by ubiquitous intelligence officers. In public and private service there was a tendency to measure people by their devotion to the régime instead of their fitness for the work. If there was not a pervasive sense of fear and critics were sometimes outspoken in public places it was because the happy-go-lucky Egyptian people were at once obedient to authority and resistant to propaganda.

Criticism in 1958 was prevalent, particularly among the rich people and those who had worked closely with British and French firms – in short, among those who suffered most directly – but criticism was by no means universal even among the rich. The son of the pasha was adjusting himself to the new system and learning to make money with such wealth as was left to his family, and new opportunities came his way by the departure of foreigners. The country still consisted of a small class of well-to-do people and the mass of very poor, and the latter were content with the régime. Further, criticism of the régime was not always criticism of President Nasser and his close associates. There were complaints of the return of corruption to government departments, of favouritism of young officers, and of unfair discrimination against Copts, but there was no suggestion that the ruling group was corrupt.

The nationalisation and 'Egyptianisation' of foreign firms after the Suez affair was in part a reprisal and in part the fulfilment of the national aspiration to be rid of all foreign influence, but Nasser was already formulating his concept of the rights of private ownership which was to lead to their severe limitation. He came to the conclusion that the economic difficulties of the country were due in no small measure to the reluctance of private firms to collaborate. At the same time, ambitious public planning, which called for more funds for the development side of the budget than could be produced by taxation or borrowing, led him to cast covetous eyes on private profits. The practical considerations were reinforced by the conviction that workers should have their say in the conduct of the firms they worked for and led him to two conclusions: that private capital should not be able to control or influence government policy and workers should be represented on Boards of Administration.

On 11 February 1960 a decree was issued nationalising Bank Misr, a firm which had widespread commercial and industrial connections. It was totally Egyptian, having been brought into being in a patriotic effort to limit by financial and commercial means the further extension of foreign enterprises and was therefore highly thought of in public opinion; but the Government disliked its investment policy. On 24 May the 'reorganisation' of publishing houses was announced and was in effect the nationalisation of the Press, for government-appointed boards were put in charge of the newspaper houses. The people were dismayed by both these acts, in the first case because they affected an institution they had been taught to admire and in the second because they had great affection for their Press, which had been closely identified with the national struggle at every stage. Not even under the British had the independence of the newspapers been so completely under government control.

Public omnibus companies were also nationalised in May and

wholesale pharmaceutical houses in August.* Then, in July 1961, a further ninety-eight were nationalised, 50 per cent of the shares were compulsorily purchased in ninety-one companies, any private shares exceeding the value of £10,000 in any individual holding were bought out in another 159 companies, and it was decreed that the State controlled any firm in which it held more than 25 per cent of the capital. The Boards of Administration were reorganised to include workers and government representatives. Thus, in accordance with the constitution, private ownership still existed; but it was very much diminished and had been deprived of all say in the control of industry and commerce – or in its own defence.

Although these extensive nationalisations were partly due to the need to get funds for the development budget they were the beginning of Egypt's rapid transition to socialism.

In April 1963 all cotton ginning and exporting firms were nationalised; in June all pharmaceutical factories and distributing firms, and a miscellaneous group of forty-five factories were closed down for 'dereliction in production'; in August 200 industrial firms were nationalised, and in November another 175. In the end, almost the entire private sector had been eliminated: banks, insurance companies, transport, exporting and importing firms, all mining and manufacturing, and the wholesale trade were under public control.

The cotton and stock exchanges were closed. All that remained outside were landholdings up to 100 acres, some sectors of the retail trade not absorbed in the government co-operatives or the larger nationalised stores, and urban property; but in all these fields there were severe government controls, such as limits on crop rotation, marketing, and rents in agriculture, and regulations controlling prices, purchases and profits in the retail trade. In due course a complex of Public Organisations was built up to control firms and industries. It was decreed that 25 per cent of all profits should be distributed among the workers, and to parallel the land limit in agriculture it was decreed that no one should be paid more than £5,000 a year. Taxes, which were negligible when the revolution took place, were raised several times and made steeply progressive until the top income group was paying 90 per cent.

* These nationalisations did not apply to the Northern Region of the U.A.R. – Syria. The 1961 nationalisations applied to both regions.

## II

President Nasser gave ideological form to his revolution in a lengthy Charter of National Action in May 1962. It was the product of his heart-searching after the break with Syria in the previous year, but the ideas it expounded had been taking shape gradually in his conduct of the State. Early in 1961 the theory of 'the return to the revolution' was debated in the Press by two confidants of President Nasser and it set the stage for the sweeping nationalisation decrees of July. As these decrees helped to precipitate the Syrian revolt the policy as expounded in the Charter was a cause rather than an effect of the collapse of the United Arab Republic.

The nationalisations created widespread disillusionment and discontent in Egypt, to which the failure in Syria added its quota, creating fears – and in some quarters hopes – that the régime would be overthrown. There was in the autumn of 1961 a growing conviction that Nasser had lost his grip on unknown political back-room boys who, in alliance with the administration, were wielding arbitrary power. In the twilight of freedom no man felt free, not because he thought that the Government wished his enslavement but because the weapons of the executive power seemed to be wielded by unknown hands. The French trial was an example. Late in 1961 military intelligence arrested the French resident Mission, and some Egyptians with them, against the advice of the Ministry of the Interior. For the outside world the trial was a judicial farce, but it was no joke for Egyptians, who saw that merely for mixing with foreigners they could be arrested, suffer detention, trial, and public ignominy, and escape a long term of imprisonment only if, by some hairbreadth chance, such as the end of the Algerian War in the French case, a change occurred in the political context of the trial.

By a frank exposition of the national difficulties made to a preparatory People's Congress in January 1962, Nasser began to recover his ascendancy over the minds of the Egyptians. His address did not convert people wholesale to support for the régime, but it did make sense to many and reassured them that he was aware of faults in the system and in control. His Charter of National Action carried the point further by directly condemning excesses of executive power. As no one supposed he was castigating himself he was presumed to be pointing to the executants, seen and unseen, who surrounded him and, whatever doubts remained about socialist planning, it was felt that he was trying to establish some democratic control of the country's affairs.

His Charter, presented to a National People's Congress in May, was the most ambitious effort in his persistent search for a political structure within which the revolution could evolve. It proposed to turn Egypt into a workers' and peasants' democracy by peaceful means and declared that the will of the people must have authority over the executive: 'democracy means the sovereignty of the people'. Nasser said that workers and peasants should be elected by direct vote to half the seats in all popular institutions.

Further: 'The freedom of the loaf of bread is an inevitable guarantee of the freedom of the election ballot'. The utter dependence of the Egyptian masses on the ruling class before the 1952 revolution had made voting a farce and democracy had been a façade behind which they were mercilessly exploited. It was the first principle of the Charter that now the worker must be free from exploitation and given the opportunity to share fairly in the national wealth.

The second principle laid down that in order to give the worker this freedom, reaction must be deprived of its weapons, prevented from exploiting the government, and liquidated. The remaining alliance, of peasants, workers, soldiers, intellectuals and national capital, would then be free to form the Arab Socialist Union which, according to the third principle, would be the vehicle of popular authority. The Union would have the task of creating political machinery for the formation of a new political leadership, and this, in turn, would guarantee collectively the 'revolutionary upsurge'. The fourth principle stated that popular organisations, such as trade unions and co-operatives, should play an important part in establishing a true democracy. The Press, 'freed from the domination of economic interests' by the law of 1960 (which transferred ownership to the National Union), would become the property of the Arab Socialist Union and thereby 'an extension of the freedom of the people'; this was the fifth principle, which declared criticism and self-criticism to be important guarantees of freedom.

The principles governing the economic policy of the State did not differ in essentials from the system inherent in the nationalisation laws of July 1961, whereby the control of capital, private and public, was vested in the State. The aim of economic management was unchanged: to expand and direct the capital of the country in a way that would ensure its rapid development and raise the standard of living of the people. President Nasser firmly supported birth-control in order to slow down the rapid rate of population growth and thus help the economic development.

The social principles seemed to imply new laws. 'Justice . . . cannot be an expensive commodity beyond the reach of the citizen. Medicine must be cheap and available to everyone. Educational curricula must be reviewed "in a revolutionary manner". Laws must be redrafted to serve the new social relationship of political democracy.'

President Nasser portrayed himself in a new role as one of the 'teacher people – the makers of civilisation', to whom he referred in the Charter several times. His task was to lead the workers, peasants, soldiers and intellectuals along the road of revolutionary Arab socialism. He prophesied that the revolution would extend to the Arab world and lead to the overthrow of kings and sheikhly rulers, and in due course spread through Africa; but, said the Charter, the revolution could not be imposed on others. Egypt would only provide the example and the experience.

The Charter did not mean the abandonment of his power at home. The return to democracy, whatever it might eventually mean in practice, was based on the prior elimination of all opposition; only the mass of assenting people would be free. The Charter presupposed that peasants, workers, soldiers and intellectuals would support the revolution or could be educated to do so, but if they did not they would not be allowed to modify the revolutionary plan. His democracy was democracy within the revolution, not against it. Those people who were believed to have reason to oppose the régime were 'isolated', that is, deprived of the right to participate in the democratic process, and were not even allowed to vote for representatives to the National Congress of Popular Forces, to which the Charter was presented.

It was not until December that the Statutes of the Arab Socialist Union were formulated. They attempted to secure widely based democracy by indirect elections not notably different from the method used by the National Union in both Egypt and Syria, and were described as 'laying down a formula by which the mass of the people will be represented through the pyramidal structure of the union, the broad base of which will lie in the small towns and villages'. The Union was supposed to approve an electoral law in May 1963 and the new parliament to meet on 23 July, but it was not until March 1964 that a new constitution was adopted. It was not markedly different from its predecessor, and Aly Sabry, who had been virtually Prime Minister (as president of an Executive Council which had been appointed six months earlier), was given the title as well as the authority. Field-Marshal Abdel Hakim Amer was appointed First Deputy President and therefore Nasser's heir-apparent. The newly elected National Assembly nominated Nasser for re-election as President in January 1965, and in March his term of office was renewed for six years by a referendum which gave him no less than 99·999 per cent of the votes.

The ·001 who voted against him must all have been plotting, for in August he told a gathering of Egyptian students in Moscow that a big Moslem Brotherhood plot had been broken. Four hundred were arrested for conspiring to murder him, other Ministers, and Western ambassadors. When some of the charges were announced in November they also included fourteen communists of the pro-Chinese faction who would not accept Moscow's instruction to co-operate with a régime which had persecuted them.

There was, indeed, considerable discontent. The wealthy people who had been dispossessed were naturally opposed, but, in addition, lawyers, accountants, traders, brokers, almost the entire 'middle class', had been impoverished by nationalisation. Then in 1964 the Government's very successful efforts to keep prices steady began to break down and the rising cost of living deprived the agricultural and urban workers of many of the benefits they got from the revolution.* The extra wages they obtained from building or manning factories were spent on necessities, mainly food and clothing, until the national cupboard was bare; the Government had not enough foreign exchange to buy from abroad; the co-operatives were no longer able to keep pace with demand, and a black market, notably in meat, rapidly developed. The peasant farmers killed their animals to make a quick profit in this sellers' market and so impoverished the countryside. The workers were no doubt still less poor than they had been before the revolution. If they could now seldom afford to buy meat, they had formerly not been able to buy any except for feast days, but when they judged their lot it was by yesterday not a decade earlier, and they were accordingly discontented. In October 1966 popular unrest broke into the open for the first time when dock workers at Port Said went on strike against wage cuts.†

When speaking of development plans in the first years of the revolution, President Nasser had said that this generation should not pay the full price for the well-being of the future, but hard facts had changed all this, and to the National Assembly in January 1965 he said that 'we should steel ourselves to further sacrifices now that this

---

* According to the International Monetary Fund, the price Index rose from 100 in 1963 to 113 in 1965, but from 1961 to 1963 the Index fell from 102 to 100 (1958 — 100). Prices held firm from 1958 to 1963 but rose sharply after 1963.

† The *New York Times* reported that, according to informed sources, the leaders of the wildcat strike were arrested and soldiers and naval men unloaded vessels at the port.

generation has chosen to bear its historic mission'. The loss of American wheat supplies was clearly going to make the coming months critical and Prime Minister Aly Sabry exhorted the people to save half a day's pay a month in order to take some money off the market, but the people, who had never had enough money to acquire the habit of saving and had inherited a distrust of governments of all types and creeds, did not respond.

Hard facts had to be faced at last. On 29 September Aly Sabry resigned and Zacharia Mohieddin became Prime Minister and Minister of the Interior. As an expert in security and the scourge of both communists and Moslem Brothers, he repaired the weakness in the intelligence organisations that had allowed the plots against the régime to get so far, but his main task was to undertake the unpopular measures required to save the economy. He decreed massive increases in taxes and the prices of manufactured goods, announced increases in supply of consumer goods, and said he would 'let the law of supply and demand work'; in short, he would let prices rise to their natural level.

It was a peculiarity of the situation that both the middle class, who had been impoverished, and the better-paid workers, who had profited by higher wages, had money they could not spend, for there were hardly any imported goods on the market, domestic manufactures were in short supply, they could seldom get permission or the foreign exchange to holiday abroad, and there was very little they could invest in except government bonds, which they did not want. (On one occasion, Zacharia Mohieddin allowed a big store to import £20,000 worth of luxuries such as expensive French perfumes and they were all sold in a matter of hours.) They were, therefore, able to absorb the taxes and the higher prices, however reluctantly. The mass of poor workers who paid the extra piastre on necessities felt the pinch and at their cost the worst of the crisis passed. When Zacharia Mohieddin relinquished the premiership to Suleiman Sudki in 1966, the supply position, if not satisfactory, had improved.

## III

These economic difficulties bear witness to the self-evident fact that it is extremely difficult to raise living standards in a country with limited resources or to satisfy a conservative people during the revolutionary process. Nevertheless, the class structure has undergone radical change since the revolution. The gulf between rich and poor still exists but is neither as wide nor as sharp. This is due not only to the impoverishment of the rich. Industrial development has created new population groups, including a managerial class; agrarian reform has increased the number of small farmers and the new land brought into production by irrigation from the High Dam will add to their number; new industries have established a new urban population of unskilled and semi-skilled workers with high living standards and a growing group consciousness. The country has taken a long, if unsteady, step towards socialism. 'The freedom of the loaf of bread' may still be far off but the effort to achieve it is being made. The trouble remains that there is still not enough bread.

Although President Nasser assumed more power himself after the defeat by Israel the political organisation is unchanged and reflects a desire to find a democratic form. His executive power was and is so complete that he is not an absolute dictator only to the extent that he limits his own authority. He handpicked the Presidential Council and through it he controlled the Council of Ministers and he could dismiss the Prime Minister or the Ministers, so little was changed when he became Prime Minister himself except that there was no one to dismiss him by constitutional means. The National Assembly is largely a sounding board of public opinion but in theory it can still reject decisions of the Presidential or Executive Councils and force the President to submit his veto to referendum. This has never happened and is unlikely to, but its discussions have often been critical and illuminating, and the structure of the Government itself leaves areas of semi-independent action to Ministers and the Executive Council.

President Nasser makes no apology for the authority he retains, for he has always contended that centuries of total subservience and lack of education have so unfitted the Egyptians for democracy that much time and training are required to repair the deficiency. It is from the grass-roots of government, the villages, town and provinces, that he hopes to inculcate the democratic method, by the participation of the people in local councils. The councils in the twenty-five governorates and the cities administer the public utilities and the social services, passing to village councils the conduct of the social services. At all levels, governorate, city and village, the various Ministries are represented, so that the central Government is still dominant, but it benefits in turn from knowledge of local needs and the councillors acquire experience.

The functions of the Arab Socialist Union, of which Nasser is now the leader, are more difficult to define. It replaced two earlier efforts to create the one party of a one-party system, the Liberation Rally and the National Union, but its organisation is more clearly defined.

It, too, has a pyramidal structure, from the 6,912 basic units of town and village, to the Basic Unit Committee, the Provincial District Congress, the General National Congress and finally the Supreme Executive Council over which Nasser now presides. Its broad function is to define the ideological context of Arab socialism within which the Government will work, much in the manner of the Communist Party in Soviet Russia, and its Supreme Executive Council is reputed to have considerable influence with the President. Its representatives sit on all the local government councils as watch-dogs for the revolution, and their power to impeach from behind the scenes is widely resented. It preserves in itself the principle that criticism must be within the revolution, not against it.*

It remains true that local councils and the Union have involved large numbers of people in the running of the country who would never have been permitted to say a word about it, and with all their defects they are providing the opportunity of democratic development. Whether this opportunity will ever be fulfilled will depend on the central executive's desire to achieve democracy.

* It was probably the influence of the A.S.U. which touched off an 'anti-feudalist' witch-hunt in 1966. In April the murder of a village official of the Union was attributed to 'feudalist' revenge. Twenty-five committees studied it, Field-Marshal Abdel Hakim Amer was put in charge of an anti-feudalist commission, and in the first wave 89 landowners had their properties seized. The A.S.U. found 'pockets of feudalism' everywhere.

## Chapter 15

# In Search of Welfare

I

THE EXTENSION OF social welfare services in Egypt is impeded by the fact that the mass of people who most require it cannot afford to pay for it. The Government has long desired to create a national health service on the British model, for example, but it is quite impossible for the working people to contribute from their small wages the amount necessary to run one, and taxation of the relatively few people in the high-income bracket cannot satisfy the budgetary demands of this and other welfare services.

The foreign policy of the Government, which has involved it in the war in Yemen, heavy propaganda costs, and diplomatic expenses out of proportion to the country's needs, has not helped. Despite these obstacles, both inherent in the country's condition and self-created, much has been done since the revolution to raise society from its backward state. It is now well on its way towards free, universal education, the health services have been improved, the status of women has been raised, workers' rights strengthened and cultural activities encouraged. Expenditure on social services has increased by about 150 per cent since 1952 and now constitutes approximately one-fifth of the ordinary budget.

Ever since the Egyptian national movement accused Lord Cromer of deliberately restricting education it has put it in the forefront of its programme, recognising that the renaissance of the country could not be achieved otherwise. Nor do objective observers of the Egyptian scene disagree. Charles Issawi states that 'Egypt's human resources have been hardly tapped relatively to those not only of advanced but even of comparatively backward countries. . . . Indeed in certain respects, notably literacy, some Asian countries such as Ceylon, Burma, Korea and Malaya, which are well behind Egypt economically, have a distinctly higher social level'.*

Backwardness in education was largely due to the inability of past governments to keep pace with the growth of population, despite substantial efforts to do so. The £350,000 allocated for

* *Egypt in Revolution*, published in 1963.

education in 1906 rose to £22 million in 1949–50, and in the following year Taha Hussein, as Minister of Education, raised the allocation to £28 million. Since the revolution, however, expenditure on education has increased remarkably, rising to £41 million, about 13 per cent of the national budget, in 1962–63, and to £111 million (including scientific research) in the estimates for 1966–67.

The rewards for this effort still appear meagre, for compared with 82 per cent illiteracy in 1937, there was still 72 per cent illiteracy in 1954 and about 70 per cent in 1966. Nevertheless, the vast school programme will soon greatly reduce this figure. In 1952 only 45 per cent of children of elementary school age received any education, but by 1960 65 per cent were attending school. A plan to give universal elementary education by 1964 could not be fulfilled, but the figures continue to increase, and it is expected that the target will be achieved by 1970. If so, it will be in spite of the extremely high population increase, as represented by the actual numbers of children at primary schools: 1,392,741 in 1953 as compared with 4,294,823 in 1966. From the very outset of the revolution the Government built a standardised, cheap primary school at the rate of one a day, reaching a record figure of 372 in 1954, and there are now 8,000.

From the reservoir of primary scholars the students are drawn for the higher studies in accordance with a plan laid down immediately after the revolution by which the six-year primary stage is followed by a three-year preparatory stage and then a three-year secondary stage, at the completion of which there are final examinations to entitle the student to enter universities or other institutes of higher education. Compulsory education terminates at the end of the primary education, and the pupil can only advance beyond by passing an examination. The Government aims eventually to extend compulsory education to preparatory schools.

In 1964, when there were 3,130,000 in the primary schools, there were 403,500 receiving preparatory training and 141,500 in the secondary stage. Of the secondary students, no less than 110,000 proceeded to the universities; in 1966 the number of university students totalled 130,000. The proportion of graduates to the total population is eleven times higher than in Britain and must be one of the highest in the world. English is very much the second language throughout the education system, and those taking science courses at the university do their specialised studies in the English language.

There were three universities in Egypt before the revolution: Cairo University, which was a private institution until taken over by the Government in 1925, Alexandria University, which was founded by the Government in 1942, and Ain Shams, in the Cairo suburb of Heliopolis, which was founded in 1950. In 1957 Assuit University was opened, and then in 1961 the ancient university of Al-Azhar was extended to include secular faculties.

The reform of Al-Azhar was one of the more notable developments, for this university was the foremost, orthodox centre of advanced Islamic education in the world. Its rigid conservatism had been for decades the target of Islamic reformers, from Mohammed Abdou to Taha Hussein, but no government felt strong enough to tamper with its antiquated system until President Nasser decreed that it should be modernised. The decision was in keeping with his radical attitude to religion, but there were other reasons for his decision to change it: he needed more graduates in secular subjects for his development programme, and the many foreigners who through the centuries had come to Al-Azhar were no longer in search of Moslem obscurantism, of which it was a distinguished exponent. Nearly 5,000 foreign students who come to Cairo annually now desire a modern, even technical education, in place of Islamic theology which had been Al-Azhar's sole fare for a thousand years.

In addition to the universities there are about forty institutes of higher education under the direction of the Ministry of Education, which provide specialised studies but, even so, the higher educational system has not met the needs of Egypt since the revolution. The curricula had been designed for a country with very little industry, but after 1960 the requirements of industry became the most pressing need. In 1966 the National Planning Institute reported that the country was going to be totally unable to execute its plans unless it rapidly increased the supply of personnel with the necessary training, calculating that the shortage of semi-skilled and skilled workers and technicians would be respectively 440,000, 139,000 and 213,000 by 1970, and 655,000, 759,000, and 373,000 by 1980. President Nasser thereupon established a committee to examine the problem and, as a result of its decisions, 30 per cent of the preparatory pupils will be directed to industrial training to become semi-skilled workers, 25 per cent will be sent to technical secondary schools to become skilled workers, 25 per cent will be sent to specialised technical schools to become technicians, and only 20 per cent will proceed to the ordinary secondary schools. It is argued that as almost all these people get their advanced education at the Government's expense, it lies within the rights of the Government to direct them to the studies which most suit the needs of the country. Nor can there be much question of the wisdom of this decision, for the immense expense of Egyptian education has for years been used to produce civil servants, lawyers and journalists in super-abundance while the requirements of what is virtually an industrial revolution were not met.

A Ministry of Education publication stated that the major aim of the primary school is the provision '. . . of adequate and sufficient opportunities for children of school age to achieve an integrated and well-balanced development, physically, mentally, socially, emotionally and spiritually. This school also aims at the creation of good citizens who are proud of Arab nationalism and are able to partake in life in a democratic socialistic society and to participate in practical activities, such as agriculture and industry, after a short period of relevant training'. This statement accurately expresses the intention of the system, but in doing so also reveals a defect normal to authoritarian régimes: the creation of good citizens is equated with absolute devotion to the revolution, and from the earliest stages the pupil is indoctrinated by all possible means, from the singing of patriotic songs to the rewriting of history.

The vocational and industrial training centres which are an increasingly important part of urban life have counterparts in the countryside in the Combined Rural Centres, but the centres have a much broader purpose in that they include ante-natal clinics, classes in preventive medicine and health clinics. They also have rural craft schools which provide agricultural training and education in cottage-type industries. Although the idea for these centres dates back to 1940, the first serious effort to develop them was made during the Wafd Government in 1950, but in 1951 there were still only 126 in existence. Fifteen years later there were nearly 700 serving about 1,300 villages. This great advance has been achieved by government finance and centralised control, but localised management is encouraged.

## II

Although women have not reached equality with men in the matter of education, considerable progress has been made in that direction. The percentage of girls to boys in the primary and preparatory stages has risen from approximately 25 per cent in 1952–53 to just under 50 per cent in 1963–64. Fewer girls than boys proceed with their education beyond the compulsory stage; less than a quarter of the pupils at secondary schools are girls, 39,451 out of 180,896, but most of them who do continue go right through to the universities. Each year sees an increase in the number of girls at school; for example, between 1961 and 1964 the percentage of girls in the secondary school population rose 2 per cent.

Women are now helping to fight illiteracy, for a great many of them take up teaching in primary schools. Their assistance would be even greater were it not for family traditions, which break down only slowly. They still tend to marry young and have children early in marriage, with the result that family necessity or the prejudice of the husbands against working wives quickly cuts short their careers. This is more noticeable at the lower social levels; educated women of the upper-working and middle classes are having smaller families, and many of the wives continue in employment to help maintain the new living standards of their families. At the lowest level, primary education makes little difference to the woman's lot, for she usually shares her husband's work, bears his children and labours in a crowded and comfortless home until she is prematurely old and sick.

Nevertheless the rapid expansion of education for women is an outstanding example of their emancipation, and if the benefits have not reached the poorest of them it is because economic circumstances still make it impossible; and even in their case, the radio, the spread of literacy, and education in birth control which eventually will release them from unceasing child-bearing, will ease their domestic servitude. The daughters of upper working-class parents now often go to work in offices, schools, restaurants, and see no harm in attending co-educational schools, so that the concept of seclusion from men (which, however, never existed among peasants) has collapsed in the towns.

Women also now take part with men in athletics and are active in voluntary organisations such as the Red Crescent. There are more Girl Guides than Boy Scouts.

The veil is rarely seen in Egypt. Polygamy is limited to a minority of the most ignorant people and the theologians try to convince the public that, if permissible, it is certainly not favoured in the Koran. The divorce rate, however, has risen to about three in every ten marriages and among the highest in the world, even though it is still difficult for women to initiate and secure divorce – an inequality which their organisations are campaigning to remove.

In the towns, marriage is developing more and more on the Western model, but this can put women at a disadvantage under Islamic law. Whereas in the case of divorce they are often in a better position than Western women because they have always been able to retain their own property and to transact their own financial affairs, and they have no dowry to lose, as it is paid by the man;

in matters of inheritance they are only entitled to half a son's share in the paternal estate and they receive only a small fraction of the estates of their husbands or sons. As the new status of women breaks down the paternal system of the family, by which women were cared for by the menfolk throughout their lives, the Islamic inheritance laws often leave widows in financial difficulties.

Syria and Lebanon gave the vote to women before Egypt, but since 1956 the Government has made a deliberate attempt to bring them more and more into public life. They are encouraged to stand for the National Assembly and membership of the Arab Socialist Union, and in 1962 a woman was appointed Minister of Social Affairs.

### III

Literacy poses a special problem because colloquial Arabic is so different in vocabulary, syntax and structure from literary, or classical, Arabic that knowledge of the script is not enough to read and write, or even for full communication between uneducated and educated people. Clearly many years will be required to level up the standards of primary education before literacy in the Western sense will be achieved. There is, however, the steady development of a 'middle Arabic', the language of newspapers, the radio and the cinema, and of some modern literature, which is helping to bridge the gap and bring contemporary writing within the comprehension of more and more people.

One other difficulty of the language is its lack of scientific and technical words. For decades an Egyptian academy has sought to create the vocabulary from classical roots, but the results were frequently complicated to the point of absurdity and seldom accepted. The attempt continues, but again newspapers and magazines by repetition are establishing the common use of Arabicised Western words, so that a great many words in mechanical engineering are French or English with an Arabic suffix. The universities teach medicine in English.

In 1956 the Government formed the Higher Council of Arts, Letters and Social Sciences to encourage cultural activity and its enjoyment, and today, with its blessing, the writer, artist and composer can be wealthier than the highest officials or university professors. Top Egyptian writers can earn as much as £400 a month through various kinds of subsidies; theatrical companies are financed to keep them constantly in work; and artists are paid salaries by the State for a year or two in which they can devote themselves entirely to painting and sculpture. A permanent gallery has been opened by the Government to display their work.

Side by side with this encouragement of the creators the Government has set out to take culture to the masses who were, in the past, totally devoid of it. The quality is not high 'but one must remember that the State is trying not so much to guarantee a high standard of the arts as simply to create a taste for them'.*

No less than eighteen theatrical companies are playing in Egypt at the present time. The existence of these companies and of theatres up and down the country has encouraged the dramatists, and there is a spate of modern plays and of dramatised versions of stories. The main characteristic of younger playwrights is their realism and, if their technique is immature, they successfully portray modern Egypt and are revolutionary in their use of colloquial Arabic. There are also performances of Western plays, both modern and old, and many of the established writers, like Tewfik al-Hakim, who has been writing since 1921, are adapting their works to the new needs with great vigour.

Parallel with the encouragement of the theatres there is an immense output of books through the nationalised State publishing houses. The Higher Council and the Ministry of Culture have embarked on a scheme to produce 2,000 books under what is called the Arabic Library Scheme, the idea of which is to fill the gaps existing in Arabic literature by printing or reprinting all works, classical and modern, which seem to have permanent value. Masterpieces of foreign literature are also being translated and published.

Inevitably, this State-encouraged burgeoning of the arts has created a dialogue between those who wish to reject entirely the old traditions and those who desire to adapt them. The revolutionary régime, conscious that no art consistent with its attitude existed before 1952, is on the side of the innovators but the dialogue is nevertheless sustained by the artists themselves. This is most obvious in poetry, which had a long and revered classical tradition. 'Young poets are in revolt. They argue that traditional forms, a heritage of pre-Islamic Arabia, are not suited to present society, that old patterns of classical poetry are forced and arbitrary and can never answer to the requirements of the new, vital life. They believe that the basic principles of real poetry should be: technical freedom; that they should spring from contemporary life and concrete realities and should develop a diction based on day-to-day life; that they

* Morsi Saad el-Din. 'The Cultural Climate of the U.A.R.', *The Arab World*, Journal of the Anglo-Arab Association, Winter Issue, 1966.

should dispense with purple patches and hackneyed expressions; that they should renounce pessimism and sadness, embracing joy and optimism; that they should give up the reporting style and use more imaginative and symbolic language; and, lastly, they ask that a poem should be looked upon as an entity and not, like classical poetry, simply a grouping of beautiful lines with no development of ideas. . .*.'

The Government's support for all cultural activity springs from its conviction that a new ideology must be created for the country and this channelling of artistic expression towards nationalist ends has its price. Morsi Saad el-Din states that 'the dissemination of culture must not be equated with indoctrination; not in Egypt anyway', and it is true that much of the creative work is free of it. But the writer or painter whose message conflicted with the ideology would not be encouraged. 'In many Arab countries today', wrote Patrick Seale, 'intellectuals stand defenceless against the great power of the State. To displease the authorities is to go hungry when, as in Egypt, newspapers, publishing houses, magazines, theatres, the radio and television are in the hands of the State. But in compensation for exercising self-censorship, top Egyptian writers are pampered and well-paid.'†

The Egyptian Press is by far the most highly developed in the Arab world, with newspaper circulations of *Al-Ahram* and *Al-Akhbar* ranging between 200,000 and 300,000. Except when censorship prevents their entry, these newspapers and several of the popular weekly magazines are sold in all the Arab countries. The fact that they are licensed by the Arab Socialist Union only thinly disguises State control, which precludes them from pursuing an independent line on any of the ideological principles of domestic, foreign or Arab affairs, although they are permitted to criticise domestic matters that do not infringe the principles; indeed, it is an important part of their function to be watch-dogs for the public against infringements of the revolutionary purpose by the bureaucracy, industrial management or landowners. Like the National Assembly, they are critics within and not against the revolution. Because they reflect the revolutionary purpose of the Government in Arab affairs, they are part of the propaganda machine of the State and for that reason they are frequently censored in, or excluded from, some Arab countries.

Egypt's sound and television radio programmes are highly

---

* Morsi Saad el-Din, op. cit. He said that the modern poets are greatly influenced by W. B. Yeats and T. S. Eliot.
† The *Observer*, 12 June 1966.

developed and are equalled in programme time only by the most advanced countries. Their domestic and foreign programmes are considered by the Government to be part of the 'liberation struggle', educating people at home in the principles and meaning of Arab socialism and people abroad in the need to resist imperialism, colonialism and neo-colonialism. The foreign broadcasts pay particular attention to black Africa and are presented in more than thirty different languages. Propaganda broadcasts to the Arab world, notably the *Voice of the Arabs* programme, have considerable impact and constitute the principal vehicle for spreading 'Nasserism'. The Egyptian radio attracts a big Arab listening public because of the high standard of its entertainment programmes, which are rarely equalled by other Arab countries. Accidents of radio propagation enable many people in Lebanon and Jordan to watch Egyptian television from time to time during the year and for that reason families equip themselves with the aerials to do so.

In the entertainment field, Egypt is dominant, although Lebanon offers some competition. The Egyptian cinema, which is the oldest in the Arab region, has a near monopoly, with the result that cinemas throughout the Arab world are compelled to take Egyptian films. Its predominance, the Cairo Press, and the influence of Cairo Radio, are doing much to impose Egyptian 'middle Arabic' as a *lingua franca*.

## IV

Standards of health in Egypt are among the lowest in the world. The expectancy of life at birth is barely twenty years and nearly a quarter of the children die before the age of one year. Bilharzia, amoebic dysentery, malaria and tuberculosis continue to take their toll, and there is a high incidence of total or partial blindness caused by eye diseases such as trachoma.

Yet Egypt both before and since the revolution has tried hard to combat the problem and if the rewards have not been commensurate with the effort it is because underlying the problem of health is the poverty of the people, and that in turn is now largely due to the abnormally high birth rate. In 1951 there were only 5,200 doctors, but there were nearly 11,000 in 1966 and the output from the medical colleges continues at a high rate. Unfortunately for the country too high a proportion of the doctors remained in the urban centres, where the rewards were high, and the countryside did not benefit in proportion to their number. To overcome this the Government ordered that those doctors who secured their training at the Government's expense must work for the first five years after qualification in the rural areas. This instruction, and the Combined Centres in the villages, are doing something to correct the disparity between health care in town and countryside.

The two scourges which particularly affect the peasants are bilharzia and trachoma, and considerable progress has been made in fighting both of them. The former is contracted through a micro-organism which is parasitic on water snails and lives part of its life cycle in human beings whom it infects by penetrating the skin, then damaging the liver, kidneys and bladder. This illness weakens and substantially reduces the efficiency of the sufferer. In recent years a big campaign has been waged against it from 168 medical units and many other related organisations, by which four million people are treated yearly, but even greater success has been achieved by destroying the snails themselves with chemicals placed in the ditches where the snails live. The percentage of the population infected has been reduced from 60 per cent to 37 per cent since 1952. In the case of trachoma, from which about 87 per cent of the population suffered to a great or less extent at one time, and which sometimes led to blindness, modern drugs and better hygiene have reduced the number of sufferers by three-quarters.

Malaria is almost totally restricted to Southern Egypt. Although it is not as serious a scourge as bilharzia, an epidemic during the last war decimated villages, and control is constantly necessary. The Government has allocated £23 million for an eleven-year campaign to eradicate it. Progress has also been made against tuberculosis, largely by inoculation although in this case permanent long-term success must depend on a higher standard of living.

The provision of clean drinking water for the villages has made a substantial contribution to general health and would do more were it not for the peasants' preference for the 'rich' Nile water, a preference which only time and education can eradicate. In 1936 there was no potable water outside the towns, by 1952 it had been provided for two million peasants, by 1957 for nearly six million, and it will very soon be available for the entire population.

## V

The panic execution of the two workers' leaders at Kafr el-Dawar in the first days of the revolution did not reflect the true character of the régime which from the outset regarded itself as on the workers' side and the trade unions as allies. For a time the activities of the Moslem Brothers and communists within the unions impaired the relationship, but in the Neguib crisis of 1954 the unions rose in defence of the revolution. Since 1961 various decrees have given workers a share in profits and representation on the boards of companies, and guaranteed their proportion of members in the Arab Socialist Union and the National Assembly.

One of the first acts of the revolutionary Government in 1952 was to give many unorganised workers the right to join unions and membership rose from just over 125,000 in 1952 to about 600,000 in 1965. As urban workers are organised on a company basis the number of unions continues to increase as industrialisation progresses, but the law that only workers can be members prevents the intrusion of professional politicians or even the establishment of professional union leadership at the national Federation level. The Government, which regards the union movement as within the revolution, does not permit its emergence as an independent political force and it works in close association with the Ministry of Labour, referring to it trade disputes that would give rise to direct industrial action in more liberal countries.

In return the Ministry does its utmost to support the unions, with the result that the Labour Courts, to which disputes with employers are referred, tend to favour the worker. In the beginning this corrected the balance in a country where the employee had no defence against a bad boss, but it was carried too far, until it became extremely difficult for a private employer to dismiss a bad workman. This is of less significance now in that by far the greater part of the industrialised labour force is employed in nationalised or controlled industries. Nevertheless the unions' association with the Ministry has been helpful in many practical directions; together they have worked with the I.L.O. and with Egyptian labour attachés at the embassies abroad to improve working conditions.

Individual contracts of service were decreed in 1953, notably by the imposition of a basic Labour Law which determined minimum wages and maximum hours, guaranteed compensation on dismissal or retirement and minimum periods of sick benefit during periods of illness. In 1955 the Workers' Insurance and Provident Law was promulgated under which employers and workers contribute to a fund from which indemnities and pensions are drawn by the workers, thus ensuring that benefits no longer depend on the ability of employers to pay. On retirement, a worker draws a part of the sum to which he is entitled as capital and the remainder as pension. Another law of 1953 compelled employers of more than one hundred people to provide basic medical services for them. Subsequent laws established an industrial inspection service, a thirty-six-hour week for youths between twelve and fifteen years of age, and an apprenticeship training system under the auspices of the Ministry of Labour. The nationalisation laws of 1961 stipulated that workers should be represented on the boards of companies and that 25 per cent of the profits should be distributed among the employees in cash or welfare services.

Agricultural workers constitute about 55 per cent of the Egyptian labour force and they have not benefited to anything like the same extent by these laws, largely because the conditions of work and employment are very different. For example, child labour under twelve years of age is forbidden but cannot be imposed on farm labourers who take their entire families into the fields at certain times in the year. They are permitted to organise themselves into trade unions, which they were not allowed to do before the revolution, but they have taken very little advantage of the law because unions do not fit into village life. They have still virtually no protection, whereas the urban workers have acquired benefits and a degree of security that were unknown before the revolution. The gains of the peasants come from sources outside the labour laws, such as the Combined Rural Centres which provide some basic health services and craft training for both sons and daughters, and the rent controls imposed under the Agrarian Reform Law. It remains true, however, that the peasant relies still to a large extent on voluntary communal self-help, which is traditional in the villages, to see him through most of the crises of his poverty-stricken life.

The Government, working through the governorates and co-operative credit societies and with the assistance of some of the big nationalised undertakings such as the petroleum refinery at Suez and the State Railways, has executed many important housing projects in Cairo, Alexandria and other main towns. Many slums in the two cities have been eradicated and replaced by blocks of cheap flats, but there is still a shortage of houses for the better class of worker who is often driven to the illegal expedient of paying 'key money' in order to find somewhere to live. Controlled rents, which favour the tenants in possession, prove a disadvantage to the people, particularly young people getting married, as landlords try to make a substantial profit when any house or apartment falls vacant. Here again the villagers have had little benefit, because there are too many of them; they are crowded into a small space and other land is too valuable for building; and, in any case, they like to live with their animals, which are their principal capital.

## Chapter 16

# In Search of Wealth

I

THROUGHOUT KNOWN HISTORY the Egyptian people have depended for their well-being on the Nile and have fed well or gone hungry according to the care they took of it. The annual flood coursed through their rainless land to irrigate the fields and for thousands of years there was little change in the system whereby the flood water was held by mud walls on the low-lying land of the valley and then freed to flow to the sea when it had deposited its silt and soaked the soil.

When British engineers completed the first Aswan Dam in 1902 they made the first real advance on the pharaonic system of basin irrigation by storing some of the flood water for use in the spring of the year when the river was low, so enabling two or three crops to be grown annually on the land which was given the stored water. The Dam has twice been heightened and the river brought increasingly under control by many other works, large and small, all the way northwards from Aswan. There are barrages at Esna, Nag Hammadi and Assuit, all of which serve the same purpose as the Mohammed Aly barrage: that of raising the level of the river to supply the irrigation canals. In 1939 the Mohammed Aly barrage was abandoned in favour of two barrages built close by on the Rosetta and Damietta branches of the river, and other barrages were built on the branches in the delta. The delta is served by three main canals which are equipped with regulators to control the flow into the web of lesser channels and irrigation ditches.

There is an efficient and intricate administration, whose engineers measure the Nile with accuracy and control its flow to every corner of the cultivated land. It is orchestrated with hundreds of creaking iron gates, from the double-bass of the sluices at Aswan to the squeak of the metal sheets in the ditches, all of which rise and fall separately or in grouped unison as the irrigation system calls the tune. Come kings, go kings; through riots, civil turmoil or revolution, the work goes on day by day, month by month; and through the length and breadth of Egypt, millions of farmers and peasants and their animals work to the rhythm of the waters. The principle of life on the Nile is in that sense unchanged since the time of the pharaohs; wheat has given way to cotton as the main crop and the works are more complicated – that is all.

Since the Mohammed Aly barrage was made to function properly in 1890 the whole of the delta has been converted to perennial cultivation, and Middle Egypt, between Cairo and Assuit, is almost entirely perennial. In Upper Egypt there are still about a million acres of basin land, although here too irrigation has been improved by better control of the water and the use of wells and pumps. The six million acres under cultivation provide about ten million cropped acres by perennial cultivation; and there have been improvements in drainage, an important factor in the perennial system.

The land reform which the revolutionary Government introduced in 1952 improved the distribution of wealth by giving land to about 80,000 families comprising about half a million people and controlling the rents of about four million tenants. Another experiment in social betterment was started in the desert on the western fringe of the delta in 1953, when about 1,200,000 acres were marked out and named Liberation Province. For this dual experiment in land reclamation and collective farming, which was unknown to the highly individualistic Egyptian peasant, about 14,000 peasants were employed at high wages and in good living conditions, and the latest mechanical equipment was brought in to blitz the desert. But this was extravagantly costly and limited by lack of water. Neither land reform nor collective farming could of themselves add to the national wealth beyond the limits of available water.

The weakness of the system of Nile control lay in the fact that the Aswan Dam could only control the water within one year. It could not supplement the supply in a year of low flood nor entirely prevent damage to the farmlands in periods of excessive flood. Messrs. Hurst, Black & Simaika, of the Egyptian Irrigation Service, proposed in volume seven of their mammoth work *The Nile Basin* that there should be a system of century-storage based on the control of the flow from the great African lakes, Victoria and Albert, so that the waters of a year of big supply could be held to make good the supply in a bad year. Britain and Egypt reached agreement with other riparian countries on such a scheme in 1949, the first result of which was the building of the Owen Falls Dam just below the exit from Lake Victoria. It was all-embracing, providing for works along the length of the Nile and the cutting of a canal through the Sudd, a swampy region in the Sudan where much Nile water was lost, but even the best estimates assumed twenty-five years for the completion of the programme. It was doubtless the best possible plan for Nile control but it did not meet the urgency of Egypt's case.

It is the irony of Egypt's situation that the highly developed Nile valley, giving some of the best crop yields in the world, has failed to keep pace with the growth of population since about 1910. The process began in the nineteenth century. There was an acre for every inhabitant in the time of Mohammed Aly but only three-quarters of an acre at the end of Ismail's reign. The Aswan Dam and perennial cultivation arrested the process for a few years, for in the first decade of this century, when there were 12 million people fed from eight million acres of enhanced fertility, the country was probably more prosperous than it has ever been since. By the time the revolution occurred there were only two cropped acres for every seven people. Dr. Meunier, of Alexandria University, calculated in 1951 that the *per capita* income of the country was in real terms 39 per cent less than in 1913, and Professor Charles Issawi stated in 1963 that 'during the last few decades the volume of agricultural production has failed to keep pace with the population, in spite of much technical research and improvements of methods of cultivation'.*

The fact that Nile development can never again keep pace with population is at the root of Egypt's economic problems. Experts calculated that 7·5 million acres was the maximum area that could be cultivated from the Nile, but it is now thought that cheap electricity will make it possible to lift water to higher levels and cultivate a larger area not exceeding a total of ten million acres. Meanwhile population is increasing at an alarming rate. It was seven million in 1882, 13 million in 1917, 27 million in 1962, 30 million in 1965, and is increasing at a rate of 700,000 a year. It is clear, therefore, that the well-being of Egypt no longer depends on agriculture alone, although that is vital. It must also industrialise and do its utmost to limit the growth of population.

The military Government abandoned the Great Lakes storage scheme in favour of a scheme mooted earlier for a High Dam south of Aswan to provide a reservoir for multi-year storage, which would bring an extra million acres under cultivation, extend perennial cultivation to the basin lands of Upper Egypt, and provide electric power. It had the advantage that its construction would be within Egypt's frontiers and entirely under the Government's control; and it would enable the Government to control the flow from one year to the next and to plan the crop system in advance for the country's own needs and the export trade. This plan became the corner-

* Charles Issawi, *Egypt in Revolution.*

stone of the country's long-term planning and constituted the first advance on the system of Nile control since the building of the first Aswan Dam.

As this is being written the High Dam is nearing completion. It is one of the great dams of the world: a rock-fill structure two and a half miles long and rising 365 feet above the river level. Behind it there is forming Lake Nasser, the biggest man-made lake in the world, which stretches 344 miles upstream, reaching 124 miles into the Sudan and submerging every habitation, including the whole town of Wadi Halfa, in its basin. After allowing for about 14 million cubic yards of water loss through evaporation, it will provide 72 million cubic yards of additional water for Egypt and 24 million for the Sudan. The lake is released northwards through a diversion channel on to the sluices of the old Aswan Dam, which regulates the supply of water to the valley to the north. In addition twelve mammoth turbines in the diversion channel, each of 175,000 kilowatts, will generate ten milliard kilowatts of electric power.*

During the first five-year plan which ended in 1965 the Government reclaimed or developed 500,000 acres, but, using water from the High Dam, it plans to reclaim 150,000 acres a year for the next seven years. The Government is also making a systematic study of rainfall, underground water and soil with a view to the development of areas outside the reach of Nile water. The biggest of these projects is in the western desert where hundreds of workers, supervised by engineers and geologists, have been at work since 1960 to create a New Valley by raising underground water along a line of five oases, stretching from Dakhla to Siwa. The region was fertile in Greek and Roman times, and Roman wells in the Kharga and Dakhla oases are among the 120 restored to use.

It was an essential part of the High Dam concept that the time taken to build the Dam should be used to industrialise the country as far as possible, the theory being that the extra production made possible by the Dam would just about keep pace with the growth of population and that industrial production would thereby constitute a net gain in national wealth. This concept was falsified by the fact that political and financial difficulties delayed the start of work on the Dam until 1960 and the growth of population was much more rapid than expected. Further, the start of work on the Dam coincided with the calculated extension of public ownership, so that the economic progress of the country now must be measured largely in terms of the socialised State beginning with the five-year plan from 1959–60 to 1964–65.

* See *High Dam at Aswan*, 1965, by the author.

The first few years of the revolution were economically an extension of the preceding system and were notable for the encouragement given to foreign and domestic private enterprise. Nationalisations before 1960 were imposed largely for non-ideological reasons, such as the seizure of British and French concerns after the Suez invasion, of the Misr undertaking because of dissatisfaction with the Bank Misr investment policy, and of the Abboud industries because of tax evasion.

Dr. Galal Amin of Ain-Shams University, Cairo, states: 'The argument in favour of the adoption of socialism in Egypt could briefly be put as follows: An underdeveloped country can achieve both a more equitable distribution of income and a higher rate of growth when the means of production are predominantly publicly owned, since the state is capable of realising a higher rate of saving and investment, and of directing investment into channels which are more productive from the society's point of view'.*

There has been equalisation of income, but it has been mainly achieved by greater employment rather than by higher real income for the working classes. The share of wages in national income rose from 42·8 per cent to 46·7 per cent during the five-year plan; but whereas the money wages of industrial workers rose by 22·8 per cent the official cost-of-living index for the five-year period rose by 23·2 per cent. On the other hand there were more than 1,300,000 additional workers in employment, an increase of 22·2 per cent as against a 15 per cent increase in population and an increase in employment between 1947 and 1960 of just over 10 per cent. Both in urban and rural areas there has been a substantial increase in public services, such as education and health, which is not reflected in the wages share in national income, and agricultural workers have gained by redistribution of land and reduction of land rents. By comparison, income from other sources such as property and trade has declined. It follows that there has been an equalisation of income since the socialist policy was embarked on.

There has also been a higher rate of economic growth. The real *per capita* income remained steady at £E45 between 1952–53 and 1955–56, then rose to £E50·3 during the next four years and then to £E59·8 in 1964–65. The Gross National Product also increased by just under 7 per cent in the years from 1956 as compared with an increase of under 1 per cent in the preceding four years.

The rate of national investment increased rapidly during the

* In an unpublished paper to the Department of Middle Eastern Studies at London University. This and a similar paper by Dr. Bent Hansen of California University were most useful assessments up-to-date to the autumn of 1966.

five-year plan, from £E171 million in the first year to £E364 million in 1964–65. There was, however, a decline in investment from the peak reached in 1963–64, probably caused by the difficulty in maintaining the level of foreign credits and the decline of stocks due to shortage of foreign exchange, and the decline is, therefore, almost certainly a continuing factor. There is almost no private investment, for the public sector provided 94 per cent of gross investment in the year 1963–64. Domestic saving has, if anything, shown a slight decrease since 1956.

The lack of adequate domestic saving and the inability of Egypt to increase its foreign borrowing point to a probable failure to maintain the level of investment for planned national growth, and this is perhaps the most crucial factor in Egypt's economic position. It stems from the failure to find the correct equation between the socialist concept of the greatest good of the greatest number and the economic facts of life. Given the principles on which the revolution is based, it was extremely difficult for the Government not to offer the workers a share of the revolutionary gains. Thus, the provision of employment became a purpose in itself and the avoidance of unemployment a perpetual effort, to such an extent that unwanted workers could not be discharged and were often moved to other tasks where they were equally useless. Government servants were shuffled about from one department to another merely to keep them in work.

The restoration of the national investment ratio demands restraint of domestic consumption and there is no evidence that adequate steps will be taken to achieve this. The Mohieddin Government of 1965–66 raised taxes, increased the prices of manufactured goods, and allowed consumer goods to find their natural price levels, steps which contributed substantially to the 20 per cent increase in the cost of living between mid-1964 and mid-1966, but the policy was not pursued consistently. The maintenance of high employment and the total failure of the Government to persuade the population to save are two major impediments to investment.

Over the plan period the investment in agriculture was probably exactly as planned. Actual investment is given as 16·7 per cent of the plan total instead of an estimated 20·5 per cent; but the High Dam is listed separately, and in speeding the completion of this project the actual investment was 6·1 per cent of the total instead of the planned 2·9. If the proportion of High Dam costs for the power installation is deducted the balance must bring agricultural investment to the planned 20·5 per cent.

The rate of growth from this investment, however, fell far below both the average for the plan as a whole and the estimated growth of agriculture itself; the planned growth overall was 7 per cent and of agriculture 5 per cent, but the actual agricultural growth was 2 per cent. The slow return natural to agricultural investment and in particular from the High Dam, which is expected to produce about £E235 million increase in the national income when its full benefits are realised in 1972, accounts to some extent for the disappointing returns from agricultural investment but not for the faulty estimates of the planners.

Similarly the investment of industry has been almost exactly as planned, but if power is left out of account the average annual growth rates were little more than half of the target. The fact that the plan as a whole came near to achieving its intended 7 per cent annual growth is therefore subject to serious qualification by the failure to reach the targets in both agriculture and industry, upon which the future prosperity of the country is predicated.

The increased capacity for electrical production, which was already set high in the plan – a 14·7 annual growth – exceeded even this rate by 4 per cent. As a result the annual output rose from just over 2 million kilowatts to nearly 6 million kilowatts. This is long-term investment of importance in a country which lacks power supplies, and the Government, looking beyond the big hydro-electric works at the High Dam, had German engineers to study in 1966 an even greater scheme for the otherwise useless Qattara depression in the western desert; the general idea is to cut a canal from the sea to the depression and use the natural fall of water to generate electricity.

This higher growth in electrical power and in construction and services brought the plan close to its overall target rate; for the latter two sectors show growth averaging between 8 and 9 per cent a year, although the planners had actually provided for a slight fall in the rate of construction. The Services section of the national income also includes the revenues of the Suez Canal which were considerably higher than expected, but, in contrast, the increase in the government labour force and the substantial overseas service pay to 70,000 troops in the Yemen were considerable and unproductive factors.

The development plan has not altered to any major extent the preponderance of agricultural products, mainly cotton, in the export trade, of which they constitute about 75 per cent. Apart from exports of cement, which are worth about £E1 million, the principal manufactured exports are cotton yarn or fabrics. Nor have the requirements of the country itself been met by domestic production; the imports of cereals are more than three times the value of the only cereal export, rice, and the country is importing maize and many other commodities which it never did before.

Egypt has not been able to contribute much towards its capital and consumer imports, and the interest and repayment of its loans, from new production resulting from its investments in development. This is not surprising, given the abnormal increase in population and the time taken to recoup from investments, but it has produced a major crisis of foreign payments. There was a deficit of £E76 million on the balance of payments for the five years, which was £E126 million worse than originally planned. The Yemen War and the ravages of the cotton worm in the year 1961–62 contributed to the difficulty, but the root of the problem was deeper; the ravages of the cotton worm can be controlled and the Yemen War will end some day, but the development plan itself was out of balance. Nor are there signs that balance will be achieved in the current plan, for the Government, although proposing an even higher rate of investment, seems unwilling to impose the drastic restraint on public and private consumption which would make the investment rate possible.

President Nasser has himself admitted that his economists believed that the first ten years of planning should be extended over twenty years and that he insisted on ten years because the population increase would otherwise nullify the benefits of development. He pointed to the High Dam, 850 factories, an urban working population increased by three million, and a national wage bill that had risen from £E349 million in 1952 to £E770 million in 1964 as the reward for his efforts.

But almost all this extra money went to ordinary working men who spent it on the necessities of life, such as food, clothing and medicines, and sufficient priority in planning was not given to providing the consumer goods which would absorb it. It was no doubt desirable for the future to build a steelworks or a motor-car factory, but in the meanwhile the people building the factories or working in them did not eat iron bars or wear a car. The inevitable happened: the people emptied the shops with their new money and prices rose.

The Government attempted to control the rise of prices by the introduction of co-operatives, with the result that there developed an official and a free market. Meat could be bought at about 3s. 6d. a lb. in the co-operatives but cost 10s. in the free shops. This produced long queues at the co-operatives and a deal of corruption among those who found ways of switching official supplies to free shops or favoured customers.

The effect on the countryside was opposite to the nation's needs. Improvident peasants who could get nearly 10s. for a chicken decided to kill it instead of keeping it for eggs, and the farmer killed cattle that could have provided milk; and the shortage of milk in turn led to a shortage of cheese. For the real problem was food, the supply of which depended on Nile water and, being limited by it, was not easily increased. The Government was forced to import maize, which it had never done before, and became one of the largest importers of wheat. Until 1965 the United States helped greatly by selling nearly £E50 million worth of wheat a year against Egyptian currency, but in this matter of buying from abroad Russia, the benefactor, became a serious problem. Half of Egypt's cotton crop, by far the most important export, was mortgaged to Russia for arms, the High Dam and factories. Further, every factory needed its spare parts and raw materials. The chronic shortage of foreign exchange has therefore been the effect of many factors at work.

Since 1955 there has been a growing trade deficit and this, combined with foreign exchange commitments, has led to a spectacular fall in reserves. They declined from $467 million in 1955 to $31 million in April 1966, and short-term liabilities were much greater than the latter figure. At 31 July 1966 Egypt had drawn $253 million from the International Monetary Fund, which was almost 170 per cent of its quota. Towards the end of 1964 it was calculated that the short-term debt to Western banks and financial institutions was about £71 million, nearly half of it overdue, and that trade and payments agreements with Eastern bloc countries were overdrawn by about £77 million. In October 1964 the gold cover for the currency was £E60 million, but in December Egypt sold gold valued at about £13 million in Zurich, which was approximately the amount of cover released by an effective devaluation of the currency in 1962. In September and October of 1966 another £10 million of gold was sold.

Because the greater part of the income from cotton must be delivered to the Eastern bloc countries under barter and other agreements the Suez Canal is the main source of Egypt's transferable foreign currency. Since 1957, when the Canal was reopened after the nationalisation of the Suez Canal Company, it has earned about £450 million sterling, and transit receipts in 1965 were worth about £E86 million, having risen to that figure from £E51·5 million in 1961 when the first stage of the widening and deepening programme was completed. Whereas in 1957 the Canal could only take ships up to 30,000 tons with 35 feet draught, it can now take ships up to 55,000 tons with 38 feet draught, and the Government plans further development which will enable ships of 100,000 tons dead weight and with 48 feet draught to use the Canal. Essentially the object of these programmes is to make it worthwhile for big oil tankers to continue to use the Suez route instead of circling the Cape. Many other improvements have been made to enable the Canal to handle the 20,000 ships which now use it annually.

The discovery of an oilfield in the western desert holds out hope that Egypt may at last become a substantial oil-producing country, perhaps eventually rivalling the growth of the industry in neighbouring Libya. This discovery in the autumn of 1966 was the first ever made west of the Nile; all Egypt's oil production has been in the Sinai, the Gulf of Suez and the Red Sea coast, where the geological structures yield only small quantities. The estimated reserves of all fields were about 80 million tons until the Morgan field was discovered in 1965 in the Gulf of Suez, with reserves estimated between 200 and 400 million tons. Egypt has only recently become a net exporter of petroleum products, but with the annual output of the Morgan field rising to 10 million tons a year, the annual export surplus should be about 12 million tons in 1970. The western desert field holds out much bigger promise however, and may transform the whole situation before that date.

## II

No one has been more frank about the economic difficulties than President Nasser himself. In a speech on the thirteenth anniversary of the revolution he confessed that Egypt was engaged on a development programme far beyond its own capacity and, what was more, paying for it herself. He made the point that Israel was given money but Egypt was only lent it and therefore had to repay its loans. But, he contended, there was no alternative to this policy, for with the population increasing at an extravagant rate the country was doomed unless it maintained the momentum of progress. His speech reflected his determination to maintain his course, in development, in social revolution, and in the Arab world and beyond.

A serious impediment to the successful execution of development planning is the lack of trained management and of labour with the required skills, and the failure of the bureaucracy to meet the immense burdens which the socialist system has placed on it. These problems are recognised by the Government, which has formed an organisation to train managers, made plans to send a high proportion of secondary school pupils to technical schools, and is surveying the government service; but these efforts will not bear early fruit.

The delay in announcing the second development plan indicates that the Government is conscious of the problems and failures of the first, notably in the conflict between the short-term gains of labour and long-term national growth. The decision to raise taxes and the prices of some essential goods in 1965–66 points to a desire to encourage growth.

The preliminary figures of the second plan provide for a gradual rise in domestic savings from the 12·7 per cent of the first plan to 22 per cent in the fifth year of the second, and a rise in money wages of 36·5 per cent, instead of 60 per cent as in the first plan. It is also proposed that the annual average of gross investments should rise from £E302·6 million to £E452·3 million. There are clearly difficulties in the way of all these targets, although the income from the High Dam and the oil strike in the western desert might prove substantial factors on the credit side.

The effort to improve the lot of the ordinary Egyptian, by social welfare, increased employment and, where possible, higher living standards, is manifestly justified, for they had been greatly neglected. Nor can it be doubted that herculean efforts are required to provide for the 700,000 extra mouths there are to feed each year; Egypt is like Alice's queen: it has to run very fast in order to stay in the same place. The pre-revolutionary régime did not make any effort commensurate with the needs of the country, and would undoubtedly have escaped Nasser's present difficulties by living tranquilly on the mass of deepening poverty.

What is in question is President Nasser's ability to pursue successfully all of his policies at the same time: to expand agriculture and industry, maintain high employment levels and social benefits, fight a war in Yemen, conduct a revolutionary policy throughout the Arab world, maintain a propaganda machine comparable to that of a great power, and to fight imperialism, real or imagined, in Africa or anywhere else he can find it. The cost on all counts is high both in money and lost friends.

Agriculture still gives Egypt a capacity to survive economic difficulties because the mass of the people are hardly touched by them. As the Middle East correspondent of *The Times* pointed out in 1957: 'The fundamental strength of Egypt's economy is its broad base of individual poverty. Nine out of ten Egyptians live today, as they have always done, at subsistence level; and when a man is already on his back it is difficult to knock him down'. The position has not markedly changed since, and neither has the fact that the economy cannot easily support large-scale capital development; its one crop economy puts it at the mercy of the world market and the weevil, its rate of domestic capital formation is low, and widespread poverty deprives industry of an adequate domestic market.

Egypt's development programme depends on foreign loans and aid, which have come from many sources, but mainly from the United States and Russia, which have each contributed about $1,000 million It is improbable that foreign support will continue at the high levels of the first five-year plan and in that case the only way to maintain the investment ratio required for the plan will be to take tough measures to cut back domestic consumption: by taxation, diminished welfare, reduced public spending and the like. Such a policy is so foreign to the desire and intention of the Government that one doubts the efficacy of recent efforts in this direction; but it is certain that there cannot be development on the scale planned and consumption at the present level.

Only by the most stringent controls is there any foreign exchange in the trading account. The *Pravda* correspondent in Cairo stated that Egyptian officials admitted that the country's economy was in a parlous state because the bulk of Egyptian exports had to be bartered for machinery from communist countries and little was left to earn foreign exchange. Soviet military aid, estimated to amount to $700 million, contributes to the problem, although the editor of *Al-Ahram* stated in his newspaper on 31 December 1965 that Egypt only paid between £E6·5 million and £E10 million annually for these arms purchases. President Nasser has himself admitted that some of the factories built under the development programme are not working, or working at half-capacity, because the foreign exchange for raw materials and spare parts is not available. This means that these factories are not helping to repay the loans with which they are built and are therefore augmenting the difficulties.

## III

Since the seizure of the Suez Canal Company in 1956 completed the independence for which the people had struggled for nearly a century, the economic plight of the country was the one essential problem. Apart from the need to maintain adequate defences against Israel, almost all other aspects of Egyptian policy have been to some extent artificial and have often produced dangerous contradictions. Egypt's economic and defence policies after 1954, which were justifiable in themselves, helped to establish the Soviet position in the Middle East, but the union with Syria, in the guise of pan-Arabism, was designed initially to defeat the Levant Communist Party, which was the instrument of Soviet policy. Above all, President Nasser appeared to forget that power is politics. On the one hand he conducted a bitter struggle against Britain, although it was obvious that the decline of British power would mean the progressive decay of British positions in the Middle East and, at best, he could only hope to expedite the process a little. On the other, he pursued the revolution in the Middle East, with the result that he increased instability without the power to impose a new order in the place of the old.

In the event, the military build-up for defence against Israel also proved a waste of wealth and effort. Most of the material was destroyed in four days of warfare in which Egypt proved incapable of holding Israel, much less of recovering any territory for the Arabs, and she is now paying for weapons she does not possess. The cost of war must have been considerable, the replacement and maintenance of new arms even on the most advantageous terms was an additional burden the country could not easily bear, and the loss of income from the Suez Canal at the rate of £2 million a week and from tourism further weakened the foreign exchange position. The efforts that maritime nations and international oil companies were compelled to make to manage without the Suez Canal may do long-term harm to canal business and therefore to Egypt, which is more vulnerable than the countries penalised. Although it would be wrong to exaggerate the ill-effects of the war, they must impede development and eventually compel a rethinking not only of the economic situation but of its political context.

It is self-evident that the maximum of foreign goodwill, trade and aid are necessary for the successful pursuit of Egypt's economic plans. The dilemma of President Nasser has been that the policies have brought him into conflict with too many states: with Britain, for a long time with France, with Belgium, Portugal, West Germany, the United States and, briefly, with Russia. In consequence Egypt is not trusted by many Western countries which might individually be incapable of contributing much to Egypt's economic plans but which in the aggregate could have been of great assistance. He considered all concessions to friendly powers as political strings; thus it was a gross offence for the United States to *suggest* that he might change his attitude to the Congo rebels. He chose to fight the good anti-imperialist fight and at the same time to push on with his development plans, and Egypt's ties with Russia are the result. In a speech on 21 November 1956, when British, French and Israeli troops were still on Egyptian soil, President Nasser promised that Egypt would maintain political and ideological independence; would remain free of 'marxism, fascism, racialism, colonialism, imperialism and atheism, all of which, incidentally, are of European origin', and would not become a satellite of any power; but the combination of ambitious economic planning with an aggressive foreign policy has brought his Egypt closer to economic dependence on the Soviet bloc than she ever was on the Western powers.

The connection remains economic, not ideological, on Egypt's part; but not on Russia's. The collaboration of the Egyptian Communist Party with the régime was decided upon and recorded in Moscow and is no mean political string when related to substantial economic ties. Debts must eventually be paid, and the coin of Soviet Russia in the last resort is political. To consolidate the independence of his country, President Nasser must re-establish the balance of his economic non-alignment; and it follows that the Western powers must respond with trade and aid. An adjustment of policy is required on both sides, for Egypt needs the West, and the West cannot have a successful Middle Eastern policy without Egypt.

Twice before attempts were made to pull up Egypt by her shoe-straps. Mohammed Aly came into conflict with the Powers and was forced to capitulate. The Khedive Ismail mismanaged and wasted his wealth and was compelled in the end to yield to his creditors. President Nasser has been at pains more than once to reject the comparison with Ismail on the grounds that Egypt's current debts built factories whereas Ismail threw his money away. In fact, Ismail did a great deal for his country and the proportion of wasted wealth was perhaps no greater than Egypt now wastes on excessive propaganda and diplomatic services and on military operations.

President Nasser does not see the problems in these terms, for to him independence is indivisible and it is the duty and the self-interest of Egypt to support the liberation struggle wherever it occurs. Those who say that his policy is dictated simply by the desire for self-aggrandisement misjudge the man and his sense of mission. The question at the end of 1966, however, is whether the economy or the mission will crack first.

Essentially it is a problem of the management of the revolution, for politically Egypt will never again be as she was before 1952. Though Nasser were to die tomorrow and there were new upheavals, the revolution which he has carried so far, which has made great social gains for the mass of the people and established new principles of social life, would not be ended. There might be a pause, there might be a change, but Egypt would not turn back.

## Chapter 17

# War with Israel

THE ECONOMIC development of the Arab world and the attempt to reconcile tradition with material progress and social welfare is the fundamental problem of the region and commands the attention of every thinking Arab. A considerable part of urban Arab opinion believed that President Nasser's efforts to this end, his propagation of Arab socialism, his attempt to overthrow 'feudal rulers' and destroy 'imperialist influence', expressed his primary purpose in the region, and the extreme left-wing of Arab opinion would not have sacrificed any of this purpose in order to recover the part of Palestine lost to Israel. Even Nasser behaved as though the liberation of Palestine could wait.

Palestine remained—and remains—the great emotive force in Arab politics nevertheless, and the majority of Arabs believed that it was his inescapable duty as supreme leader of the Arabs to take back their land from Israel. What other duty could he have? They regarded imperialism as an enemy because they believed it had lost them Palestine, the liberation movement not as applying to vague territories in Africa and Asia but to Palestine, and the Arab revolution as a means of uniting their peoples to reconquer Palestine. Many leaders had pandered to popular passion by making promises no one expected them to fulfil but with Nasser it was different. The barometer of his reputation rose and fell with the measure of his ability to defend Arabia against Israelis and ultimately to defeat them.

Towards the end of 1966 his reputation was at its lowest ebb because dissension within the region was at its worst. The rift between the monarchies and the 'progressive' states was complete and was reflected in bitter divisions of opinion in each Arab country, so that no one could see what good could come of it either in social and economic progress or in defence against Israel. Intelligent Arabs, even Palestinians, were saying in private that they had lost their country for good.

It was in this climate of opinion that Israeli land and air forces attacked Samou and another village in the Hebron region of Jordan on 13 November, inflicting severe damage and loss of life.

The apparent inability of the Arab States to defend themselves provoked the most bitter recriminations between those who blamed Jordan for not admitting troops of the United Arab Command earlier and those who blamed Egypt and Syria for doing nothing to help, in the course of which it was forgotten almost everywhere that it is impossible to defend every village along the whole Jordan frontier all the time. The Jordan Government was most incensed against Syria which was outspoken in its demands for immediate war to defeat Israel and which permitted the free-lance guerrillas to train on its soil and raid Israel when its own army command was so torn by political dissension that its ability to fight was in doubt.

The guerrilla raids had precipitated the Samou attack but Israel was rightly censured at the United Nations for the strength and viciousness of her riposte. The Israeli Government was also criticised at home and abroad for attacking Jordan, whose Government had done its best to prevent the raids, while the real culprit was Syria. When trouble switched to the Syrian frontier at the turn of the year it was widely concluded that this had become the danger point, although the spring sowings in the Huleh plain had provoked incidents every year. A severe Israeli air attack on Syria in April, the deployment of strong Israeli forces near the frontier and a statement by Mr. Eshkol which seemed to confirm Arab fears that Israel was preparing to attack Syria brought the matter to a head.

The position was difficult and dangerous for President Nasser because he had a defence agreement committing him to military support of Syria, and even more so because his unique position demanded that he either take charge of Arab policy in the approaching crisis or abdicate his leadership of the Arabs. He tried to restrain Syria whose preemptive bids in patriotism were partly responsible for the situation but the April air raid showed that there was no reciprocal restraint in Tel Aviv and the attempt failed. He was in a weak position because his frontier was protected by the United Nations Emergency Force, which he had admitted during the 1956 Suez crisis despite the fact that Israel had refused to have it on her side of the frontier, and during the Arab Defence Committee meeting after the Samou attack the Jordanian delegates had taunted the Egyptians that they had little right to criticise Jordan's failure from behind a U.N. screen. The Egyptian spokesman replied that UNEF would be ordered to withdraw when the time was opportune. Arab opinion was even more critical of President Nasser over his failure to support Syria during the Israeli air attack in April and was swinging round to the view that the Arab States would once again back down in face of Israeli threats.

President Nasser felt compelled to act but he did so at two points where he could argue the greatest right and might satisfy Arab opinion without provoking war; it was brinkmanship of the most extreme kind but there was nothing else he could do except start a war himself. He closed to Israel the Strait of Tiran, which gave access to the Israeli port of Eilath at the head of the Gulf of Aqaba, and he ordered the U.N. force to leave the Sinai, thus eliminating the two concessions he had made at the time of his military defeat in 1956. There can hardly be any question that the force was only there by permission of the Egyptian Government which had the right to tell it to leave at any moment and although the Strait of Tiran posed a more difficult problem it is probable that an international court would have found in his favour. The passageway had been opened to Israeli shipping by force in 1956 and might reasonably be closed by force in 1967; the port of Eilath whose existence raised the question of rights of passage was an Arab village seized by Israel after the armistice agreements with the Arab States; Israel was not at peace with the Arabs; and Egypt, Jordan and Saudi Arabia, the three other states on the gulf, did not recognise her existence. No other case concerning international rights of passage that might be cited had comparable complications, for the issue was essentially political, not legal. It involved the right of the United Nations to create Israel on Arab soil and condone the expansion of her territory by force, and the rights of Arab States to refuse to accept her existence.

Nevertheless, Nasser must have known that his claims would have no meaning for Israel, which would be bound to seek to reopen the strait by force if the Powers failed to do so by diplomacy. He clearly calculated that the United States and the Western powers in general would restrain Israel from going to war and to that end proclaimed that he had no further action in mind. By expelling the UNEF force he emphasised the danger of war and his readiness to face it but this was probably intended only to increase Western pressure on Israel. At no time during the fortnight preceding the outbreak of war did he show any fear that the Western powers would force the strait or that international maritime opinion would compel him to reopen it to Israel.

He must have felt sure that his army could at least hold Israel if the worst came to the worst but Egypt's position was by no means a happy one. His relations with Jordan, whose small but efficient army could give useful support in the early days of any war, and with Saudi Arabia, which had money to spare if necessary, were embittered by long months of wordy conflict. Relations with Syria, however cordial on the surface, were at best lukewarm and the leadership of the enthusiastically patriotic Syrian Army had been decimated over several years by political upheavals. The Iraqi Army was second only to Egypt's in strength but was 500 miles away across the Syrian desert. The Egyptian Army was itself as strong in Egypt as it had been before its involvement in Yemen but there were still reckoned to be about 40,000 seasoned troops there. These were not conditions to inspire confidence in fast, effective and united Arab action, and in the event only Jordan put a large enough force in the field quickly enough to suffer heavy losses in support of Egypt.

President Nasser no doubt realised that the Palestine problem overrides all dissension and it was quickly apparent that popular support for his action was so strong that no government dared stand back from his commitment. King Hussein quickly settled all doubts on this score by piloting his own plane on a spectacular flight to Cairo where he signed a defence pact that committed his army to the hilt. The doctrinaire socialists of Syria regarded this pact between Nasser and the 'imperialist stooge' of Jordan as wrong and King Feisal of Saudi Arabia may have regarded the manner as too flamboyant a gesture to the enemy of yesterday but the Arab world as a whole had no doubt that to forget enmities and join forces against Israel was right and proper. Even Ahmed Shukairy, President of the Palestine Liberation Organisation, who a few days before had called for King Hussein's overthrow and death, felt constrained to fly back with him to his homeland.

The recovery of Nasser's reputation in the Arab world happened overnight with his declaration closing the Strait of Tiran. The common people spoke of him as though he were a god and even his enemies were fulsome in his praise all the way from Casablanca to Bahrein. Only a hard-headed few paused to ask whether the calculation of his risk and ability to defeat Israel was correct. Within a matter of days the realisation that his action might precipitate the long-awaited war with Israel inspired confidence and not fear, for it was quickly deduced that President Nasser would never have risked the military challenge unless he were sure that this time the Arabs could win. The statements of Nasser himself were relatively restrained and cautious but these were discounted as an essential political gambit, an example of his astuteness. The Arabs became so convinced that more was intended than the closing of the strait that even a pacific victory that left him with its control would have seemed a let-down.

Whether Nasser himself began to feel that greater victories were at hand may never be known but certainly some of his generals, commanding the most powerful force that Egypt had ever possessed, began to hope that Israel would attack and told journalists so. An official at the Department of Information declared that if she did so the Egyptians would be in Tel Aviv in two days. Elsewhere the Arab objectives differed from country to country and even person to person, ranging from the destruction of Israel to simply holding the Strait of Tiran. As the war drew closer, President Nasser told members of the National Assembly that he had gone back to the position of 1956 (by closing the strait) and 'God willing' would go back to the position of 1948, which could mean confining Israel within the partition frontiers voted by the United Nations in 1947 and was certainly understood by the Arabs in that sense. It was a widely held view that he would at least regain the land bridge across the Negev to Jordan, and Palestinians of 'revolutionary' persuasion believed that he would then create a Palestine republic consisting of the West Bank of the Jordan and the Negev.

These were dreams destroyed in a few hours of war. At about seven a.m. GMT on 5 June Israel launched its Mirage and Mystere transonic jets at subsonic speeds across the Mediterranean under the Egyptian radar screen and turned them in from the West on the Egyptian airfields where 200 MiGs were destroyed on the ground and the runways put out of action. Before the day was out another one hundred Egyptian planes had been destroyed and in strikes in Syria, Iraq and Jordan about one hundred planes were wrecked. The Arab forces, deprived of air cover, were beaten before they started. As the record of the blitzkrieg was put together it became clear that Egyptian forces in the Sinai and Jordanian troops on the West Bank of the Jordan fought with courage, often fanatical courage, but were pounded to pieces from the air. Some Kuwaiti, Iraqi and Saudi contingents reached the front but the war was over before the main body of the Iraqi army, the only force that could have had importance, reached the front.

The war was between Israel on one side and Egypt and Jordan on the other, for Syria took no serious part until the fifth day when the defeat of Jordan and Egypt was complete. *The Sunday Times* reported on 11 June: 'Through the week, Syria's extremist government managed to combine the most bloodcurdling public attitude with the least vigorous military posture. The Israeli Army, busy with Sinai and Jordan, coolly left the armed kibbutzim to hold off the threat to the north—and they succeeded. Then, on Thursday, the day after the Jordanian collapse, the Syrians began to step up their artillery fire'. Whatever may have been the reason for Syria's slowness in entering the war, the Israelis were not willing to let her get away with it and launched a savage and bloody attack that struck deep into the country and captured the commanding heights over the Israeli plains from which Syria had shelled the villages. The sufferings of Syria were slight compared with Jordan but the Israeli attack was launched after the cease fire and could not be sustained for long in defiance of it.

The victory of Israel was complete. She held the whole of Sinai, including the south-eastern tip at Sharm el-Sheikh which command-ed the Strait of Tiran, the whole of the West Bank of the Jordan as far east as Jericho, including Arab Jerusalem and the Old City, Ramallah, Nablus, Jenin and Qalqilya, and had driven the Syrians away from the vulnerable northern frontier. The victory was so sweeping and Israel absorbed so many Arabs that if she kept all gains she was in danger of becoming a bi-racial state, but soon the pattern of Israeli policy became clear as thousands of refugees from the West Bank of the Jordan streamed across the river and no one was allowed to return. Although Arabs firmly believed always that Israel desired to take the rest of Palestine none in his heart believed that so great a disaster could be allowed to happen.

President Nasser was compelled to take the blame for the defeat because in the final count he had precipitated the war, whatever earlier causes were created by Israel and Syria, and the Arab people had followed him blindly and with faith. History will almost cer-tainly record that the war was not determined by individual courage which was equal on both sides but by faulty planning and strategy in Egypt where the main strength of the Arabs lay. Not to anticipate the Israeli air-strike from the West must be one of the most remark-able aberrations of intelligence in the history of modern warfare.

He offered his resignation and withdrew it in response to an outburst of public feeling which must have surprised him after such a calamitous defeat. It is true that outside Jordan few Arabs, and certainly not the Egyptians, understood the extent of the failure, but the more important factor was that no other leader commanded the minds of the Arabs so completely. His replacement seemed so impossible that the Arabs handed back to him the task of saving something from the wreck.

Many Arabs blamed the United States and Britain for the defeat on the basis of an Egyptian report that their planes had supported the Israeli forces. It had its origin in an incomplete radar record by the Ajlun station in Jordan of planes over the Mediterranean. They were soon known to have been Israeli but the report was given credence because the first Egyptian statements made King Hussein the source of the information. King Hussein promptly put the record straight but other Arab broadcasting stations, notably those of Egypt and Syria, continued to broadcast the untruth and did immense harm to Arab relations with both countries at a time when the Arab States needed all the international support they could get.

The Soviet position was not much better, although for other reasons. Such is the strength of feeling about Palestine that even arch-conservatives who hated the very thought of Russia began to see in Russia their hope of victory. 'Kosygin will not let Nasser down', they said. 'You pro-Israel Western countries are neutralised by Soviet power'. When defeat was apparent and Russia supported the unconditional cease-fire at the United Nations, Arab disillusionment was so intense that the Egyptian Government, with no other major country to turn to for support, was compelled to dampen popular anger. The Western powers suffered most severely: some of the Arab countries broke diplomatic relations, oil-producing countries cut their supplies of oil, and plans were prepared to boycott their commerce; but disappointment with Russia may eventually have more long-term effects on Arab and Egyptian foreign policy by emphasising the fact that *all* great powers pursue their own policies in the end.

Domestic conditions might also play their part. Defeat in war only confirmed what was becoming daily more evident in economic affairs, that Egypt's problems are so immense that it requires wide and tolerant international relations if she is to preserve her independence, that she cannot afford to crusade for other people when she has too many of her own to feed. Whether the lesson has been learnt remains to be seen but hard facts may compel rethinking of policies that have harmed both Egypt and the Arabs in the end.

# BIBLIOGRAPHY

# Bibliography

*The Middle East*, W. B. Fisher, London, 1950
*History of the Arabs*, Philip K. Hitti, London, 1956
*The Arabs in History*, Bernard Lewis, London, 1950
*The Encyclopaedia of Arabic Civilisation*, Stephan and Nandy Ronart, Amsterdam, 1959
*The Middle East in World Affairs*, George Lenczowski, New York, 1952
*Communism and Nationalism in the Middle East*, W. Z. Laqueur, London, 1956
*The Arabs*, Anthony Nutting, London, 1964
*Egypt*, P. G. Elgood, London, 1935
*A Family in Egypt*, Mary Rowlatt, London, 1956
*Ibrahim of Egypt*, P. Crabbites, London, 1935
*Modern Egypt*, Earl of Cromer, London, 1908
*Secret History of the English Occupation of Egypt*, Wilfrid Scawen Blunt, London, 1895
*The Making of Modern Egypt*, Sir Auckland Colvin, London, 1906
*The River War*, Winston S. Churchill, London, 1899
*The Redemption of Egypt*, W. Basil Worsford, London, 1899
*The Truth About Egypt*, A. Alexander, London, 1911
*The Expansion of Egypt*, A. Silva White, London, 1899
*England in Egypt*, Alfred Milner, London, 1904
*Founders of Modern Egypt*, Mary Rowlatt, Bombay, 1962
*Bankers and Pashas*, David S. Landes, London, 1958
*Samuel Shepheard of Cairo*, Michael Bird, 1957
*Ferdinand de Lesseps*, Charles Beatty, London, 1956
*New Egypt*, A. B. de Guerville, London, 1905
*Lord Cromer of Egypt—A Retrospect*, George Kirk, Offprint from *Harvard Library Bulletin*, 1958
*Egypt Since Cromer*, Lord Lloyd, London, 1933
*Egypt*, George Young, London, 1927
*The Awakening of Modern Egypt*, M. Rifaat Bey, London, 1947
*The Arab Awakening*, George Antonius, London, 1938
*Islam and Modernism in Egypt*, Charles C. Adams, London, 1933

*A History of Land Ownership in Egypt 1800–1950*, Gabriel Baer, Oxford, 1962

*The Nile*, H. E. Hurst, London, 1952

*The Sudan Question: The Dispute over The Anglo-Egyptian Condominium 1884–1951*, Mekki Abbas, London, 1952

*The Sudan's Path to Independence*, J. R. S. Duncan, Edinburgh, 1957

*Turkey*, G. L. Lewis, London, 3rd Edition, 1965

*The Decline of the West in the Middle East*, republished from Albert Hourani, *International Affairs*, January and April 1953

*England and the Middle East*, Elie Kedourie, London, 1956

*The Middle East, A Political and Economic Survey*, Sir Reader Bullard (Editor), 3rd Edition, Oxford, 1958

*Al-Azhar*, Bayard Lodge, Washington D.C., 1961

*The Middle East in the War*, George Kirk, Oxford, 1952

*The Middle East, 1945–1950*, George Kirk, Oxford, 1954

*The Ideas of Arab Nationalism*, Hazem Zaki Nuseibeh, New York, 1956

*Arab-Turkish Relations and the Emergence of Arab Nationalism*, Zeine N. Zeine, Beirut, 1958

*The Intellectual Origins of Egyptian Nationalism*, J. M. Ahmed, Oxford, 1960

*Egypt in Search of Political Community*, Nadav Safran, Oxford, 1961

*Nationalism and Revolution in Egypt*, Christina Phelps Harris, The Hague, 1966

*Arab Nationalism and British Imperialism*, John Marlowe, London, 1961

*Egypt in Revolution*, Charles Issawi, Oxford, 1963

*U.N. Reviews of Economic Conditions in the Middle East* (annual)

*The Moslem Brethren*, Ishak Musa Husseini, Beirut, 1956

*Land Reform and Development in the Middle East*, Doreen Warriner, London, 1957 and 1962

*Old Ills and New Remedies*, Eva Garzouzi, Cairo, 1958

*Nasser's New Egypt*, Keith Wheelock, New York, 1960

*High Dam at Aswan*, Tom Little, London, 1965

*Egypt in Transition*, Jean and Simmone Lacouture, London, 1958

*The Modern Middle East*, Ed. Richard H. Nolte, New York, 1963

*Britain's Moment in the Middle East*, Elizabeth Monroe, London, 1963

*Four Aspects of Egypt*, John Marlowe, London, 1966

*The Soviet Union and the Middle East*, Walter Z. Laqueur, London, 1959

*The Philosophy of the Revolution*, Gamal Abdel Nasser, Cairo (also published as *Egypt's Liberation*, Washington D.C., 1955)

*Revolt on the Nile*, Col. Anwar El-Sadat, London, 1957

*Egypt's Destiny*, General Neguib, London, 1955
*Nasser of Egypt*, Wilton Wynn, Cambridge, U.S.A., 1959
*Nasser, The Rise to Power*, Joachim Joesten, London, 1960
*Gamal Abdel Nasser et son équipe*, Georges Vaucher, Paris, 1959
*The Boss*, Robert St. John, New York, 1960
*The Egyptian Army in Politics*, P. J. Vatikiotis, Indiana, 1961
*The Suez Canal—Facts and Documents*, Cairo, 1956
*Suez—Ten Years After*, six broadcasts on the B.B.C. Third Programme, July/August 1966.
*The Record on Suez*, Reprints from the *Manchester Guardian*, 1956
*The Road to Suez*, Erskine B. Childers, London, 1962
*The Suez Canal Settlement*. Documents 1956–1959, Ed. E. Lauterpacht, The British Institute of International and Comparative Law, London, 1960
*Middle East Crisis*, Guy Wint and Paul Calvocoressi, London, 1957
*100 Hours to Suez*, Robert Henriques, London, 1957
*The Suez Canal*, A Selection of Documents relating to the International Status of the Suez Canal Company, 30 November 1854–26 July 1956. Reprint of a special supplement to *International and Comparative Law Quarterly*, 1956
*Documents on the Suez Crisis*, 26 July to 6 November 1956, London
*The World Today* (Monthly) R.I.I.A.
*Mideast Mirror* (Weekly), Regional News Services (Mid-East) Ltd.
*International Affairs* (Quarterly), R.I.I.A.
*Foreign Affairs* (Quarterly), New York
*National Bank of Egypt*: Quarterly Reports
Annual Reports of President Nasser's Speeches. Dept. of Information, Cairo
*St. Antony's Papers*, Oxford

# INDEX

# Index

285